W9-BLL-614

BACKROADS & BYWAYS OF

MONTANA

BACKROADS & BYWAYS OF
MONTANA

Drives, Day Trips
& Weekend Excursions

SECOND EDITION

JEFF WELSCH AND SHERRY L. MOORE

THE COUNTRYMAN PRESS

A division of W. W. Norton & Company

Independent Publishers Since 1923

Copyright © 2016 by Garden Angel Enterprises, Inc.
Copyright © 2011 by Jeff Welsch and Sherry L. Moore
Photograph on page 14 © Leigh Anne Meeks/Shutterstock

All rights reserved
Printed in the United States of America

For information about permission to reproduce selections from this book, write to
Permissions, The Countryman Press, 500 Fifth Avenue, New York, NY 10110

For information about special discounts for bulk purchases, please contact
W. W. Norton Special Sales at specialsales@wwnorton.com or 800-233-4830

Book design by Chris Welch
Manufacturing by Versa Press

Library of Congress Cataloging-in-Publication Data

Names: Welsch, Jeff. | Moore, Sherry L.
Title: Backroads & byways of Montana : drives, day trips & weekend excursions
/ Jeff Welsch and Sherry L. Moore.
Other titles: Backroads and byways of Montana
Description: Second edition. | Woodstock, VT : The Countryman Press, 2016. |
Series: Backroads & byways | Includes index.
Identifiers: LCCN 2015049399 | ISBN 9781581573503 (paperback)
Subjects: LCSH: Montana—Tours. | Roads—Montana—Guidebooks. | Scenic
byways—Montana—Guidebooks. | Automobile travel—Montana—Guidebooks.
Classification: LCC F729.3 .W46 2016 | DDC 917.8604—dc23
LC record available at http://lccn.loc.gov/2015049399

The Countryman Press
www.countrymanpress.com

A division of W. W. Norton & Company, Inc.
500 Fifth Avenue, New York, NY 10110
www.wwnorton.com

10 9 8 7 6 5 4 3 2 1

How This Book Works

This isn't just a book about the best driving tours in Montana. It's also about capturing Montana's essence through twelve primary drives plus a Glacier National Park bonus drive, each revealing a different portrait of the Treasure State's wide range of landscapes, communities, and personalities.

Our routes are all over the Montana map, literally and figuratively. Some are included for insights into local and historical culture, such as the Big Sky Backcountry Byway and The Warrior Trail in eastern Montana. Some are on well-maintained paved roads and some are on gravel or dirt that could be impassable after a hard rain- or snowstorm. Some, such as the breathtaking Beartooth All-American Highway near Yellowstone National Park and the Going-to-the-Sun Road in Glacier National Park, aren't backroads or even byways per se, but are included because no book about Montana would be complete without the scenic tours.

At the beginning of each chapter, you'll get the basics about the designated drive—where it starts, mileage, estimated time, highlights, and how to get there. You'll also get an overview of the area and its significance in Montana's history, geography, and culture. We then complement most chapters with a short story about a relevant topic and tips for the best lodging, dining, and bars on the route. And at the end, in case the tour has whet your appetite for more, we add a nearby "Detour" with its own brand of character and charm.

Based on feedback from readers, in every chapter except "The Warrior Trail" we have added one or two short "Side Tracks" that are mostly on dirt or gravel and decidedly off the beaten path—backroads in every sense of the word. Also new: two additional chapters, one on the Blackfoot Valley between Missoula and Wolf Creek, the other a loop through the picturesque ranch country of the Musselshell Valley beginning and ending in Lewistown, the geographic center of Montana.

In this book, we think you'll find Montana backstories you won't see anywhere else. For instance, do you know about The Little People of the Pryor Mountains? The Blackfoot Challenge? The impacts the film *A River Runs Through It*—simply known as "The Movie" in parts of Montana—has had on the region? The little town on the eastern prairie that briefly changed its name to "Joe" to capitalize on the name of a former National Football League quarterback of some renown?

For consistency's sake, we get you to the start of each route from points on or near Interstate 90, the busy (by Montana standards) freeway bisecting the state from east to west. We chose to start each drive in a community where essential amenities are available. Naturally, in many cases you'll be coming from a different direction and can plan accordingly.

We include attractions, scenic vistas, points of interest, lodging, and dining that help tell each tour's story. Because driving in Montana frequently requires an overnight bag, we've also included our "Best Places to Bunk." For our twelve primary routes we have listed a cost guide for dining and lodging (dining based on the average price of a lunch or dinner entrée). We also offer insights into signature menu items and try to note whether eateries are open for breakfast, lunch, and/or dinner. Hours can vary according to the seasons, days, and sometimes even the whims of owners, so call ahead—or take your chances as part of the adventure. Our lodging and dining price guide is as follows:

Lodging		Dining	
$:	$75 and under	$:	$10 or less
$$:	$76–125	$$:	$11–20
$$$:	$126–199	$$$:	$21–30
$$$$:	$200 and over	$$$$:	$30 and over

These routes are mostly rural and often have limited dining options. When asked what foods they're known for, a strong majority of owners and servers responded "our burgers." And it's true that from border to border we ate dozens of brawny, juicy, handmade hamburgers, some with secret ingredients. Though a few restaurants are known for their culinary skills, this isn't a fine-dining guide. Eateries were chosen for many reasons—sometimes quality, sometimes character, sometimes location, and sometimes because it's the only game in a remote town. In many cases all of the above apply.

Lodging options reflect similar diversity. We have covered upscale accommodations as well as motor-court motels for those on a budget. We have also added a category called "Alternative Bunking" for anyone driving an RV, camping, or wanting to have a one-of-a-kind experience in a Forest

Service lookout or cabin. Though much of Montana has wonderful dude and guest ranches, we omitted some appealing all-inclusive places simply because the concept of staying in one place for a week doesn't align with driving the backroads and byways.

To the best of our knowledge, all lodging and dining listings are open year-round unless otherwise noted.

Montana is famous for its colorful bars, taverns, and saloons, so we give them a nod, too, in the category "Best Bars." Though each bar is unique in its own right, we have highlighted a few for each route based on their history, character, food options (sometimes), and the overall vibe we felt when stopping to converse with locals and visitors. A word to the wise: many rural establishments in Montana only accept cash.

One other note: you'll notice frequent references to the seven Indian reservations that help give Montana much of its character. Throughout the book, we refer to the people who live on these small remnants of their historical territories as "Indians" instead of "Native Americans." From our experiences in the region, this is their preference, along with "Native," and we have made every effort to honor it.

To fully absorb the flavor of this state of treasures and appreciate what you're about to experience, we encourage you to first read the introduction and following chapter on Montana's wide-ranging geography, history, and culture. This should provide ample background for the memorable journeys you're about to undertake.

Happy trails!

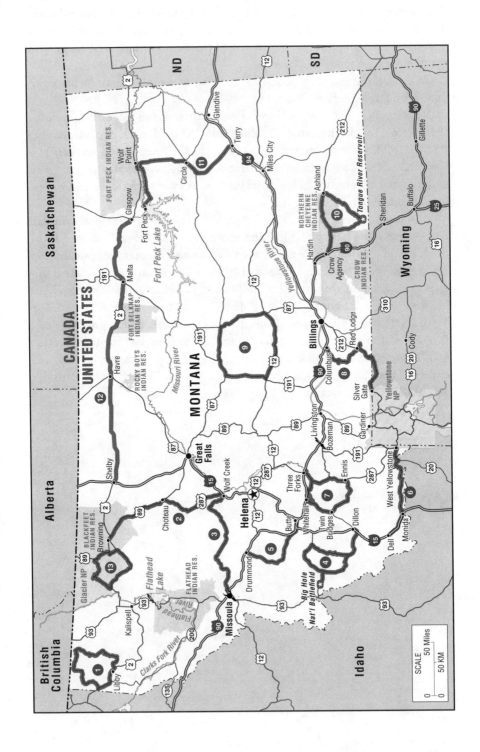

Contents

Introduction

Think of Montana, and images of snowcapped mountains, pristine free-flowing rivers, and weathered cowboys traversing vast prairies astride proud horses likely come to mind. After all, these portraits are the core of the Montana mystique, captured in the lilting prose of the late Ivan Doig and A. B. "Bud" Guthrie, the vivid paintings of C. M. Russell, the gritty black-and-white images of Evelyn Cameron, and the breathtaking cinematography of *A River Runs Through It, The Horse Whisperer,* and *Legends of the Fall.*

Certainly, this is the romanticized Montana, and yet these snapshots offer an alluring dose of accuracy as well. Even today, more than a century after the open-range era that emblazoned the Old West's image in the American psyche, visitors can participate in an actual cattle drive, cast a caddis or nymph to glistening pools full of fat wild trout, watch magnificent herds of wild elk on the march, and marvel at brawny mountains in every direction. In many respects, Montana is still a raw, rugged, and wild place—even as well-heeled cowboys and ranchers from elsewhere flood river valleys and mountain resorts in the western half of the state. They're all yearning to reconnect to a bygone era that's probably more myth than truth.

Yet it's still possible to experience the Montana of popular mystique, especially if you're willing to leave behind the well-traveled highways that cater to the whims of tourists and newcomers. It's on these backroads and byways where the adventurous can best see why Guthrie dubbed Montana "Big Sky Country." You'll also recognize the evolved definition of the term "Treasure State." After a century of drawing deep upon rich reserves of minerals, timber, rangelands, and fossil fuels, Montana's nickname now better describes the state's scenic, cultural, and natural wonders as residents and visitors work to protect what's been lost elsewhere in America.

Once away from the hum of Missoula, Kalispell, Billings, Great Falls, and Bozeman—still small by eastern standards but veritable metropolises in a state that barely surpassed 1 million residents in 2012—you'll find a remarkable variety of landscapes and cultures.

Did you know, for instance, that Montana has a temperate rain forest? The hardy, rugged loggers and farmers of the cool, damp, and gray Yaak River Valley in the northwest corner of the state certainly can tell you about it.

Did you know that Montana is dotted with semiarid deserts? Lest you doubt, check with the ranchers near Bridger in the south-central part of the state and at Hot Springs up in the northwest, where annual rainfalls in a good year are about the same as in Tucson, Arizona.

Did you know that a state famed for rivers also features the largest freshwater lake in the western United States? Growers of cherries and other fruits are forever grateful for the fertile soils and moderate climes around Flathead Lake, one of the purest bodies of water of such scope and size in the world.

Did you know that Montana has seven Indian reservations, all on the same wide-open spaces—albeit a fraction of their historical lands—where indigenous peoples once hunted bison and other wild game? Drive across the reservation lands of the Crow, Northern Cheyenne, Blackfeet, Cree, Assiniboine, Sioux, Salish, Kootenai, and others, and it doesn't require much imagination to envision Indians on horseback atop coulees and ridges, silhouetted against a cobalt sky.

With a state so huge and diverse, it's a challenging task to pare down a list of compelling back roads and byways to a mere handful. After all, at 147,000 square miles, Montana is surpassed in size only by Alaska, Texas, and California. It's at least an 11-hour drive across the state from east to west, and that's only by going at the maximum speed of 75-mph—80 in some places as of 2015—on I-90.

In *Backroads & Byways of Montana*, we have detailed a collection of memorable drives that reflect the many geographic, historical, and social faces of Montana. You'll meander amid towering fir and spruce in the foggy shadows of the northwest corner. You'll practically touch the stars atop the broad shoulders of the Beartooth Mountains, on a highway once dubbed the most beautiful road in America by CBS newsman Charles Kuralt. You'll be smitten with the untamed Rocky Mountain Front, where grizzly bears can sometimes still be spotted on the prairie.

You'll step back 150 years to the unspoiled Centennial Valley, a critical Greater Yellowstone Ecosystem migration route for such iconic wildlife species as wolves, grizzly bears, wolverine, moose, and elk. You'll watch the sun set beyond the Bitterroot and Beaverhead in the upper Big Hole Valley, where you might hear the wailing ghosts of Nez Perce women and children who perished in a futile 1877 pursuit of freedom. You'll traverse the same Big Blackfoot riverbanks that Norman Maclean made famous in his novella *A River Runs Through It,* which was so powerful in capturing our imaginations that the movie of the same name changed the face of western Montana almost overnight.

You'll discover where to enjoy the best dining along these routes, whether it's savoring local beef, bison, or lamb under the watchful eyes of trophy elk mounts in darkened saloons or harder-to-find vegetarian fare in eclectic settings. You'll find out where to draw a draft of locally produced microbrews or traditional domestic lager while gazing at century-old backbars hauled up the Missouri on steamships. You'll have choices of lodging ranging from primitive to cowboy lux. And along the way you'll find out about things to do and see, and how to enjoy the many faces of Montana's attractions.

Oh, and we'll throw in a few trout streams and mountains along the way, too.

A Montana Primer

History, Geography, and Driving

In our ethnocentric world, the calendar shows Montana's birth date as November 8, 1889, when after 25 years as a territory the state was welcomed into the union by proclamation of President Benjamin Harrison. The truth, of course, is that the scenic, cultural, and spiritual wonders of Montana really began to take shape about 100 million years ago, when the Rocky Mountains were born and converted what had been shallow seas, swamps, and plains into the dramatic geography we see today.

Anyone familiar with the fiery turbulence that lurks just beneath the earth's surface at Yellowstone National Park understands the violent genesis of the region. The Yellowstone supervolcano has experienced major eruptions three times in the past 2.2 million years—the last about 700,000 years ago. They were the most dramatic forces during a period in which molten rock pushed upward in what is now western Montana, creating the mountain ranges for which the state is named and famed. The mountains' mostly north–south orientation can be attributed to tectonic plates grinding, folding, and thrusting from the west, pinching the land so that it was forced upward rapidly along faults. Over time, wind, rain, snow, and ice have eroded the mountains and carved deep river valleys.

The first significant life forms were the dinosaurs that roamed the swamps and plains about 150 million years ago, before the Rockies were formed. Fossilized bones and eggs have been found everywhere east of the mountains, from Choteau on the Rocky Mountain Front to the small canyons and plains of eastern Montana. To paleontologists, Montana is a geological treasure trove, and the distant presence of dinosaurs has created a bounty reflected in museums across the state. Energy companies also covet the dinosaur legacy. Oil, gas, and coal are abundant beneath the surface where the mountains meet the plains, and the countryside is sprinkled with oil and gas wells all the way to the Bakken Formation under eastern Montana and western North Dakota.

As far as historians can tell, the first humans came to present-day Montana from what is now Russia during the last Ice Age, which ended approximately 11,000 years ago. They hunted the woolly mammoth and avoided the saber-toothed cat for several thousand years after the glaciers retreated, eventually dispersing when the land became too arid to provide enough game for subsistence. Shortly after, another group of tribes arrived, this time from the west and south. They, too, eventually disappeared, leaving a human void that wasn't filled until about 1,000 years ago.

HISTORY

A common misconception is that Montana tribes such as the Sioux, Assiniboine, Crow, Northern Cheyenne, Blackfeet, Flathead, Kootenai, Kalispell, Gros Ventre, Arapaho, and Nez Perce roamed the plains and mountains unfettered for thousands of years until their worlds were abruptly shattered by migrating white settlers in the 1800s. Truth is, their heyday in Montana probably lasted about 250 years, from the time the Flatheads arrived around 1500 until the tribes were banished to reservations by the late 19th century. The earliest evidence of modern-day tribes connects to the Crows and dates to about 1150. The Sioux, pushed west by the advancing Europeans, sought refuge on the inhospitable plains of the Dakotas and eastern Montana before they were subdued in 1876.

French fur traders began trickling into the region as early as the 1740s, but the defining moment of the European invasion was the 1804–06 Lewis and Clark expedition that began in St. Louis, Missouri, and crossed Montana east to west en route to Fort Clatsop, Oregon. Some of the most memorable reports from the expedition occurred along the Missouri and Yellowstone Rivers in what is now Montana. Ironically, the expedition was probably saved from disaster by a Native woman named Sacagawea, who guided the group across the imposing Bitterroot Mountains along the backbone of the Rockies in the winter of 1805. While Lewis and Clark historical markers are ubiquitous in Montana, the single remaining tangible evidence of the corps is preserved under glass on a small sandstone butte called Pompey's Pillar, along the Yellowstone River east of Billings. There, Captain William Clark etched his name and the date he camped there amid the cottonwoods beneath a butte he named for Sacagawea's son.

The Lewis and Clark trek eventually brought a flood of immigrants, most of them homesteaders with visions of wide-open spaces where they could raise crops amid lush shoulder-high prairie grasses and get rich from gold nuggets gleaming in the rivers. Reality was quite a bit harsher. Homesteaders lured by pie-in-the-sky advertisements by railroad companies suffered through brutal winters and scorching dry summers, which caused many to abandon their dreams and leave their sod and wood houses. The frontier Montana epitomized by the so-called open range era of cattle ranching was short-lived as well. This mystical time began in 1866 when Nelson Story drove a herd from Texas to Montana on the Bozeman Trail—the film *Lonesome Dove* was based on this journey—and paved the way for others to follow. The open-range era lasted about two decades, effectively ending during the wicked winter of 1886–87, when half the state's cattle perished due to the lethal combination of overgrazed lands and unrelenting blizzards.

The mining boom in the southwest part of Montana Territory was fleeting as well. Gold was discovered in a mountain creek near Helena in 1858, and subsequent finds over the next few years brought men with picks and shovels by the thousands. Silver and copper also were unearthed. Such towns as Virginia City, Nevada City, Bannack, Garnet, Granite, Coolidge, Southern Cross, and Elkhorn rose from the piney hillsides overnight and became tawdry centers of drinking, carousing, and lawlessness. When the mines played out, the miners departed. The ghostly remnants of many of those towns, some of them still well-preserved, stand as an eerie testimony to a rags-to-riches-to-rags legacy.

Two other migrations are significant in Montana's pre-1900 history: the journeys of the missionaries and the spread of the railroads. In the 1830s, Jesuit priests were invited west by Native tribes, reputedly for spiritual instruction, though many historians suspect the Indians were looking for more tangible items such as guns, food, and medicine. In any event, many missions are scattered on tribal lands throughout Montana, including St. Mary's near Stevensville south of Missoula, St. Ignatius on the Flathead Indian Reservation of northwest Montana, and St. Xavier on the Crow Indian Reservation southeast of Billings. It was at these missions that basketball was introduced to the tribes, and the game has become almost a religion on reservations across the state, thanks to the unfettered freedom it represents.

The first railroad, the Utah & Northern, didn't arrive until 1880. Three years later, the Northern Pacific brought Montana's first access to a transcontinental line. Then came the Great Northern across the Hi-Line. Spurs were built, and cattle towns sprang up much like gold towns. The ability to ship cattle to the Midwest, East, and South created vast wealth for cattle barons.

Life still isn't easy in Montana. Winters are long and cold even as the climate seems to warm. Until the 1990s, the economy ebbed and flowed according to the wildly fluctuating values of natural resources. Every boom, from the gold rush of the 1860s to the energy frenzy after 9/11, to the current oil and gas bonanza in the Bakken formation in far eastern Montana, has ended with a bust—or at least an anxious slowdown. Today, Montana is cashing in on another natural resource: its natural beauty and wildness. With the increasingly frenetic pace of life on both coasts and in metropolitan areas, Montana has become a destination for people seeking one of the few places where wide open spaces and vestiges of yesteryear remain. The good news is that the old axiom "you can't eat the scenery" no longer rings true. Modern technology allows many businesses to locate wherever they choose, and innovative companies are discovering that a great way to lure the best, brightest, and most passionate workers is to locate in communities like Bozeman, Missoula, and Whitefish, where just outside the office there is immediate access to an unparalleled quality of life.

GEOGRAPHY

Not surprisingly, given its size, Montana is a state of many distinct regions. In general, residents divide the state into two halves: western Montana, with its rugged mountains and cool rushing rivers, and eastern Montana, known for its plains, canyons, and warm meandering streams.

Within that division are six more regions, largely created by the state's tourism bureau but nonetheless relevant. Some are the size of small eastern states, and all are composed of subregions worthy of their own names.

YELLOWSTONE COUNTRY in southwest Montana features the burly mountain ranges and pristine trout streams of travel brochures and famously includes the three percent of Yellowstone National Park that lies in the Treasure State. The Beartooth Highway and Centennial Valley drives in this region are featured in this book.

GLACIER COUNTRY in northwest Montana tends to include the most densely forested areas of the state, complemented by the jagged peaks and jewel-like lakes of Glacier National Park. This area is traversed by the Going-to-the-Sun Road and Yaak River Country tour.

GOLD COUNTRY in western Montana offers forests, broad picturesque valleys, and the remnants of once-flourishing mining and logging economies. The Anaconda-Pintler Scenic Route, the Vigilante Trail, and Big Hole Valley driving routes all wind their way through this area.

RUSSELL COUNTRY is largely characterized by undulating prairies rising gently to abrupt meetings with walls of mountains, most strikingly on display at the confluence of the plains and the vast Bob Marshall Wilderness. The Rocky Mountain Front is a highlight of this region.

MISSOURI RIVER COUNTRY is Montana's windswept northeastern corner and features mile after mile of wheat fields, farms, and the Missouri River

MAILBOXES ALONG THE RURAL ROUTE NEAR RED LODGE

John Baker

Breaks. The Hi-Line bisects this part of Montana as well as Russell Country, and the Big Sky Backcountry Byway and the Musselshell route enter this area, too.

CUSTER COUNTRY is marked by the wide-open spaces of southeastern Montana, where the term *"big sky"* comes to vivid life amid coulees, prairies, sunsets, and Montana's most famous Indian country. The Warrior Trail covers a corner of Custer Country.

DRIVING IN MONTANA

As much as anywhere in America, it's imperative to be prepared when driving in Montana. In winter, Montanans know to drive with everything they need to spend a night on the side of the road. That includes matches, candles, water, sleeping bags, blankets, boots, gloves, and plenty of warm clothes. With a warming climate, winters aren't as harsh as the old-timers remember them, but 20 degrees below zero isn't uncommon. Winds whip across the plains and down mountainsides, creating blinding conditions in a heartbeat. The Rocky Mountain Front, from Browning in the north to Livingston

Montana Dept of Transportation

DEEP SNOWS MAKE PLOWING THE BEARTOOTH HIGHWAY A LENGTHY CHORE IN MAY

in the south, is renowned for its winter Chinooks, serving up wind speeds of up to 70 mph and scouring the valleys of snow. Even the most beautiful autumn or spring day can turn on a dime. Snow can fall in any month in Montana, and snowstorms in June and September are not aberrations. In 2015, for example, the mountains received a good dusting in late July.

If you want some weather certainty, plan your vacation between mid-June and late September. A typical summer day in much of Montana begins with blue skies in the morning, some afternoon clouds, an isolated thunderstorm or two around dusk, and then evening clearing. Even summer provides its challenges, though. Traffic can be heavy, with campers and motor homes clogging roads in the more tourist-oriented places.

An old joke is that there are two seasons in Montana: winter and road construction. Patience is a requirement, even in these wide-open spaces. Late-afternoon thunderstorms are common in the summer and can rapidly turn a dirt road into impassable gumbo. If you're on a remote gravel road, you can easily get stuck. With its dry air, Montana's 90-degree days become 45-degree nights. It's no surprise that the most precipitous 24-hour temperature plunge in recorded US history—100 degrees—took place in Montana in

1916, at Browning on the Blackfeet Indian Reservation. Nearly as dramatic was the 84-degree drop in 12 hours at Fairfield in 1924.

In the old days, Montana was so big, broad, and lightly trafficked that many highways didn't require speed limits. "Reasonable and proper" was the rule. Today, all roads have speed limits, topped by the newly minted 80 mph signs on the three interstate highways. Two-lane rural state and county highways typically have a 60 to 70 mph speed limit. With these speeds and the monotonous countryside, be wary, especially at night. Drunk driving and fatigue-related fatalities are categories where Montana has the dubious distinction of high national rankings.

Once upon a time, watching your fuel gauge was critical in Montana because distances between towns are great and many stations close after dark. Paying at the pump with credit cards has improved this situation, but some of the roads featured in this book have 60, 70, 80, or more miles between stations. Luckily, Montana's fuel costs typically are slightly below average compared to the rest of the country. Speaking of costs, Montana is one of five states that doesn't charge a sales tax, so it's a great place to buy that log bed or antler chandelier you've always wanted.

LIBBY HAS A PROUD BUT CHECKERED MINING AND LOGGING HISTORY

1

FORESTS AND FREE SPIRITS
The Yaak River Country

LIBBY/REXFORD/YAAK/TROY

ESTIMATED LENGTH: 175 miles
ESTIMATED TIME: 5 hours to 2 days
HIGHLIGHTS: Forest fire lookouts, Kootenai Falls, Libby Dam, Lake Koocanusa, Yaak River Falls, Turner Mountai Ski Area
GETTING THERE: Take the St. Regis exit from I-90 and double back on MT 135 to a meeting with MT 200. At the junction of MT 200, go west and keep following the Clark Fork through Paradise and Plains to Thompson Falls, which is a great place for a meal or snack break (see Detour). Continue northwest through Belknap, Whitepine, Trout Creek, and Noxon to MT 56. Turn north toward Troy and Libby, passing the turnoff for the towering conifers at Ross Creek Cedars Scenic Area. From there, it's 20 miles to US 2 and the beginning of Yaak River Country.

OVERVIEW

Whatever accessories are on your checklist for travel through the Yaak River Country, be sure to include a book by the valley's most famous former resident: author Rick Bass. The most obvious is *The Book of Yaak,* but our favorite is *Winter: Notes from Montana*, about spending a long winter amid the mist, curling woodstove smoke, and eclectic folks in the state's most mystery-enshrouded corner.

Bass eloquently explains the Yaak's appeal, which stems not just from its literal and figurative distance from anywhere, but also from what its thick forests and foggy mountaintops leave to the imagination. Though it's true that Lincoln County is sparsely populated—the "56" on its license plates reflects that at one time Lincoln was the least populated among the state's

56 counties—it also doesn't feature the wide open spaces and distant snow-capped mountains for which the state is most famous. Secrets are easier to keep in the Yaak. Along the Yaak River Road, narrow two-track driveways disappear into the shadows, leaving passersby and even delivery folks to guess what lurks amid the darkness of thick lodgepole, white pine, western larch (also called tamarack), and Douglas fir stands. In some cases FedEx drivers are simply instructed to leave packages "on the orange X."

Aside from the lights powered by a grumpy diesel generator at the Yaak's once-notorious Dirty Shame Saloon, electricity didn't arrive here until 1963. And many families here still live "off the grid," without electricity or plumbing. The river starts in British Columbia as the Yahk, exchanges the *h* for a second *a* as it crosses into the United States, and begins an alternately swift and meandering 45-mile southward journey toward a meeting with the brawny Kootenai River below US 2. The Yaak's serpentine path suggests anything but its name, which is Kootenai for "arrow." At its midpoint, the river passes through the valley's largest community, Yaak, where some of the valley's 500 or so aging hippies, loggers, and Forest Service employees emerge from the woods and unwind at the Yaak Mercantile.

Where once the forest was abuzz with the whine of chain saws and the thunder of logging trucks, now a conservation ethic has begun to take root, championed by the likes of Bass and others who are trying to preserve the last vestiges of America's vanishing old-growth forests. Remnants of clear-cuts and old logging roads are still obvious in country that's 90 percent forested, but today such towns as Troy, Eureka, and Libby are increasingly orienting themselves toward outdoor recreation and catering to visitors who come to hike a remote mountain trail, hunt a trophy bull elk, or perhaps photograph an elusive wolf slipping in and out of the shadows.

The Yaak River Country route traverses a gravel mountain pass, traces either shore of the caterpillar-shaped Lake Koocanusa, and includes a piece of the relatively populous US 2, the country's northernmost coast-to-coast highway.

HITTING THE ROAD

Assuming your journey starts at the junction of US 2 and MT 56 just outside Troy, head east toward Libby first. Within 5 miles is the most awe-inducing natural wonder on the loop: **Kootenai Falls**. The Kootenai River funnels through a rocky gorge that the Kootenai Indians worshiped as the center of their universe. Other great waterfalls of the Pacific Northwest have been inundated by dams, but today visitors are transfixed by the spectacle of 50,000 cubic feet of water per second thundering unfettered through the S-shaped canyon. Take a walk over the swinging bridge just downstream

WATERS TUMBLE OVER THE YAAK RIVER FALLS BETWEEN TROY AND YAAK

from the cascading whitewater, too. If the falls look familiar, this is where Meryl Streep used her river guile to outwit the evil character played by Kevin Bacon in the 1993 movie *The River Wild*.

For a longer hike with more exertion, stop another 6 miles past the Kootenai Falls parking area at the **Scenery Mountain Lookout Trail**. Turn right on Cedar Creek Road and drive 3 miles to the trailhead. The last half of the 5-mile hike is on the arduous side, but the views looking south from the lookout into the Cabinet Wilderness are impressive.

Back on US 2, it's a few more miles into **Libby** (pop. 2,691), a deceptively attractive town of 3,000 with a checkered history. A quarter century after a company called W. R. Grace began mining the mineral vermiculite, a Seattle newspaper ran a series investigating an extraordinary number of deaths due to related asbestos contamination. The town is still reeling (see sidebar). Don't let this sad legacy stop you from spending a few days here, though. Libby could use both morale and economic boosts. Besides, its people are cheerful, the Cabinet Mountains backdrop is dramatic, and the fishing on

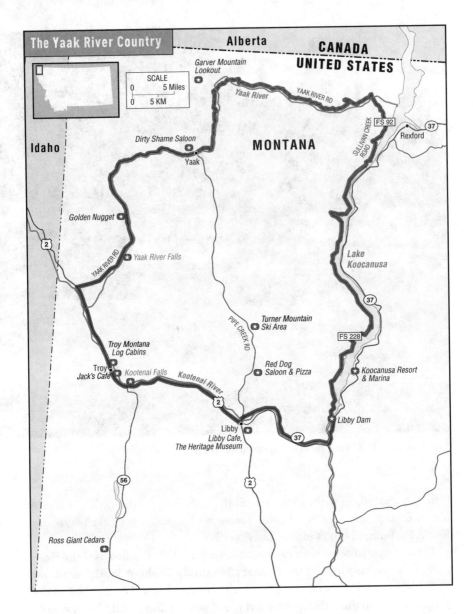

The Yaak River Country

the Kootenai between the town and Libby Dam about 17 miles upstream is as exceptional as it is intimidating. The state record rainbow trout, a whopping 33-inch football weighing 38 pounds, was caught just below the dam, and Montana's largest native whitefish, a 5-pounder, was landed in the same stretch. Check out the **Heritage Museum** (406-293-7521, summers), which captures the area's rich mining, logging, railroading, and American Indian history, among other topics.

The first stop after leaving Libby on MT 37 is the massive **Libby Dam** and its informative visitor center (406-293-5577, summers). At 422 feet high and

3,055 feet long, the dam creates **Lake Koocanusa** (KOOtenai River, CANada and USA), a caterpillar-shaped body of water that backs up for 90 miles, nearly half of the upper reaches pushing into British Columbia. The structure, completed in 1972, was built to tame the mighty Kootenai's spring flooding and also provide hydropower. Guided tours are available in the summer.

From Libby Dam, there are two choices for continuing the journey northward along Lake Koocanusa, between the Salish and Purcell mountains.

Libby Still Reeling from Asbestos Scare

Looking at Libby, with its forested hillsides and dramatic Cabinet Mountain Wilderness backdrop, it's difficult to imagine that this visually arresting community on the banks of the Kootenai River could be the site of the nation's first and only public health emergency. Yet that's just the case, thanks to the town's ongoing issues with vermiculite contamination from an unusually toxic form of asbestos from a nearby mine that closed in 1990.

From the 1920s to 1990, the Libby mine on Zonolite Mountain, 6 miles north of town, produced up to 80 percent of the world's vermiculite. However, Libby and nearby Troy suffered from an extraordinarily high rate of such lung diseases as asbestosis or the lethal mesothelioma because of a fine white dust that coated the mine workers and, when the winds blew right, blanketed the entire town. Just how serious the health issue was didn't fully become public until 1999, after an investigative report by the *Seattle Post-Intelligencer* and then a one-man crusade by a terminally ill miner named Les Skramstad. Nearly every family in this valley of 12,000 people has been directly affected. They have contracted diseases in many ways, ranging from direct contact with contaminants experienced by the miners to wives inhaling dust off of laundry and kids playing on vermiculite-coated piles near the baseball field.

This led to a massive cleanup, and in 2002, Libby was added to the Environmental Protection Area's list of federal Superfund sites. In the past decade, more than 1,100 residential and commercial properties have been cleaned up, with more still needing help. In 2009, the EPA declared a health emergency, stating that the job was far from over and that the residents of Libby needed more help to recover from a decades-long tragedy. Another $130 million was made available for medical aid and cleanup.

Is it safe to spend time in Libby today? Depends on whom you ask. The tragedy has divided the town between those who are angry and those who fear economic devastation due to the asbestos stigma. Certainly, a great deal of cleanup remains, but a 2008 EPA study showed that the air in Libby is safe. Passing through town or using Libby as a base to explore the Yaak/Koocanusa region is no cause for concern. And the resilient people who have suffered all these years will appreciate your support.

LAKE KOOCANUSA, WHICH STRETCHES INTO CANADA, IS KNOWN FOR BOATING AND FISHING

MT 37 hugs the eastern shore, and the less-traveled FS 228 winds through pines on the west side. Both are paved and equally scenic. If you're not in a rush, take FS 228. In winter, there is no choice—FS 228 is closed once the snow flies. To find lodging and dining, take MT 37. Five miles north of the dam is **Koocanusa Resort & Marina** (406-293-7474, Apr.–Dec.), which offers cabins, 81 RV sites, camping, a restaurant, and a small general store. The resort is best known for its annual Salmon & Trout Derby, which pits anglers in a competition to land the biggest kokanee salmon and rainbow trout.

About 45 miles north of Libby, a bridge crosses the lake. If you're needing a break, continue for about 6 miles on MT 37 into **Rexford** (pop. 149), which was once on the banks of the Kootenai River but was moved 2 miles to its current location in 1974 after rising lake waters flooded the original town site.

Once back down to the bridge, your navigational skills will be tested. Cross the lake and turn right on Sullivan Creek Road—also FS 92—and follow the shoreline about 3 miles before veering west and beginning an ascent into the wild Yaak River country. A well-maintained gravel road climbs over a modest pass, where it remains FS 92 and also becomes the Yaak River Road. As you descend, you'll meet the tumbling waters of the Yaak from the right. At this point, you're less than 4 air miles from the Canadian border, and you might even come across a border patrol agent in a telltale white truck with green markings. When the road bends south, FS 276 juts off to the west toward **Garver Mountain Lookout,** one of four such towers in the area available as a recreational rental. If you're into roughing it a bit, these are unforgettable experiences.

After following the Yaak through private lands, look on the right for a pioneer cemetery amid the pines. Headstones dating to the late 1800s poke from a carpet of pine needles and are scattered widely around an American flagpole. The gravel road continues past an occasional private residence to the junction at **Yaak** (pop. 248), home to the **Yaak River Tavern & Mercantile** (406-295-5159) and the "World Famous" **Dirty Shame Saloon** (406-295-5439), now open year-round. The tavern's back deck serves up pastoral views of the lazy river and a nearby trail leads to trout fishing that remains solid despite decades of logging.

TROY'S LOCATION IN THE MOUNTAINS BELIES ITS ELEVATION

Heading south on the Yaak River Road, the first cascade of **Yaak River Falls** is easily seen from the highway and is quite photogenic. More interesting is the lower drop, where water slides down a flat slab of rock at about a 30-degree angle. Some of the exposed rock here is 1.5 billion years old. Also visible are the remnants of a mining bridge. Built in the 1880s as a route to the now-defunct mining town of Sylvanite, it was the first bridge across the Yaak.

After winding through the woods past many of those mysterious gravel two-track driveways, the Yaak River Road ends at US 2. Turn east to **Troy** (pop. 957), where the signs boast "Lowest in Elevation, Highest in Recreation." Set amid the pines and firs, Troy is the last Montana town before the Idaho state line on the Kootenai River, which collects a goodly portion of western Montana's waters. At a decidedly un-Montana-like 1,880 feet above sea level, Troy has relatively mild, albeit damp, winters.

Returning to Troy means you've completed the loop.

Best Places to Bunk

LIBBY: Libby has a few small motels that are comparable in providing adequate overnight stays, but the **Venture Inn** ($$, 406-293-7711) rates above-average marks. For the B&B experience, congenial hosts Keith and Ellen Johnston have the clean-as-a-whistle **Huckleberry House** ($$, 406-293-9720) on Main Avenue, with four rooms to choose from and their famous "huckle-licious" breakfasts starring huckleberry French toast. A few miles out of town, the **Bobtail Lodge B&B** ($$, 406-293-7175) has the creatures to go with the comforts, from wild deer and turkeys to domestic peacocks and laying hens that contribute to the farm-fresh breakfast. For a more secluded getaway, **Moose Ridge Cabin** ($$, 406-293-3960, May-Oct.) is in a pretty wooded area off US 2, about 14 miles southeast of town. It sleeps up to four, but is most comfortable for a couple.

YAAK: The hunting and fishing-oriented **Yaak River Lodge** ($$/$$$$, 406-295-5463) is a busy place down the road a piece from the two bars that make up the entire town. The lodge has six inviting suites, a communal flop-house with bunk beds on two floors, and a private fishing cabin open only in the summer that sleeps twelve. The lodge is situated on the banks of the river, just downstream from town.

SIDE TRACK

Pipe Creek Road (37 miles)

This is the Yaak River country of lore. Once you make the right turn at Yaak and cross the bridge, you're off the grid for more than 30 miles all the way to **Red Dog Saloon & Pizza** just north of Libby. The road is a single paved lane through dense thickets of fir, pine, larch and cedar, and the residences visible through the tangle range from primitive to comfortable. There's no cell service, so locals monitor traffic on CB Channel 22.

Along this route you're likely to see more deer or grouse than pickup trucks. Find the right local at the **Yaak Tavern** or **Dirty Shame**, and they'll tell you this is the best road for spotting Bigfoot. About five miles after crossing the river at Yaak, turn left at the mailboxes (Viral Lake Road) and go about another five miles to an open meadow where you'll find one of the resident Sasquatches, in all his glory, standing upright in a field. Don't panic: he hasn't moved in years.

Aside from the few homes and a camp for troubled kids that crop up, this drive is all about enjoying the utter stillness and unmistakable scents of conifers, especially cedar. The road carves a trough through towering trees and along the mostly invisible South Fork of the Yaak River until it reaches the Yaak Summit, marked only by spray paint in the road.

Descending toward Libby, you'll pass the junction for **Turner Mountain Ski Area**, whose lone lift provides access to twenty-five varied runs, with a 2,110-foot vertical drop from a summit elevation of 5,952 feet. It isn't Whistler, Sun Valley, Vail, or even Bozeman's Bridger Bowl, but Turner is among the most remote ski areas in America, so crowds are light. And at $37 for a full-day lift ticket (2014–2015), it's also light on your wallet.

The isolation of this area is epitomized by its lone interpretive site. Even if you *don't* blink you might miss it. Approaching the junction of Forest Service Road 336, just before the road becomes two lanes with yellow center stripes, keep a lookout on your right side. In a small, over-grown clearing you'll notice a weathered brown Forest Service sign with fading white letters. It explains the story of the first national Christmas tree to come from Montana, a 75-foot Engelmann spruce harvested here and presented to President Eisenhower in 1958. Even though it's less than 50 feet from the road, you'll either need binoculars or to scramble down the embankment through the scrub brush to read the sign—and good luck finding the stump that's supposedly still there.

THE HIGH POINT ON THE OFF-THE-GRID ROAD BETWEEN YAAK AND LIBBY

Soon after, the road widens you'll arrive at the Red Dog and Libby, which will seem like a metropolis after spending time in the Yaak.

TROY: **Troy Montana Log Cabins** ($/$$, 406-295-5810), on a slight perch about a half-mile west of town, has four clean and comfortable cabins, two that sleep up to eight and two others that are slightly smaller. All four have all the basic amenities. A fifth cabin has three bedrooms, two bathrooms, and a Jacuzzi tub.

Alternative Places to Bunk

TROY: The **City of Troy** ($, 406-295-4151) seasonally rents a five-person yurt on the Kootenai River for $50/night. Bring your sense of adventure along with your bedding, food, and dishes. **Kootenai River Campgrounds** (406-295-4090, May-Oct) has five tent sites and 25 RV sites in the pines on the river. They also have four cabins with bedding, electricity, and a fridge; three of them sleep two for $35/night and one larger one sleeps seven for $60. By the way, they haven't raised their prices in years!

FOREST SERVICE CABINS/LOOKOUTS (Reservations: 877-444-6777 or www.recreation.gov.): You've heard of rooms with a view? For views with a room, rent a forest fire lookout tower. In the Kootenai National Forest (406-293-6211) there are more for rent than on any forest in the Pacific Northwest—nine in all, including seven accessed from the Yaak-Koocanusa Route: The 45-foot-high **Yaak Mountain Lookout** ($35/sleeps four) near Troy, 41-foot **Big Creek Baldy Lookout** ($40/sleeps four) near Turner Mountain Ski Area, 40-foot **Mount Baldy/Buckhorn Ridge Lookout** ($35/sleeps four) west of Yaak, and 40-foot **Garver Mountain Lookout** ($35/sleeps four) northwest of Yaak. For cabins, primitive **McGuire Mountain** ($25/sleeps four) off MT 37 between Libby and Rexford has views of Lake Koocanusa and the Purcell Mountains, the spacious **Upper Ford Ranger Station** ($50/sleeps seven) just northeast of Yaak is accessible year-round on pavement, and **Webb Mountain Lookout** ($35/sleeps five) is a cabin 10 feet off the ground with views of Lake Koocanusa as well as Glacier National Park's highest peaks. Most lookouts and cabins are equipped with spartan beds, mattresses, and propane cook stoves. Some cabins are equipped with bathrooms, but the towers only have separate one-holers. These are extremely popular, especially in summer. It's wise to book well in advance.

Best Eats

LIBBY: The only town on the route with the usual fast-food suspects, Libby also provides some diversity. The best breakfast stop in town is the **Libby Café** ($, 406-293-3523, B/L), popular for its Montana Muffins (which can be shipped back home). Like many bakeries in Montana, the Libby Café takes advantage of the state's most famous local berry: the huckleberry, which only grows in the wild. **Red Dog Saloon & Pizza** ($/$$, 406-293-8347, D, closed Tuesdays in winter), north of town on the way to Turner Mountain Ski Area, is a quintessential community gossip, peanut shells on the floor kinda bar and eatery—with decent pizza to boot. The menu has a wide variety and everything's tasty. They're always busy, so you might have to park on the other side of the road. Also worth a try is the rustic **Antlers** ($$, 406-293-6464, B/L/D), which has a little bit of everything American.

TROY: Jack's Café ($, 406-295-4352, B/L) does little on the exterior to coax you in (and offers nothing special on the interior, for that matter). Oh, and the owner, Kathy, who's been cooking there since the 1960s, can be a bit crusty. But can she ever cook! And you won't believe the prices. Breakfasts are what you'd expect—no trimmings, but they cost around $5. Friday night prime-rib dinners bring folks out of the woods. If you show up late, you're probably out of luck and will just have to come back for breakfast.

YAAK: If it's deep fried deliciousness you're after, you'll find it at the **Yaak River Tavern and Mercantile** ($, 406-295-4706, L/D)—steak, chicken, fish, gizzards, pickles . . . you name it. And then there's the nachos (chips or tots), fries dripping in cheese 'n chili, flatbread pizzas, and even green salads. If you're lucky there'll be a pot of homemade soup or smoked and grilled specialties such as brisket or ribs. No matter what they've got cooking, you won't go away hungry, and you might get to hear about the latest Sasquatch sighting from the regulars unwinding on the wagon wheel bench out front. An outdoor music stage adds to the experience.

Best Bar

Time was, the **Dirty Shame Saloon** (406-295-5100) was one of the roughest, toughest, gnarliest bars in all of Montana. Loggers, shut-ins, gritty Forest Service workers, tattooed bikers, and even airmen from the now-defunct Yaak Air Force Base stumbled into the remote bar after hours, all looking for a stiff drink and, in many cases, a fight. The saloon's name was reportedly coined by one of the airmen who frequented what was then called the Yaak

THE DIRTY SHAME SALOON IN YAAK REMAINS WORLD-FAMOUS DESPITE BECOMING MORE GENTRIFIED IN RECENT YEARS

iver Lodge. It was, he said, "a dirty shame" that the place looked nothing like an actual lodge. Another legend has it that the great boxer Joe Louis once ordered a scotch at the bar, and when told they didn't have it, he reputedly replied, "That's a dirty shame." Why—or if—Joe Louis was actually in Yaak is lost to the dustbin of history. These days, John Runkle, owner of the Yaak River Lodge, owns "The World Famous Dirty Shame." He bought it out of foreclosure after the previous owner, a Maryland preacher, ran into some legal issues back home. Much to the chagrin of many locals, he had completely tamed the place, turning it into a family-friendly bistro—a theme that didn't align with the names carved into the planks, the bullets embedded in the walls, and a onetime owner who liked to shoot pool balls off the table with a pistol. Runkle is determined to restore a semblance of its previous unfettered heyday, minus the gunplay. Included in the plans are the return of the annual Crawdad Festival, Halloween costume galas, Monday night football parties, and re-emphasizing Harley Davidson orange.

DETOUR: ONE FOR THE ROAD

The Clark Fork Valley
St. Regis to Troy

ESTIMATED LENGTH: 134 miles
HIGHLIGHTS: Quinn's Hot Springs Resort, Noxon Reservoir, Ross Giant Cedars
GETTING THERE: St. Regis is about an hour northwest of Missoula on I-90. Take the MT 135 exit and begin the journey along the Clark Fork as it winds through the mountains toward its eventual end in Idaho's Lake Pend Oreille.

The official name of the broad river that serpentines through forests of ponderosa, lodgepole, larch, fir and spruce is the Clark Fork of the Columbia River, because Arlo Guthrie's famous hard-working river is its ultimate destination. The Clark Fork begins its life as Silver Bow Creek in Butte and collects enough mountain water while following I-90 to become a behemoth by St. Regis, where it leaves the interstate and briefly backtracks to the east before renewing its commitment to reaching Idaho. The entire drive is picturesque and is dotted with friendly little communities that beckon with cafés, ice cream stands, and inviting mom-and-pop motels.

St. Regis (pop. 319) is an old logging and mining community where the St. Regis River finishes its descent from the Bitterroot Mountains to the Clark Fork. Today it is playing well as a jumping-off point for tourists headed north to Glacier country and the Flathead region. Its primary claim to fame is Montana's largest flea market, which takes place over Memorial Day weekend. Popular for folks gassing up for the I-90 climb toward Lookout Pass on the Montana-Idaho border is the St. Regis Travel Center, which features a large trout aquarium.

MT 135 cuts for 25 miles through a weak spot in the Coeur d'Alene Range on the St. Regis-Paradise Scenic Byway toward **Paradise** (pop. 210), which sits at the junction of two railroads, the Clark Fork and Flathead Rivers, and three mountain ranges. Just before Paradise is **Quinn's Hot Springs Resort** (406-826-3150), which has six pools (including four soaking pools) in a pine-studded setting with 10 pet-friendly cabins (some with Clark Fork views), a lodge, suites, tavern, and a restaurant. Quinn's, open all year, is also known for its Montana Baroque Music Festival each July.

At Paradise, the road meets MT 200 and the Clark Fork becomes brawny with the addition of the Flathead River's waters. From here, you'll explore a series of logging and railroad communities that have evolved to exploit the numerous outdoor-recreation options in their backyards. Five miles up the road is **Plains** (pop. 1,064), once called Wild Horse Plains because Indians wintered their horses here. Plains has an appealing assortment of cafés, an ice cream stand and a charming little motel called the **Dew Duck Inn**. Signs along the highway caution travelers to look for bighorn sheep that cling to the rocky ridges of the Cabinet Mountains and occasionally wander onto the highway. The best place to see these majestic mountain creatures is

A MOOSE COOLS OFF IN THE MEANDERING BULL RIVER

SOME OF THE GIANT RED CEDARS AT ROSS CREEK ARE MORE THAN 2,000 YEARS OLD

the **Koo-Koo-Sint Bighorn Sheep Viewing Site**, a pullout with interpretive signs along the road near a field where the sheep frequently linger. Prime viewing time is in the autumn, when as many as 100 bighorns congregate. If you're lucky, you'll see rams in the annual rut battering each other with their distinctive curled horns, all in an effort to impress the neighborhood ewes.

Thompson Falls (pop. 1,338) was built for logging at the edge of a natural falls on the Clark Fork. Once upon a time, residents forced trains to stop here by putting logs on the Northern Pacific Railroad tracks. Now a dam has mostly inundated the falls and the locals are subtler, coaxing tourists to stop along the main drag using their cafés—especially **Minnie's**—and appealing lodging, and plenty of quaint shops for browsing. Just outside of town, **Thompson Falls State Park** is in a shaded, pleasant setting along the river, perfect for a picnic, fishing for trout in the small pond, or to camp as a base for exploring the surrounding mountains. If you're inclined to make this a more leisurely drive, leave MT 200 at Thompson Falls before the highway crosses and river and take Blue Slide Road as it slithers along the north bank.

Another 22 miles down the road is the recreation haven of **Trout Creek** (pop. 242), which marks the beginning of Noxon Reservoir. Trout Creek is a busy little place with a couple of marinas where motorboaters launch onto the fishing-rich waters of the reservoir. Nightlife here revolves around the cleverly named **Naughty Pine Saloon** and a St. Louis Cardinals-oriented sports bar with indoor and outdoor seating called the **Way Side** that's known for its homemade pizza dough and special sauces. The bartender/cook once lived in Seattle and has brought a taste of the Emerald City—veggie-oriented entrées, for instance—to Trout Creek. The **Lakeside Motel & Resort**, which has a bar, cabins for rent above the reservoir, and a restaurant popular for its steaks and fried chicken, is constantly abuzz with activity.

At Trout Creek, MT 200 re-crosses the reservoir and passes a U-pick blueberry farm hidden in the hills before arriving at the turnoff for **Noxon** (pop. 218). It's a lengthy drive across a one-lane bridge to the town, which is out of sight and out of mind for most tourists. Noxon does have a general store, tavern, and a grill open for lunch and dinner. Back on MT 200, for a supper-club atmosphere, there's the **Hereford Restaurant & Cocktail Bar**, a dark log structure tucked amid tall cedars. The menu runs the gamut from handcrafted pizzas, nachos, and wings to rib-eye steaks. And at Heron, which marks the junction with MT 56, or Bull River Road, the **Big Sky Pantry** has fresh-baked breads, cookies, desserts, ice cream, deli sandwiches, and farm-to-table meals.

Turn right on Bull River Road and follow the river as it winds along the western flanks of the Cabinet Mountains, providing periodic spectacular views. Look for moose in the meandering Bull River. Just before Bull Lake, you'll arrive at the turn for the 100-acre **Ross Creek Cedars Scenic Area**, which boasts 1,000-year-old trees with trunks as thick as 12 feet in diameter. Tucked in a gulch in what passes for a rain forest in Montana, these western red cedars clearly are survivors, having emerged unscathed from the scorching fires of 1910 and staring down flames again in the scorching summer of 2015 before Mother Nature provided 11th-hour clemency. The trees along the flat 1 mile-long interpretive trail are nearly as impressive as California's redwoods, and so are the thousands of human-made cairns rising from logs, bare ground, and the river rock course of Ross Creek. The road into the cedars is one lane but paved with pullouts. Bull Lake has a couple of campgrounds and lodging options, including the rustic and affordable **Bull Lake Guest Ranch**. Enjoy the views of the Cabinets the rest of the way to the junction of US 2 and Troy.

THE MISSOURI RIVER NEAR CRAIG IS A FLY FISHERMAN'S PARADISE

2

ON THE EDGE OF WILDERNESS

The Rocky Mountain Front

WOLF CREEK TO BROWNING

ESTIMATED LENGTH: 136 miles

ESTIMATED TIME: 6 hours to 2 days

HIGHLIGHTS: Milford Colony, Sun River Game Preserve, Old Trail Museum, Pine Butte Swamp Preserve, Teton Pass Ski Area, Miller Colony, Two Medicine Dinosaur Center, Egg Mountain, Museum of the Plains Indian, Scapegoat and Bob Marshall wilderness areas

GETTING THERE: From I-90, go north on I-15 out of Butte through Helena to the US 287 and exit 2 miles north of Wolf Creek. This is what Lewis and Clark referred to as The Gates of the Mountains. Upon leaving the freeway, you'll cross a strip of the Rocky Mountain Front into the prairie and the beginning of a drive that bobs all the way to Browning on the Blackfeet Indian Reservation.

OVERVIEW

The Rocky Mountain Front technically stretches from the Canadian border near Glacier National Park to northern New Mexico, but for the most part, only here can you see the great American prairie as it once was—sweeping, undulating, often-unscarred native rangelands rising gently to meet the sheer walls of the Northern Rockies and rugged Bob Marshall Wilderness, known simply to locals as "the Bob." This is the country of A. B. Guthrie, the famed author of westerns who lived outside Choteau. The region is so striking that it stirred a rare coalition of locals—ranchers, Blackfeet, business owners, recreationists, politicians, and even some energy companies—to protect the Front from oil and gas drilling as well as subdivision, so that it would retain its rugged character and all that comes with it for current and future generations. In late 2014, nearly forty years after the seeds of protection were first conceived, the Rocky Mountain Front Heritage Act was signed into law, ensuring that a roughly 100-mile strip from East Glacier south to Rogers Pass would be safe from exploitation. About 67,000 acres were added to the wilderness system, but the act also created a 208,000-acre special conservation zone set aside for traditional uses such as motorized recreation, timber thinning, and grazing, and has elements that help family ranchers remain on the land.

The movement began in 1977 when Pendroy taxidermist Dusty Crary and Choteau elementary schoolteacher Gene Sentz started Friends of the Front, with the support of ranchers and sportsmen who feared that encroaching energy development would end their way of life—as it already had in parts of New Mexico and Colorado. Their concerns were heard by Lewis and Clark National Forest supervisor Gloria Flora, who had the rare courage to ban drilling on the Front at a time when her brethren were rubber-stamping leases across the West. Because of those efforts, and because of the care that multigenerational cattle-ranching families have had for an unforgiving landscape where Chinook winds come howling off the mountainsides at up to 100 mph, people are living, working, and playing in harmony with nature here. And you get to immerse yourself in a rare world.

The Front has some of the nation's best intact wildlife habitat and is home to the second-longest elk migration in the United States. Grizzlies wander the foothills. In recent years, some have occasionally sauntered more than 100 miles across the plains to the Missouri River between Great Falls and Fort Benton, the first time in a century that the great bear has been seen on the edge of the Missouri Breaks.

The Rocky Mountain Front byway starts in ponderosa pines near the Gates of the Mountains at Wolf Creek and ends in rolling sage country just east of Glacier National Park in Browning, site of the Blackfeet tribal headquarters. Along the way you'll pass through the charming ranching and outdoor recreation communities of Augusta, Choteau, and Dupuyer. While Choteau was Guthrie's home, Dupuyer is the setting for many works by the acclaimed Western author Ivan Doig, who died in 2015. It'll take some discipline to resist the urge to gaze out the driver's side of the car toward the jagged Wailing and Castle Reefs, especially at sunrise and sunset.

Lodging and dining are available, but consider gearing up in Helena before you start. Take a tour of the state capital—its decor captures the essence of Montana's heritage as well as any building in the state.

HITTING THE ROAD

As you come north from Helena on I-15, you're on what was once a toll road through a pine canyon between Fort Benton and Helena. Today, **Wolf Creek** (pop. 510) is a jumping-off point for fishing the trout-rich Missouri River and Holter Lake.

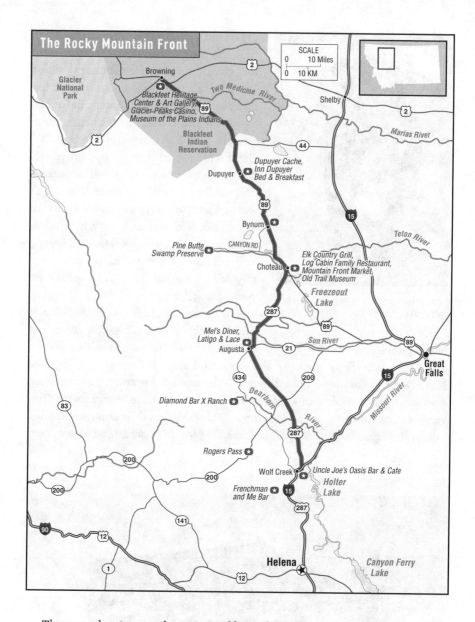

The Rocky Mountain Front

The route begins 2 miles past Wolf Creek at US 287 (Exit 228). The highway immediately begins a gradual rise out of the pines through the Front, denoted by rolling grass prairie, pine ridges, coulees, and periodic streams, starting with the Dearborn. Amid grazing cattle, look for mule deer and pronghorn antelope—the second-fastest land mammal in the world—in the 27 miles between I-15 and the junction of MT 200 at Bowman's Corners.

Coming into view in the west now are such limestone peaks as Blowout, Table, Steamboat, and Lone Chief, which rise from the **Scapegoat Wilderness Area**. Just past Bowman's Corners is the 12,000-acre **Milford Colony**, one

TWO HUTTERITE CHILDREN FROM THE MILFORD COLONY FROLIC IN RAINWATER

of 50 Hutterite communities across Montana and the state's oldest. The Hutterites (or "Hoots," as they are commonly called locally) are a self-sufficient, independent, and peaceful people of Eastern European descent who live simple agricultural lives similar to the Amish and Mennonites. Colonists frequently venture out to sell baked goods, produce, turkeys, chickens, and crafts in rural communities. Don't worry about feeling intrusive, despite an eerie lack of discernible activity. Follow the signs for fresh vegetables and fryers, and eventually a welcoming party, usually led by young boys in colorful suspenders, will greet you.

For the next 75 miles, wildlife, history, and western personalities are the name of the game. **Augusta** (pop. 309) is a sweet little cottonwood oasis near the Sun River, with great views of the Rockies. **Latigo & Lace** (406-562-3665, Mar.–Dec.) is a made-in-Montana gem with fine arts, pottery, photography, a wide array of books, an espresso bar, and a great deal more. Near Gibson, west of Augusta, is the **Mortimer Gulch National Recreation Trail**, a moderately challenging serpentine trek that features grassland views. This

THE OLD GILMAN BANK BUILDING IS NOW A PRIVATE RESIDENCE NEAR AUGUSTA

THE GILMAN STATE BANK

area is a popular starting point for hikers wanting to cross the Bob Marshall Wilderness Area and reach the sheer Chinese Wall, "the Bob's" signature geologic feature.

Inside the wilderness is the **Sun River Game Preserve**, established in 1913 as elk summer ranging grounds to salvage what was left of herds decimated upon the white man's arrival. Thirty-four years later, with the ungulates finally thriving again, the **Sun River Game Range & Wildlife Management Area** was created on the Front Range for wintering elk. It is one of the finest places in Montana to see a big herd. If domestic four-legged critters are more to your taste, the **Augusta American Legion Rodeo** in late June is Montana's oldest single-day rodeo.

Back on US 287, the highway eases away from the Front Range, but the views remain spectacular. About 25 miles northeast of Augusta is **Choteau** (pop. 1,694), which justifiably dubs itself "The Front Porch of the Rockies." Choteau is a comfortable town that's ideal for an overnight stay to explore the heart of this region. Before leaving, visit the **Old Trail Museum** (406-466-5332, May–Sept.), a collection of frontier buildings housing artifacts dating back to eras ranging from a century ago to millions of years ago. The museum, so named because it's on the 25,000-year-old Old North Trail once used by ancestors of the Blackfeet, is part of the state's Dinosaur Trail. It also has an exhibit high-

THE CITY PARK MIGHT BE THE ONLY PLACE IN AUGUSTA WHERE HORSES AREN'T ALLOWED

lighting the life of A. B. Guthrie, Jr., the first great Western writer born and raised in Montana. Certain to elicit a double-take is the display of an old French trapper standing upright despite an arrowhead lodged in his spine.

While in Choteau, veer north on US 89, though if you're a bird aficionado, take an hour-plus detour southeast about 12 miles to **Freezeout Lake**, a key spot on a migratory flyway for prolific flocks of waterfowl. In March, as many as 300,000 snow geese and 10,000 tundra swans from points south converge on their annual journey northward to Canada and the Arctic; they return in the fall. Other fowl and raptors are there year-round. Returning to Choteau, continue northwest on US 89 about 9 miles to the junction with Canyon Road, which follows the Teton River west past Eureka Reservoir and opens up the Front to a wide variety of recreation opportunities (see Side Tracks).

As you continue on US 89, note the Hutterite **Miller Colony** before arriv-

Pine Butte Swamp/Teton Pass Ski Area: Choteau to West Fork (60 miles)

Among the many desirable options for access into the alluring mountains dominating the western skyline, the one with the most bang for your half-day buck is Teton Canyon Road about 5 miles northwest of Choteau. A highlight is The Nature Conservancy's 15,500-acre **Pine Butte Swamp Preserve** (406-443-8311, see sidebar), a vast and stunning plains wetlands complex at the edge of the mountains. For an extraordinary weeklong experience, you could arrange an all-inclusive stay at TNC's **Pine Butte Guest Ranch** ($$$$, 406-466-2158, May–Sept.) and take part in nature courses, workshops, and conservation-related activities in stunning landscapes. Teton Canyon Road is straight and paved all the way to the mouth of the canyon, and along the way there are no fewer than three designated hiking trails epitomizing the diverse terrain: **Mill Falls Trail** is an easy hike through thick forest, **Clary Coulee Trail** represents the rolling prairie landscape, and **Green Gulch Trail** combines both with a nice dose of mountains. For winter enthusiasts, the picturesque **Teton Pass Ski Area** (406-466-2209) is a small family ski area with two lifts (no lines), twenty-six runs, and 1,010 feet of vertical drop. In the summer, continue past the ski area and over a small pass where the picturesque West Fork and its smattering of summer cabins unfolds far below. On the return trip, turn south on Bellview Cutacross Road past Pine Butte. Stop at the interpretive marker, grab your binoculars and take the short hike to a ridge offering an expansive view of the swamp. If you see a foraging grizzly bear in the distance, consider yourself among the fortunate few—a mighty griz on the prairie is a rare sight indeed. Dusty Bellview Road back to Choteau offers a Guthrie-esque experience of sprawling ranches, a one-room schoolhouse, and a breathtaking rearview mirror panorama of a wall of mountains.

Recreation Road: Prickly Pear to Hardy (35 miles)

Don't let a quick glance at a map dissuade you from taking this route, despite the presence of nearby Interstate 15. Recreation Road (and, later, the Craig Frontage Road) does parallel the moderately busy freeway, but you'll hardly know it's there as you follow Prickly Pear Creek and an abandoned Burlington Northern Santa Fe Railroad spur through a pretty canyon of vermillion rock before reaching the brawny Missouri River. Highlights include the fly-fishing meccas of **Craig**, **Wolf Creek**, and **Tower Rock State Park**. Coming north from Helena, exit I-15 onto Recreation Road just past the Sieben Ranch, owned by the family of longtime Montana Senator Max Baucus. Stay on what becomes Craig Frontage Road at Wolf Creek, which has two bar/restaurants, a gas station, a fly shop offering guided fishing on the Missouri, and accompanying lodging popular among fly anglers. After Wolf Creek, forested mountain terrain immediately opens up and it's a couple of miles to the Wolf Creek Bridge over the Missouri. Two miles on gravel to the southeast is the dam backing up **Holter Lake**, which provides the explanation for the procession of driftboats and rafts you'll see on the road and the river from this point all the way to Hardy and beyond to Cascade. The dam releases water from the bottom of the reservoir—and this steady flow of clear, cool, nutrient-rich "tailwater" makes for at least 25 miles of trout fishing rivaling the Bighorn, Madison, and Yellowstone Rivers. Though the river doesn't appear to change character much, it actually has four or five distinct sections where the approach to fishing changes. A bridge crosses the river at Craig, which you'll readily notice is the hub of all of this fly-fishing activity. It has a vibrant bar/restaurant, several angling shops, and lodging. Less than five miles past Craig, the Missouri serpentines through another pretty canyon with a blend of modest year-round residences and trophy homes. The route ends at **Tower Rock**, a 424-foot-high igneous rock formation that served as an important landmark for traveling Indians. Explorer Meriwether Lewis described it as a tower in his journal in July 1805 and saw it as a gateway to the Rocky Mountains. Members of the party climbed the rock and expressed wonder at the thousands of bison on the prairie they'd just crossed. Tower Rock is a day-use area only and is worth a quick stop if you can ignore the landfill at its entrance.

ing in **Bynum** (pop. 31), a diminutive town with a giant dinosaur—in fact, the world's longest. The **Two Medicine Dinosaur Center** (406-469-2211) is home to the skeletal display of a *Seismosaurus* and also features the remains of the first baby dinosaur found in North America. The museum has regular summer hours but requires an appointment during the rest of the year. While you're there, ask about joining a dig at **Egg Mountain**, an excavated area beneath a rise on US 89 just south of Bynum. Fossilized eggs were found in ancient *Maiasaura* nests discovered there in 1983, and dinosaur bones are consistently unearthed to this day. Across the road from the museum in Bynum is the **Trex Agate Shop** (406-469-2314), which has to be seen to be believed. John Brandvold's selection and collection of rocks, gems, and artifacts is updated annually and rivals anyone's anywhere. It was his wife, Marion, who found the first nest of baby dinosaurs at Egg Mountain in 1978, five years before the paleontologists. Her life is quite a story (she died in 2014 at age 102) and it's well worth a sit and chat if you catch John, who was 20 years her junior. Like the museum, the shop has regular summer hours and is open by appointment at other times.

Angling northwest of Bynum, the highway continues its rolling course toward **Dupuyer** (pop. 86), an endearing one-blink town along Dupuyer

Creek. For goodies, the quaint **Dupuyer Cache** (406-472-3272, 11am–5pm, Wed.–Sat.) combines many of the amenities of an old mercantile, from groceries and dry goods to local honey, crafts, and wool that comes from the Big Hole Valley.

A few miles outside Dupuyer is the southern boundary of the 3,000-square-mile **Blackfeet Indian Reservation**, home to about 8,500 tribal

The Front: Where the Mighty Griz Roams the Prairie

Once upon a time, the mighty grizzly bear, king of the wilderness food chain, roamed the Great Plains by the tens of thousands. But by the late 1800s, westward Anglo expansion and a determined extirpation effort pushed the great bear into small mountain nooks, mostly in Greater Yellowstone and the Crown of the Continent bordering Canada at present-day Glacier National Park.

A notable exception is the Pine Butte Swamp Preserve, where the grizzly has continued its annual spring migrations from the expansive Bob Marshall Wilderness Area to the prairie. In 1979, The Nature Conservancy purchased these 15,500 acres of foothills, prairie, and a 500-foot sandstone butte solely to provide a lowland outlet for the grizzly, which arrives via the Teton River riparian corridor.

Grizzlies have made a solid comeback in the Northern Rockies in the past three decades, though they remained under Endangered Species Act protections as of mid-2015 because of uncertainty over the future of some of their primary food sources. Except for the Pine Butte Swamp Preserve and a small slice of the Blackfeet Indian Reservation to the north, though, they still generally aren't tolerated on the prairies.

Our willingness to live with these majestic and fearsome creatures is being tested. With grizzly numbers expanding in wilderness areas and national parks, more are wandering onto the grasslands in search of new space. Some have roamed as far as 100 miles onto the plains here. Montana wildlife officials typically trap the bears and return them to the wilds. Grizzlies are occasionally seen in creek bottoms all along the Front and have been in Dupuyer. Expectations are that grizzlies will continue to move to lower elevations in search of food, raising fears of increased conflicts between humans, livestock, and bears. When that happens, bears usually die.

At Pine Butte, the mindset is different. It's the bear's world, and humankind is to tread lightly. Spend a week here in the summer or just visit for a weekend in the spring or fall, and marvel at the idea that somewhere amid the cottonwood and juniper in a creek bottom, a grizzly is contentedly living the way its ancestors did more than a century ago.

DOWNTOWN AUGUSTA, GATEWAY TO THE ROCKY MOUNTAIN FRONT

members. The once-powerful Blackfeet, frequently referred to as "The Lords of the Great Plains," believe they were created on these lands about 6,000 years ago. The Blackfeet (it's "Blackfoot" in Canada) call themselves Piegans or Pikanni. Among Indians, they have the unique distinction of retaining their most sacred lands, though it's largely because Anglos had little use for the blustery high plains.

US 89 crosses nearly 40 miles of foothills scrubland, dipping and rising in and out of creek and river bottoms, before arriving in the Blackfeet capital of **Browning** (pop. 1,079). It can feel as if you've entered a foreign country, and in a sense you have, given that the tribes technically are sovereign. It's also obvious that times are tough for the Blackfeet. But as they undergo a cultural rebirth of sorts, Browning is becoming more hospitable. One example: where the Rocky Mountain Front drive ends, with US 89 meeting US 2, is the **Museum of the Plains Indian** (406-338-2230, $5 in summers/free Oct.–May), a must for anyone who appreciates the rich history of Native peoples. No fewer than 11 Plains tribes are represented here. The museum is under the auspices of the Indian Arts and Crafts Board, so you know you'll be getting their stories in words and pictures. The

TOURISTS CAN SIGN UP FOR DINOSAUR DIGS NEAR EGG MOUNTAIN AND EXPECT TO UNEARTH FOSSILS

A BIGHORN SHEEP PEERS AT A RARE INTRUDER ON THE ROAD TO TETON PASS

Blackfeet Heritage Center & Art Gallery (406-338-5661, Mon.–Sat. summers) is another place to get an understanding of Indian culture. The center sells jewelry, moccasins, beadwork, baskets, drums, and other Native items. In Browning, mark your calendars for the second week of July and the **Northern American Indian Days**, a four-day powwow where colorful teepees seem to extend to the horizon.

For fishermen, the Blackfeet Reservation is a paradise of lakes, rivers, and streams. Due to their belief that these waters hold mystical powers, the Blackfeet traditionally haven't fished, and so there are dozens of small lakes and potholes, eight large lakes, and nearly 200 miles of streams filled with big trout and other species. Stop in Browning for a tribal angling permit. Browning does have a few motels and restaurants, but more appealing options are in East Glacier—about 15 miles west but still on the reservation.

Best Places to Bunk

WOLF CREEK: Wolf Creek Angler ($/$$, 406-235-4350) is the place to stay if you're looking to hook into some trout. They have four detached cabins, each with railroad-themed signage prominent above the front doors. Also available are four connected motel rooms and three bungalow rooms with kitchens. Fishing supplies, guides and free advice are a roll cast away, and the parking lot is always filled with SUVs or pickups tugging driftboats and rafts. Limited lodging is available through the winter. More secluded is the **7 R Guest Ranch** ($$, 406-235-4207), a hideaway that's actually a handful of RV sites and motorcourt-esque motel rooms on gurgling Little Wolf Creek. A large country dining room is open to the public from May to New Year's Day. Rooms are dated but clean, and there are throwback resin picnic tables outside the rooms. Back in the day, owner Ron Adams was a touring singing cowboy. If you're lucky, he'll play a dinner set or two on weekends. To get there, take MT 434 northwest of Wolf Creek about 3 miles to where the gravel-topped Little Wolf Creek Road veers to the left. Take the fork and drive another 2 miles or so.

AUGUSTA: In this two-horse town, the choice with the most personality is the **Bunkhouse Inn** ($, 406-562-3387), an Old West-style hotel in a century-old structure. It has nine neat-as-a-pin rooms, each sharing the two bathrooms at either end of the hall. Aimee and Dylan Lennox have done a meticulous job of retaining the historic character of the reputedly haunted building (ask Aimee for a ghost story). The **Diamond Bar X Ranch** (406-562-3279, May–Oct.) south of town offers nine guest cabins, full equine accommodations, and a campground with RV hookups in the Dearborn River canyon.

CHOTEAU: Choices are limited, but **the Stage Stop Inn** ($$/$$$, 406-466-5900) is the most appealing, especially to families with kids, because of its indoor pool—the only heated pool within 50 miles, the hotel's managers like to say. A hot breakfast is included in their seasonal rates. It is a non-smoking, no-pets facility, but they have a dog kennel in back to accommodate the many hunters who stay in the fall.

DUPUYER: The **Inn Dupuyer Bed & Breakfast** ($$, 406-472-3241), is a century-old hand hewn log home restored and renovated specifically for lodging. Three single rooms and a two-bedroom suite each have their own bathroom. Your stay is completed by a full western breakfast, easy access to outdoor exploration and activity, and sensational mountain views.

Alternative Bunking

CHOTEAU: "Camp the Front" at **Choteau Mountain View Campground** ($, 406-466-2615 May-Oct) in one of their 49 RV sites, 20 tent sites, or three cabins ($50). In this relatively urban setting, at least by small-town Montana standards, they have running water in the camp but showers require an additional fee.

FOREST SERVICE: A plethora of Forest Service campgrounds are in the Lewis and Clark National Forest west of Augusta and Choteau, with two cabins recently added to the roster. The one-room **Kenck Cabin** ($45/sleeps six) near Choteau was built in 1924 by a local doctor/dentist. The family donated it to the Forest Service in 2003 upon the death of the last surviving son. The cabin, which has no running water or electricity, is on the National Register of Historic Places. The **West Fork Cabin** ($45/sleeps six) just past the Teton Pass Ski Area is available only in the winter, when it isn't manned by the Forest Service. As for campgrounds, **Home Gulch** (fifteen sites) and **Wood Lake** (nine sites) are 20 and 24 miles west of Augusta, both peaceful places on a lake where motorboats are prohibited. Two miles beyond Wood Lake is **Mortimer Gulch** (twenty-eight sites), which has a boat launch and is the largest of the Rocky Mountain Front campgrounds. Another 4 and 5 miles up the road are **Benchmark** (twenty-five sites) and **South Fork** (seven sites) campgrounds, both popular jumping-off points for Bob Marshall Wilderness forays. Another four campgrounds are northwest of Choteau: **Cave Mountain** (fourteen sites), **Elko** (three sites), **Mill Falls** (four sites), and **West Fork** (six sites). Elko and Mill Falls are free, and the other two offer quick access to "the Bob."

Best Eats

WOLF CREEK: Save your appetite for the **Uncle Joe's Oasis Bar & Grill** ($$, 406-235-9992, L/D), on the east side of the freeway in Wolf Creek. The grill side specializes in top-shelf food, including hand-pressed burgers with unique toppings, creative soups, and their most expensive dinner entrée: an extra-large New York steak with all the trimmings. In the dead of winter, the kitchen takes a break.

AUGUSTA: **Mel's Diner** ($, 406-562-3408, B/L/D) has serviceable made-to-order to meals, but what keeps plenty of folks coming back are the generous scoops of Wilcoxson's ice cream and the homemade pies. Mel's does serve dinner (known 'round here as supper), but only until 7 PM. Just down the street, the amiable Kerry will get you what you're hankerin' for at the **Lazy B Bar & Cafe** ($, 406-562-3397, B/L/D); she's the mother of the owner, after all. Whether it's their famous biscuits 'n gravy, a bowl of homemade soup, a fresh handmade pizza, pork riblets, or just a slice of pie, they'll get 'er done. It's located in the 1883 Augusta Hotel, which was billed as "a quiet place to meet gentlemen friends" back in the day.

CHOTEAU: Despite the natural beauty of the lands to the west, the tourist trade can be sparse in Choteau. So the restaurants work together and share the limited wealth by not being closed on the same days. The **Elk Country Grill** ($$$, 406-466-3311, L/D, Mon.–Sat.) is a favored spot for a sizzling steak, elk medallions, or a seafood entrée accompanied by homemade soup, a bottle of red wine, and a slice of pineapple upside-down cake or fresh-baked pie for a finish. For lunch, give the Indian taco a twirl. The **Log Cabin Family Restaurant** ($$, 406-466-2888, L/D, Tues.–Sun.) is renowned for bison burgers, steak, a succulent walleye dinner, and a selection of 20 to 25 home-baked pies. The giant hanging flower baskets adorning the outside of the restaurant come courtesy of the owner's other business, the nursery next door. **John Henry's** ($, 406-466-5642, B/L/D Wed.–Mon.) offers large portions of classic Montana fare for modest prices. Choteau is also hip enough to have a health-food store—the **Mountain Front Market** (406-466-2684, 11 AM–6 PM Mon.–Sat.)—stocked with all the requisite healthy food and drink for a long hike into the Front country or for cooking your own meals.

Best Bar

AUGUSTA: Montana bars and taxidermy are synonymous, but the classic western **Buckhorn Bar** ($/$$, 406-562-3344, B/L/D) in Augusta takes animal wall mounts to another level. Several dozen on the log beams overhead preside over you as you chow down on their famed broasted chicken (Grandma Dellwo's secret spice blend is in the coating) and handmade Montana beef burgers. All menu items are less than $10 except for the 16-ounce rib steak with baked potato and salad, for just under $18. The Buckhorn opens at 8 AM and closes at 2 AM, making it one of the few good choices in the area for early or late eats; after 10 PM, you'll have to settle for a pizza. The Buckhorn has been in the Dellwo family for four decades and is a regional icon. Before it burned to the ground in 1974, the kitchen was in a trailer off to the side. Now the Buckhorn is in an attractive and intimate log building, complete with a photo on the wall of Grandpa Dellwo's smiling face. He seems to be saying: "Life is *all good* in Montana."

WOLF CREEK: Like a good pair of used waders, the well-worn and well-loved **Frenchman and Me** ($/$$, 406-325-9991, B/L/D) is an enjoyable place to unwind after a day of casting to trophy trout on the Mighty Mo. As you'll readily notice by the photos and artifacts on the walls and tables, the fishing roots run deep here. The historic cinder-block building west of I-15 was once a mercantile owned by the family of Jessie Burns, who met *A River Runs Through It* author Norman Maclean at a Fourth of July festival here and eventually married him. Norman and his younger brother, Paul, took Jessie's Hollywood brother, Neal, on a fishing adventure near here that's revisited in the movie. The mercantile eventually became a bar and, in later years, a grill was added before it evolved into the all-purpose watering hole Tim Hefner owns today. Hefner, an Irishman, never got around to changing the bar's name to reflect his heritage. He did get around to skillfully serving up favorites such as heaping plates of biscuits and gravy, the region's best broasted chicken, and a belly-satisfying rib-eye steak dinner. The ubiquitous Montana staple—burger 'n fries—is renowned and hard to beat for under 10 bucks. And Tim's mean Bloody Mary will help you quickly forget about all the big ones that got away. Beer, wine, and a full bar means you can find whatever you're angling for and, if your timing's right, you'll be treated to local musicians showcasing their talents. Also important: The Frenchman and Me is the only year-round restaurant between Helena and Cascade.

DETOUR: ONE FOR THE ROAD

The Kings Hill Scenic Byway
White Sulphur Springs to Belt

ESTIMATED LENGTH: 71 miles
HIGHLIGHTS: Spa Hot Springs Motel, Showdown Ski Area, Neihart, Monarch, Sluice Boxes State Park.
GETTING THERE: Exit I-90 just east of Livingston at US 89 and drive north through Clyde Park, Wilsall, and Ringling—of Ringling Brothers Circus fame—until you reach White Sulphur Springs.

Sometimes "scenic byway" isn't always about the scenery. Case in point: the Kings Hill Scenic Byway. Oh, there is plenty of classic Montana landscape to see. The distant Crazy, Bridger, and Absaroka mountain ranges ring the skyline, looking like so many sets of bad teeth.

Nevertheless, when the U.S. Forest Service—which owns a fair chunk of the real estate on this route—deemed the 71 miles between White Sulphur

Springs and Belt one of its "scenic byways," there was an ulterior motive. The Forest Service motto is "Land of Many Uses," and few drives in Montana display the state's three-pronged utilitarian history more than this one. The majority of the drive is through the modest Little Belt Mountains, an isolated 1,800-square-mile range that rises to more than 9,000 feet and is the first stretch of Rocky Mountains visitors see coming from the east on US 12. Surrounding the Little Belts are ranchlands with Angus cattle as far as the eye can see. Scattered throughout the pine- and fir-covered range is extensive evidence of the land's grazing, logging, and mining history. It is, in many senses, a snapshot of Montana.

The Forest Service wants you to understand and, hopefully, appreciate an extractive legacy that is waning in favor of recreational and aesthetic values on public lands. Kiosks at both ends of the route describe the hum of industry that once echoed across the hillsides. Distant checkerboard hilltops with young stands of lodgepole pine surrounded by mature trees reveal a timber industry gone silent. Rusted and splintered remnants of mining operations are visible from the road at once-booming Neihart. Cattle and periodic gas wells show that the utilitarian age isn't completely over. Even the recreation here tends toward the motorized: snowmobiles in the winter, all-terrain vehicles in the summer.

That said, don't be dissuaded by the lack of jaw-dropping vistas. There is plenty of charm here. In addition, if you're national park-hopping between Yellowstone and Glacier, this is both the most direct and most intriguing route. It offers the healing waters of the **Spa Hot Springs Motel** at White Sulphur Springs, where you can soak away the aches of a hard day and then literally enjoy pizza and a movie at the same time at **Stageline Pizza**. At Kings Hill Pass, it also features **Showdown**, the oldest continually operating ski area in Montana. Heading down the north side, **Neihart** and **Monarch** are the living remnants of the area's mining days. As you emerge from the mountains, **Sluice Boxes State Park** offers a peek into mining history and, when the water levels are right, a thrilling whitewater ride reminiscent of the log flumes at amusement parks.

At the end of the route is the little community of Belt, which has recovered from the demise of the coal mining industry and a devastating train derailment in 1976 to become a charming evening getaway for residents of Great Falls. The **Harvest Moon Brewing Company** in Belt is admired regionally for the microbrews (most notably the Beltian White) offered in its tasting room and elsewhere. For dinner, try the **Black Creek Brew Pub.**

3

A RIVER RUNS THROUGH IT

The Big Blackfoot

MISSOULA/BONNER/POTOMAC/OVANDO/
LINCOLN/WOLF CREEK

ESTIMATED LENGTH: 120 miles
ESTIMATED TIME: 3 to 7 hours
HIGHLIGHTS: Milltown Dam project, Lubrecht Experimental Forest, Blackfoot Challenge, Rogers Pass, river recreation, wildlife viewing
GETTING THERE: Drive east from Missoula on I-90 through Hellgate Canyon to East Missoula and Bonner. Exit the freeway at Bonner on MT 200.

OVERVIEW

To put it in the words of the Blackfoot Valley's most famous native, the writer Norman Maclean, all things really do merge into one here—and a river really does run through it. The Blackfoot exemplifies all that is Montana: Top-shelf outdoor recreation on the Blackfoot and in the mountains flanking it. Spectacular wild landscapes, including the densest population of grizzly bears on private land. An extractive tradition of mining, logging, and agriculture has supported livelihoods but has also threatened to despoil a river and landscape. Longtime residents cherish the land with such uncommon passion that they decided to do something about it, ultimately creating one of the world's pioneering land management models.

The Blackfoot is where Prince Charles and Princess Diana sent one of their sons, Prince William, to escape the glare of paparazzi lights while enduring their highly public divorce. It is also where the anarchist Ted Kaczynski, a.k.a. The Unabomber, holed up in a cabin without running water or electricity and taught himself survival skills before his eventual arrest in 1996. And as if to prove nothing about the Blackfoot is average, it was on its upper reaches, at Rogers Pass, that the coldest temperature

THE BLACKFOOT RIVER WAS MADE FAMOUS BY NORMAN MACLEAN'S NOVELLA *A RIVER RUNS THROUGH IT* ever in the lower 48 states was recorded: minus 70 degrees Fahrenheit on Jan. 20, 1954.

Mostly, though, the Blackfoot is about "keeping Montana Montana"—an orchestrated effort by multi-generational ranch families, conservationists, business leaders, and government agencies to preserve a way of life that has been lost in similarly picturesque valleys such as the Bitterroot and Paradise, which have been sliced and diced into 20-acre ranchettes. This desire manifested itself nearly three decades ago out of concern for an ailing river, and can be seen today in The Blackfoot Challenge, an inspiring collaboration worth stopping to learn more about in little Ovando.

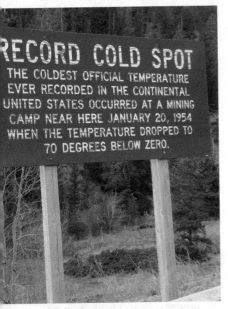

THE TEMPERATURE DROPPED TO MINUS 70 DEGREES ON ROGERS PASS IN 1954, THE LOWEST EVER RECORDED IN THE LOWER 48 STATES

Like many projects that unify strange bedfellows, The Challenge started with the recognition that most residents—liberal or conservative, private landowner or public employee, fly fisherman or bait angler—loved the Blackfoot for mostly the same reasons. And they could all agree on looming threats to their lifestyles: The possible expansion of a leaky mine at the Blackfoot's headwaters that already was fouling a once-legendary fishery. The prospect of vast timberlands being sold and developed into the aforementioned 20-acre parcels. And the likelihood of federal government intervention to save the river. They met, leaving their biases and disagreements (on wolves, for example) outside, and learned to listen and trust. The result has been an encouraging three-legged stool of economic, environmental, and quality-of-life successes, many of which are evident not by what you see (unless you know where to look) but by what you *don't* see.

Streams and trout populations have been restored. Grizzly bears, once considered a nuisance, are a source of pride, a symbol of stewardship and a reminder of just how unique this part of the world is. Even wolves are tolerated because ranchers coordinating with wildlife biologists have learned how to avoid livestock conflicts. With the reintroduction of trumpeter swans to a lake on the private Rolling Stone Ranch near Ovando, all of the wildlife species that were here when Meriwether Lewis wandered through with a small party more than 200 years ago are back on the landscape. And ranchers have discovered, perhaps counterintuitively, that working *with* nature's rhythms instead of against them is more efficient, more economical and more conducive to an improved quality of life.

The Blackfoot Challenge has been lauded as the future blueprint for successful land and water management. It is being emulated worldwide. And the benefactors are not only the people who live, work, and play in the Blackfoot, but also the people like you who get to explore its backroads and experience a naturally functioning world, as Norman Maclean might describe it, "with dew still on it."

HITTING THE ROAD

The Blackfoot backroad starts just east of Missoula, at a site that exemplifies this landscape's remarkable evolution from pristine to despoiled to pristine again. On the south side of Interstate 90 at **Bonner** (pop. 1,663), where the Blackfoot empties into the Clark Fork River, is a wide plain of stumps, gravel, and debris, with a river running through it. A few years ago, a small reservoir backed up behind the Milltown Dam here, accumulating mining toxins that arrived from more than 100 miles upstream at the Warm Springs Ponds near Butte and Anaconda.

The Milltown Reservoir complex was the largest federal Superfund site in the West due to arsenic contamination traced to as far back as a 1908 flood that spread through the years. Cleanup was made a priority in the early 1980s and the results are right before your eyes: The removal of the 100-year-old dam in 2008, the disposal of more than 3 million tons of contaminated sediments, and the restoration of natural flow and vegetation to the Clark Fork River. It'll be many years before the area around the confluence of the Blackfoot and Clark Fork returns to its pre-industrial look, but one day the only evidence of Milltown's toxic history will be spelled out on interpretive kiosks in the **Milltown State Park**, which opened in 2014.

In many ways, Bonner epitomizes the region's evolution. Once a logging town with a humming plywood mill, the community is exploiting its prime location as a recreation gateway to the Blackfoot country. Stop at **Two Rivers Memorial Park** next to the MT 200 Blackfoot River bridge and call ahead for a tour of the **Bonner Milltown History Center & Museum** (406-258-6335) to get a close-up peek into a rich history.

As you work your way out of town, you'll see more of the old and the new. The massive mill sold in 2008 and is being revamped to an industrial park with several businesses, including an aluminum trailer manufacturing facility. The new owners also bought the row of 120-year-old company-town homes on the northeast edge of town, with plans to restore and rent them.

Heading out of Bonner on MT 200, you'll meander through a pretty

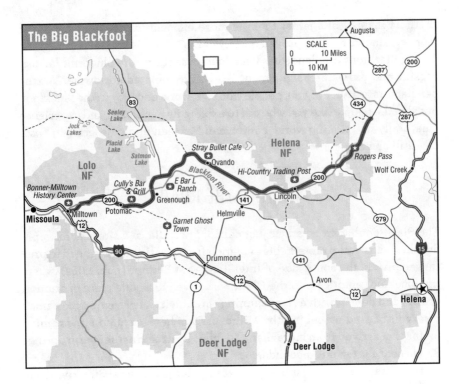

canyon with slopes blanketed by ponderosa pines. Look for bighorn sheep that come out of the hills for Blackfoot water. There are several campgrounds and river-access points for floaters along the way. Around mile post 12, look carefully for the hand-painted signs pointing over the creek and through the woods to **Steel Toe Distillery** (406-244-4567, Wed.–Sun 12–7 PM), where you can sample their whiskey and gin. At the little wayside of McNamara Bridge, **Blackfoot River Rentals** (406-244-0404) has rafts and tubes for floating the river, and also provides shuttle service. Here's where you'll need to make a decision: Continue on MT 200 for a more expedient drive through pastoral ranchlands or turn left onto the dirt and gravel Johnsrud Park Road (and eventual Ninemile Prairie Road) to stay with the Blackfoot for about 18 miles (see Side Tracks) until you rejoin the main highway at Greenough. The benefits: This is the photogenic Blackfoot of postcards and brochures, the ultimate destination for many anglers and floaters, especially fanatics of splash-and-giggle Class II–III whitewater. The downside: You'll miss **Potomac,** home to **Cully's Bar & Grill** (406-244-3100), a Blackfoot Valley fixture that reigns as the valley's top watering hole (see Best Bar).

    Greenough (pop. 250) had its brush with royalty—literally—in 1992 when the U.K.'s Prince Charles and Princess Diana sent their 10-year-old son, William, to the rustic **E Bar L Ranch** to give him a break from the attention surrounding their divorce. Owners of the guest ranch said William had a marvelous time until British tabloid media discovered his whereabouts, forcing him to flee again. The E Bar L (see Lodging) is more noteworthy locally for its conservation ethic, which provided the first roots for The Blackfoot Challenge project.

At Greenough, look for Garnet Range Road, which provides twisting, winding access to **Garnet Ghost Town** high in the Garnet Range to the south (see Side Tracks). Garnet is considered one of the two or three best examples of an intact ghost town in Montana, thanks largely to a preservation group from Missoula. Speaking of Missoula, less than a quarter-mile

SIDE TRACKS

Johnsrud Park Road/Ninemile Prairie Road (18 miles)

To fully understand why the Blackfoot River is so popular, pack a picnic, veer off MT 200 at McNamara, drive the gravel road to Barite, and watch floaters or fishers ply revered waters. The entire 18-mile drive through what is known as the **Blackfoot River Recreation Corridor** is scenic, but the best stretch for pulling over to watch rafts, kayakers, and tubers navigate Class II–III whitewater is in the first six miles after the turnoff.

Though there are eight boat launches in this short stretch, many rafters, kayakers, driftboaters, and tubers launch at Whitaker Bridge and take out at Johnsrud, ensuring they get to navigate Thibodeau Rapids, the river's most popular whitewater. Fishermen love this stretch, too, because the trout aren't as finicky as they are in some of the more placid waters of the Blackfoot above and below this canyon stretch. Despite the presence of recreationists, you'll feel as if you've entered wild country. It's a world of whitewater, cliffs, and ponderosa pines that goes right up to the river's edge—a distinct change from the beautiful but wide-open valley dotted by ranches and small communities on MT 200.

Garnet Ghost Town (24 miles)

Montana is littered with ghost towns from its mining days, but in the competition for most visited and best preserved, two emerge: Bannack near Dillon and **Garnet Ghost Town** in the Garnet Range east of Missoula. Bannack lives on as a state park; Garnet survives after three boom-and-bust eras, thanks to the Garnet Preservation Association in Missoula.

Garnet, named for brown garnets found in the mountain range of the same

(continued on next page)

name, first flickered to life when gold was discovered in the area during the Civil War. At one point, nearly 5,000 people lived in the region, but most were gone within three years when gold prices plummeted. The area was reinvigorated in the late 1800s and eventually had four hotels, a school, doctor's office, stores, and thirteen saloons serving 1,000 residents. Within a decade, though, the gold again played out. The town fell into disrepair and many buildings were destroyed by a 1912 fire.

A rise in gold prices during The Great Depression brought prospectors back in 1932, but then came World War II and the need for miners to enlist in the military. Garnet has been a ghost town ever since, having produced about $18 million in gold (at today's prices). For a time, it appeared harsh winters and souvenir hunters would render Garnet a footnote in history, but in the early 1970s the federal government decided the remaining buildings were too valuable as a cultural treasure to be lost. Since then, the Bureau of Land Management and the Garnet Preservation Association have ensured the town's future as the Garnet Historic District.

Just getting to Garnet is an adventure, whether you're coming from the Blackfoot Valley or over what was once known as China Grade from the Bearmouth area along the Clark Fork River. From MT 200, the first 3 miles are paved, but after that, the road twists and turns on gravel while rising more than 2,000 feet into the Garnets. You'll want to stop periodically and look over your shoulder at the Blackfoot Valley far below and spot the southern end of the Bob Marshall Wilderness to the north. In the winter, this becomes part of the 31.5-mile **Garnet National Winter Recreation Trail System**, with the road groomed for snowmobiles and cross-country skiing. It's especially popular among Missoula residents. Bear Gulch Road to Bearmouth is equally scenic and provides a glimpse into just how difficult it was to get mining equipment to Garnet. Authors' note: We are especially fond of Bear Gulch and Garnet, given that it's where we saw our first bear in the wild in Montana.

past Garnet Range Road and Mile Marker 22 is the turn for the University of Montana's 28,000-acre **Lubrecht Experimental Forest** (406-244-5524), an outdoor classroom for forestry and conservation students. It's a great place to learn about modern management of forests. Or stay overnight (see Alternative Bunking) and enjoy outdoor recreation, including fishing the Blackfoot, hiking, and skiing amid the pines on trails maintained by the Missoula Nordic Ski Club. For a far swankier experience in the Blackfoot, the sprawling and elegant **Paws Up Resort** (see Lodging) seems almost out of place, with its upscale log homes, spa, a restaurant with an executive chef, Wine Spectator Award of Excellence, and other all-inclusive amenities befitting Jackson Hole or Sun Valley.

Just down the road from Greenough is the arrival of the appropriately coined Clearwater River, which drains the glacial region around Seeley Lake. A gas station, convenience store, and tavern mark Clearwater Junction, while MT 83 veers north past a string of shimmering lakes through the lonely Swan Valley toward Bigfork. On the northside of MT 200 here is the 77,000-acre **Blackfoot-Clearwater Wildlife Management Area** (406-542-5542), which was created to provide prime winter range for an impressive elk herd but also is known to have grizzly bears and wolves.

After Clearwater Junction, the valley broadens and the Blackfoot River comes and goes as MT 200 points east toward the little oasis of **Ovando** (pop. 50). To the south beyond the invisible Blackfoot are the Garnet Mountains, where remnants of an intense logging history are visible, and to the north is the yawning mouth of Monture Creek, which offers a peek into some of Montana's wildest country in the form of the Swan Mountains and Scapegoat Wilderness. It is along Montour Creek where you'll find the largest concentration of grizzly bears on private lands in the lower 48. It is beautiful country for hiking, but always—always!—take bear spray.

Ovando packs a tremendous punch for such a tiny community. The Ovando-Helmville Road takes you a half-mile off the highway into a small cluster of inviting buildings, including the stately century-old **Ovando Inn,** the **Blackfoot Angler** fly shop, pottery and bead shops, and headquarters for The Blackfoot Challenge, where anybody who happens to be hanging around the office will passionately offer a brief tutorial. The **Stray Bullet Café,** owned by a fifth-generation Blackfoot Valley family, clearly is the nerve center of the upper Blackfoot and the place to go to understand what makes Blackfoot denizens tick. **Trixi's Antler Saloon and Family Diner,** named for a female trick-roper who bought it in the 1950s, is a fine place to sit on tractor-seat stools and nurse a cold one after a day of fishing the Blackfoot.

Past Ovando, the valley gradually begins to narrow. The road bends past Copenhaver Park, crosses the North Fork Blackfoot River, and arrives at the junction of MT 141 to **Helmville** (pop. 369), the sled dog racing capital of Montana, thanks in large part to prodigious snowfall. Four-time Iditarod champion Doug Swingley lives near here, as does fellow longtime musher John Barron. The annual 300- and 100-mile Montana Race to the Sky, dubbed the "Iditarod of the Lower 48," starts in Lincoln and passes north of here through Seeley Lake en route to the turnaround at Owl Creek.

After following the Blackfoot's serpentine course, MT 200 begins to climb noticeably after its meeting with MT 141. Before long, you're amid towering ponderosa pines and entering **Lincoln** (pop. 1,100) at the eastern terminus of the Blackfoot Valley. It's easy to see why The Unabomber wanted to hole up here, given the wild mountain surroundings in every direction. Lincoln

AN OSPREY NEST TOWERS ABOVE THE BLACKFOOT RIVER ON A DEAD PINE TREE

is named for a nearby gulch where gold was discovered at a time when the White House had a somewhat famous occupant attempting to end slavery. Only a cemetery remains from the original community. Today, Lincoln serves as a hub for summer and winter recreation, much of it motorized. To safely appreciate the sheer size and power of a grizzly bear, stop by the **Lincoln Ranger Station** to admire a stuffed but life-like giant that once roamed the vicinity.

Lincoln has the usual assortment of convenience stores, saloons, motels, and short-order cafés with burgers, but one standout is the **Hi-Country Trading Post** (406-362-4203) two miles west of town on MT 200. The trading post is an expansive log building with room to roam amid trophy mounts, shelves of souvenirs, regional books and art, and made-in-Montana flavors such as wild-game seasonings, jams, jellies, fudge and, of course, all things huckleberry. The store is a neighbor to Hi-Country Snack Foods Inc., which began in 1976 as a modest producer of jerky made from wild game. Rapid growth has led to a 28,000-square-foot operation that's one of the county's top employers. The trading post also serves as the official finish line for the Montana Race to the Sky.

From Lincoln, the ascent toward **Rogers Pass** becomes more pronounced. Rogers sits at a modest 5,610 feet on the Continental Divide, but there was nothing modest about January 20, 1954, when at a nearby gold camp the mercury registered minus-70 degrees—the coldest temperature ever recorded in the United States outside of Alaska. It's possible that it was actually colder, but the gauge at the camp stopped working once the temperature eclipsed its low point. The gauge monitor, a fellow named H.M. Kleinschmidt, was actually awakened in the night by the sound of cabin timbers popping from the cold. The same westerly winds that can make Rogers wickedly cold also make the area a draw for raptors, most notably golden eagles. Every spring and fall, eagles and thirteen other avian species ride the thermals on their annual migrations north and south. Birders come from all over the nation to get remarkably close glimpses of hundreds of golden and bald eagles. The sign for the viewing site is about nine miles east of Rogers Pass on MT 200.

After the viewing area, MT 200 descends onto the undulating Rocky Mountain Front where you can take MT 434 across ranchlands south to Wolf Creek or north to Augusta, or continue on to the end of the Blackfoot route at the junction of US 287 at Bowman's Corner.

Best Places to Bunk

OVANDO: Mike and Liz Raymond's **Ovando Inn** ($$, 406-793-5555) has six rooms atop a country store in a century-old building that long ago was the Cooper Hotel and Elkhorn Bar. Each room, named after a key figure in Blackfoot Valley history, features a private bath and is decorated with furnishings and art that reflect the area's history.

GREENOUGH: The **Paws Up Resort** ($$$$, 406-244-5200) is the swankiest lodging for many miles in any direction, one of those all-inclusive settings in the pines where you can come for a day, week, or longer, and never leave because all you need is on site. There are twenty-eight luxury cabins and another thirty one- and two-bedroom "tents" with bathrooms, showers, and heated floors fit for generals or kings. More befitting the classic Montana

The Big Blackfoot: 'Where all things merge into one'

In parts of southwest Montana—most notably Bozeman, Livingston, and Missoula—it is often referred to simply as "The Movie." Though the state has been a picturesque stage for dozens of films, none has been so transformative as *A River Runs Through It*, director Robert Redford's adaptation of the 1976 novella penned late in life by Missoula native Norman Maclean, who wrote eloquently about family, fly fishing, and living "at the junction of two great trout rivers in Missoula, Montana" in the early 20th century.

Expectations were modest in 1992 upon release of the film, starring Tom Skerritt as a fly-fishing Presbyterian minister presiding over a family in which his sons, Norman (Craig Sheffer) and Paul (Brad Pitt), saw "no clear line between religion and fly fishing."

Yet *A River Runs Through It* resonated because of its artistic meshing of family tragedy, the grace of fly fishing, commitment to Maclean's poetic writing, and cinematography so engrossing it won an Academy Award. The result was a migration boom to the region that continues to this day. Tens of thousands of fishermen and women came to southwest Montana brandishing fly rods and waders, a yearning to connect with a simpler era on unspoiled landscapes, and wallets overflowing with cash for the purchase of trophy log homes. The fly-fishing industry grew by sixty percent in 1992 and 1993 as flotillas of boats jammed the Blackfoot, Madison, and Yellowstone Rivers, among others.

Because the Macleans' "family river," the Blackfoot, was so despoiled by mining, logging, and agriculture by the late 1980s, most of the film's locations were on the Gallatin River south of Bozeman, on the Yellowstone River in and around Livingston, and at places in the Boulder River valley still relatively unscarred.

Thus, trophy homes sprouted up from the Paradise Valley south of Livingston to Big Sky and the Bitterroot Valley south of Missoula. Bozeman's evolution from a college cow town to the trendy, vibrant place it is today likely was inevitable, but "The Movie" certainly hastened its dramatic shift to a persona that some old-timers derisively refer to as "Boz-Angeles."

On the flip side, "The Movie" also helped with the restoration of the Blackfoot, which has improved significantly as a fishery in the past two decades. It also helped defeat a proposed mine at the river's headwaters.

Many of the movie's landmarks still stand in the Bozeman area: The ocher grain elevator where a fistfight took place, the courthouse, and, of course, the giant boulder in the Gallatin atop which a fisherman, his fly rod and line uncoiling with artistic perfection, graces the film's poster. In Missoula, visitors sign up for tours of the Blackfoot so they can explore the cabin the Rev. John Maclean built at Seeley Lake, see and smell the family's cherished river, and be "haunted by waters". A literary festival in his honor debuted in the summer of 2015 in Seeley Lake and a second is set for 2017.

Maclean died in 1990, two years before the film's release and well before he could see results that no doubt would have spawned mixed feelings. Meanwhile, Redford, a devout conservationist, was so chastened by the impact *A River Runs Through It* had on western Montana that when he returned six years later to film *The Horse Whisperer* on the Boulder River, he intentionally omitted locations in the credits.

"When I am alone in the half-light of the canyon, all existence fades to a being with my soul and memories and the sounds of the Big Blackfoot River and a four-count rhythm and the hope that a fish will rise," Maclean wrote as a prelude to the words every fly fisher has committed to heart: "Eventually, all things merge into one. And a river runs through it."

experience is the 4,000-acre **E Bar L Ranch** ($$$$, 406-244-5571), where a conservation ethic took root under first owner Bill Potter nearly a century ago. The E Bar L has a lodge for dining and communing, and a collection of cabins that look as if they were plucked straight from a hunting camp.

LINCOLN: The Hotel Lincoln ($/$$, 406-362-4822), a landmark with a colorful history dating to the area's gold-rush days of the 1870s, has had a checkered saga carrying into the 21st century. This vast log structure, with twenty-two rooms and a bathroom on each floor, was built by Leonard Lambkin in 1928. Over time, bathrooms were added to rooms and updates continued until 1999, when the total number of rooms was reduced to fourteen. It has been an open-and-shut business, reopened under new local management in 2015 with grand visions. The rooms are tiny but have attractive rustic western accents, and there's a restaurant with outdoor seating (May–Sept.) overlooking Spring Creek. If you're into the paranormal, ask to stay in Room 17.

Alternative Places to Bunk

Lubrecht Experimental Forest ($/$$, 406-244-5524): If you're looking for a place to have a group hug, the hostel-esque lodge at Lubrecht has 16 rooms that can sleep up to 34, along with a fully stocked kitchen and shared bathrooms down the hall. For a little more privacy, primitive cabins and boxcars sleep three or four. How primitive? For an extra $10, you can actually get a set of linens. The closest thing to luxury might be the apartment, which is fully furnished and sleeps up to four; check for availability, because researchers occasionally have lengthy stays there.

Best Eats

BONNER: The **River City Grill** ($$/$$$, 406-258-2758, B/L/D) is an oasis of grass and history amid the bustle of a busy truck stop just off I-90. It is housed in the century-old former headquarters of a lumber company. You'll get the standard assortment of steaks, seafood, and pastas for dinner, specialty sandwiches for lunch, and truckers' breakfasts served until 2 PM. Though not a Mexican restaurant per se, River City does have some Tex-Mex offerings and likes to showcase something called The Matador, a burrito that's distinct for its secret sauce.

OVANDO: At just about any time of day, the world's challenges—mostly agriculture-related—are being solved at the **Stray Bullet Café** ($/$$, 406-793-4040, B/L), a western-themed restaurant owned and run by a fifth-generation Blackfoot ranch family. The café has heaping helpings of what you'd expect at a gathering place for ranchers, with a twist: a "Giddy Up 'N Go" take-and-bake menu of enchiladas, lasagna, and spaghetti. Ask Colleen where a stray bullet from late-1800s cowboy revelry is lodged in the wall.

LINCOLN: At **Bushwhacker's Steakhouse and Saloon** ($/$$, 406-462-4424) and **Lambkin's of Lincoln** ($/$$, 406-362-4271) you'll get the standard Montana fare in places with distinct local personality. Locals like to gather at both, and Lambkin's is the place for eggs, bacon, and pancakes.

Best Bar

POTOMAC: The folks at **Cully's Bar & Grill** (406-244-3100, B (Sat.–Sun./ L/D) will smile when you tell them that their burger is just awful . . . good. The Awful Burger is the signature serving at Potomac's busy hub, which also has a gas station, convenience store, and full-service restaurant. That you can sit by a fireplace, shoot pool, or catch a game on the big screen is all due to Joe Johnson, who resuscitated the place after it closed in 2008, leaving Potomac without a gathering spot that had dated to when the bar was a tiny log cabin perched on a nearby hill. Johnson opened his iteration of the business in 2010, rechristening it after his grandfather's nickname, and has restored an important part of the community fabric in the process. All the burgers are hand-made; the "awful" is a thick half-pounder festooned with ham and melted cheese. Fish and chips, tuna melts, fried chicken dinners, and other beef from Diamond Bar Meats give the menu added pop. The bar is open until midnight on weekdays and until 2 AM on Friday and Saturday nights.

DETOUR: ONE FOR THE ROAD

The Swan
Clearwater Crossing to Bigfork

ESTIMATED LENGTH: 89 miles

HIGHLIGHTS: Seeley Lake, Blackfoot-Clearwater Wildlife Management Area, Salmon Lake, Clearwater Canoe Trail, Seeley Lake Game Preserve, Holland Lake Falls, Old Squeezer Loop Road, Swan River National Wildlife Refuge, Swan Lake

GETTING THERE: From the west, leave I-90 at Bonner (Exit 109) just a few miles east of Missoula and follow the Blackfoot River upstream to the junction of MT 83 at Clearwater Crossing. From the east, either turn off I-90 at Garrison (Exit 174) and go east on US 12 for 14 miles to Avon, then drive northwest on MT 141 about 33 miles to the junction of MT 200. From there, go west through Ovando for 24 miles to Clearwater Crossing. For an occasionally faster route: Remain on I-90 to County Road 271 (Exit 154) at Drummond and drive north 22 miles through Helmsville to a meeting with MT 141. Continue on through Ovando to the junction with MT 83.

Nowhere in Montana—not even in Glacier National Park—is the work of glaciers so visibly evident than along the Seeley-Swan scenic drive, a spectacular 90-mile-long corridor that could leave the unsuspecting visitor wondering if he or she had awakened in Minnesota. The towering Mission Mountains to the west and Bob Marshall Wilderness to the east quickly dispel that notion. Still, driving from the southern end of this route on MT 83, near **Seeley Lake** (pop. 1,436), has the feel of the Land of 10,000 Lakes, with one after another connected by the Clearwater River. It's called the Clearwater Chain of Lakes, and it contains anywhere from six to 24 lakes, depending on your perspective. They're popular with Montanans, especially motorboaters and water-skiers.

Even after ascending a small divide and leaving the lakes behind on the way to **Bigfork** (pop. 4,270), the Seeley-Swan carves a straight northwesterly swath through a valley that rivals the forested isolation of the remote Yaak Valley. Many Montanans think of this as the "deer route" because of the

THE FOLKS WHO NAMED THE CEMETERY IN SEELEY LAKE OBVIOUSLY HAVE A SENSE OF GALLOWS HUMOR

prolific populations of whitetails that linger near the highway, especially in the early morning and at dusk; special care is required when driving this beautiful stretch. The route culminates at Swan Lake and then Bigfork, an artsy community on the shores of giant Flathead Lake.

The route begins innocuously enough at Clearwater Crossing, where the namesake river flows into the Blackfoot. Three miles into the drive, though, the area's natural richness becomes apparent. The **Blackfoot-Clearwater Wildlife Management Area**, known simply as "The Game Range" in local parlance, is 67,000 acres of forest and grasslands with more than 3,000 wintering elk, mule deer, and whitetail deer; it's the largest Montana Fish, Wildlife & Parks wildlife area in the state. Large elk herds are visible in the fall after arriving from the Bob Marshall Wilderness to spend the winter before returning to "The Bob" in the summer.

Once you've passed the smallish Elbow, Harpers, and Blanchard Lakes, the largest of the Big Six in the chain of lakes soon comes into view on the driver's side. **Salmon Lake** has a 42-acre state park with 20 campsites and is one of the best places in Montana to see up to 200 loons. Also noteworthy here is the western larch, a common conifer tree across western Montana that turns yellow and sheds its needles in the fall. A mile past Salmon Lake is the turn for **Placid Lake**, 3 miles up North Placid Lake Road. The lake also features a state park with a campground; anglers know the lake for its prolific population of landlocked kokanee salmon. Back on MT 83, the town of Seeley Lake is the hub of the southern end of the valley, luring folks from across the West to stay in cozy cabins amid ponderosa pines and ply the shimmering waters of the town's namesake lake. For a good chuckle, note the sign on the cemetery just before arriving in town: "The Best Last Place." There are three Forest Service campgrounds on the lake, and the town has an attractive assortment of lakefront motels, cabins, lodges, and dining options to serve as bases for exploring the region.

Four miles north of town is the start of a short drive to the Seeley Lake Ranger District via the **Clearwater Canoe Trail**, identified by a sign on MT 83. The river meanders away from the highway through a peaceful willow marsh with a wide variety of birds and other wildlife; the area adjoins the **Seeley Lake Game Preserve**. No motors are allowed on the water, and after 3.5 miles of paddling, if you don't feel like making the return trip, you can always leave the canoe at Seeley Lake and hike back on a well-maintained trail. At the upper end of the Clearwater are three more lakes in short order: **Inez, Alva,** and **Rainy**. Each has fishing access, and Inez and Alva have Forest Service campgrounds. After Rainy Lake, lakes are still out there—though most of them are smaller and require some effort to reach. The largest is **Lindbergh Lake**, a 3-mile drive west on Lindbergh Lake Road. Lindbergh, which has a Forest Service campground as well, is part of the chain of lakes on the Swan River. A mile north of the Lindbergh Road turnoff is Holland Lake Road, which leads 3 miles east to Holland Lake and a 1.5-mile hike through fir, pine, and larch on the **Holland Lake Falls National Recreation Trail** to a spectacular cascade. **Holland Lake Lodge**, overlooking the lake, offers rustic lodging with dining.

Back on MT 83, the only town between Seeley Lake and Swan Lake is **Condon** (pop. 343). The Forest Service rents two primitive cabins here for folks interested in a pure backwoods experience: the Condon Work Center and Owl Creek Cabin. For lodging with a lot more comfort, there's the **Standing Stones Bed & Breakfast**. From there, MT 83 continues a forested journey through national forestlands and onto the **Swan River State Forest**, which includes a unique wildlife-viewing experience on the **Old Squeezer Loop Road**. The hiking trails near the forest's headquarters are popular among birdwatchers. Farther north on MT 83, on the southern tip of picturesque Swan Lake, is the 1,568-acre **Swan River National Wildlife Refuge**, created in 1973 as another sanctuary for migrating waterfowl.

Swan Lake is nearly 20 miles long and is known to fishermen for its kokanee, northern pike, and trout. The little village of **Swan Lake** has become popular for its more than 50 miles of groomed Nordic skiing trails and two campgrounds north of town.

After traveling the east side of the lake for 20 miles and passing through **Ferndale**, MT 83 bends left and emerges from the Swan River Valley into a congested but charming area signaling your arrival in the Flathead. Bigfork is one of Montana's favorite destination playgrounds, especially in the summer. Its picturesque setting where the river dumps into placid Flathead Lake bay has become a draw for its quaint shops, high-end restaurants with creative chefs, galleries, live theater, marina, golf, and related activities. Bigfork has envisioned this persona for itself since 1937, when a major fire gutted the Bigfork Hotel and allowed the town's fathers to rethink its future. The result was an 18-room Swiss chalet–style hotel reminiscent of Glacier National Park's lodging; it was renamed the **Bigfork Inn**, and it became a magnet for the rich, the famous, and tourists passing through.

Plan to spend a day in Bigfork. Rent a bike or kayak, book a charter boat or sailboat cruise, look for birds and wildflowers along the "Wild Mile" **Swan River Nature Trail**, play eighteen holes at **Eagle Bend Golf Club**, take in a show at the **Bigfork Summer Playhouse**, roll out a blanket for the Sunday evening **River Bend Concert Series** at Sliter Park, or picnic at **Wayfarers State Park** just south of town. Or simply wander amid the shops on Electric Avenue—named for the town's most prominent feature, a century-old hydroelectric dam on the Swan River. There is a wide assortment of lodging and dining from which to choose.

The next destination is **Polson** (pop. 4,604), on the south shores of Flathead Lake. With 180 miles of shoreline, Flathead Lake is the largest freshwater lake in the western United States. The Flathead River empties into the northern end of the lake and leaves just west of Polson, which has two fun museums and a decidedly destination-vacation atmosphere. The **Miracle of America Museum** has a transportation emphasis and is full of surprises, including a 65-foot caricature of Paul Bunyan, among its more than 100,000 items. A more traditional museum is the **Polson-Flathead Historical Museum**; it has a cluttered collection of homesteading artifacts and also boasts Nessie the Flathead Monster—the mount of a 181-pound sturgeon caught in the lake. The Port Polson Players provide a great evening diversion on display during the summers at the **Polson Theatre on the Lake**. Shoppers won't want to miss **Three Dog Down** (406-883-3696), famous for its down comforters, pillows and other items that provide warmth on those cool Montana nights.

To get to Polson, drive south on MT 35, which hugs the eastern shore of the lake and undulates through the cherry orchards for which the Flathead is famous. (If you want a wine fix, drive US 89 on the west shore to Dayton, home of **Mission Mountain Winery**.) If you want to catch the cherry trees in bloom, come early to mid-May. The cherry harvest is typically from mid-July to mid-August, and roadside stands are seemingly in every wide spot in the road.

Flathead Lake State Park is composed of six units, including Finley Point and Yellow Bay on the east side. Finley Point features a sixteen-site campground amid tall pines and cherry orchards on a skinny arm that juts into the lake—ideal for launching a boat and fishing. Yellow Bay is farther north on MT 35, and its five campsites accommodate people who come to pick the cherries in nearby orchards. Another 10 wooded miles north is Woods Bay, the last tiny hamlet before the trendy and touristy **Bigfork**.

BEAVERSLIDE HAYSTACKERS ARE HISTORIC LANDMARKS IN THE LANDSCAPE OF THE BIG HOLE VALLEY

4

THE LAND OF 10,000 HAYSTACKS

The Big Hole Valley and Pioneer Mountains Scenic Byway

DILLON TO WISE RIVER TO JACKSON

ESTIMATED LENGTH: 113 miles

ESTIMATED TIME: 6 hours to 2 days

HIGHLIGHTS: Beaverhead River, Bannack State Park, Jackson Hot Springs, Big Hole National Battlefield, Big Hole River, Pioneer Mountains, Elkhorn Hot Springs, Maverick Mountain Ski Area

GETTING THERE: From I-90, there are two ways to come at this diverse loop—both involving I-15. Start at the Divide exit on I-15 and cut through the Big Hole River Canyon on MT 43 to Wise River, where the loop begins either with an immediate left turn onto the Pioneer Mountains Scenic Byway or by continuing west along the Big Hole River toward Wisdom. Another approach is to start and finish in Dillon. Take Exit 59 three miles south of Dillon and drive west, following the signs for Bannack State Park and Wisdom. In about 20 miles, you'll have to decide whether to continue straight toward Jackson and do a clockwise loop, or veer right and follow Grasshopper Creek to go counterclockwise between the East and West Pioneers. We suggest going clockwise.

OVERVIEW

Even in the heart of summer, watching silver-tipped clouds race just overhead is enough to make a knowing Montanan shiver. The Big Hole Valley is known for extreme cold—cold air, cold water, and bone-chilling history. The air in this high mountain valley in the far southwest corner of the state is so crisp and dry that hay is safely stored in the open, stacked by the stately wood-plank beaverslide haystackers that look like giant catapults from

CATTLE, HAYSTACKERS, AND MOUNTAINOUS BACKDROPS ARE FIXTURES ON THE PIONEER MOUNTAINS SCENIC BYWAY

medieval days. The water is so brisk that the sparkling Big Hole River is home to a native population of fluvial Arctic grayling, a revered native fish making its last river stand in the Lower 48 here. And speaking of last stands: you can't help but feel a bit melancholy upon visiting the haunting Big Hole National Battlefield, where the peace-loving Nez Perce's gallant pursuit of freedom in 1877 suffered an irreparable blow along the North Fork of the Big Hole River.

This is the Big Hole country, a remote and rugged region spreading out below the backbone of the Rocky Mountains. The Lewis and Clark expedition explored this country in 1805 on its journey west—and then years later returned over Gibbons Pass west of present-day Wisdom. In fact, William Clark himself came up with the name "Wisdom," a nod to President Thomas Jefferson's foresight. The river's name was changed to the Big Hole before the 19th century was out, but Wisdom lives on in a tiny community that looks much like a setting for a shoot-'em-up western.

The symbol of the "Land of 10,000 Haystacks" is the beaverslide, invented and patented in the valley in 1910 and a staple today even as other regions evolve to more modern technology and smaller stacks. These giant wooden contraptions are responsible for the prolific large stacks of hay throughout the valley. Though many haystackers in the Big Hole are now made of metal, the technique is the same: Horses or tractors use belts to ease the hay up the slide and then flip it over into a roll the size of a small barn. For a time it appeared the beaverslide would go the way of the passenger pigeon, but it's undergoing a revival as high fuel costs have ranchers looking for more economical ways to preserve a lifestyle.

HITTING THE ROAD

We suggest starting and finishing the Land of 10,000 Haystacks/Pioneer Mountains Scenic Byway loop in **Dillon** (pop. 4,219), where you'll find all the necessary services. Dillon is a longtime ranching, logging, and mining town evolving into a place where aesthetics, wildlife, quiet recreation, and intrinsic values are of equal or greater importance to earlier activities. The upgrade of its four-year school, Montana Western, from a teachers' college to a full-fledged university, along with a gradual influx of newcomers, is changing the culture. That said, the town is in no immediate danger of becoming a Bozeman, Missoula, or Whitefish, even though the environs are just as beautiful, rugged, and appealing.

Dillon has several worthwhile stops. The **Beaverhead County Museum** (406-683-5027, Mon.–Fri.), in a log building along the railroad downtown, offers an array of pioneer artifacts, including the city's first flush outhouse toilet, a homesteaders' cabin, mammoth bones, and plenty of old mining and logging equipment. A mile northeast of town on MT 41, **Clark's Lookout State Park** (406-834-3413) is on a bluff overlooking the Beaverhead River where Captain William Clark, separated from a fretting Meriwether Lewis and his party, climbed on August 13, 1805, to survey the valley. The pair reconnected three days later at a site now submerged in Clark Canyon Reservoir south of Dillon.

To get to the loop, leave I-15 3 miles south of Dillon at Exit 59 and head west on MT 278. After traveling through sage and grass ranchlands over modest Badger Pass, with the East and West Pioneers rising dramatically to the north, you'll drop into the valley of Grasshopper Creek. Once over the pass, look for signs pointing the way to **Bannack State Park** (406-834-3413), site of the best-preserved ghost town in Montana. Turn left on Road 5, drive 3 gravel miles, and look for the turn along the creek bottom. For a few years in the mid-1860s, Bannack was the first territorial capital of Montana, thanks to a huge gold discovery there. One reason the buildings are so well-preserved is that gold was mined there as late as the 1950s. When the last miners left, the state designated Bannack a state park. More than 60 structures remain, most open to public exploration.

Back on MT 287, you'll soon arrive at the junction where the actual loop

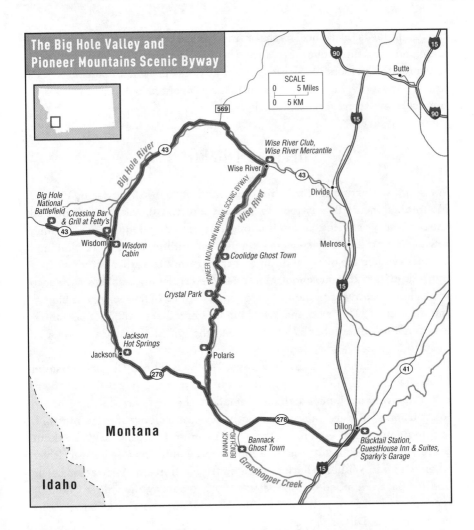

The Big Hole Valley and
Pioneer Mountains Scenic Byway

SCALE
0   5 Miles
0   5 KM

Montana

Idaho

begins. The right fork continues up the Grasshopper Valley toward Polaris and Wise River; we suggest continuing on over Big Hole Pass into the Big Hole Valley. As you cross the Big Hole Divide, sweeping views of the upper valley likely will provide the first sighting of the beaverslides and giant haystacks. In the distance are the dramatic Beaverhead Mountains.

Appearing like a dot amid the wide-open spaces is **Jackson** (pop. 134), built around its namesake hot springs. Soak in the enclosed and family-friendly **Jackson Hot Springs** (406-834-3151) mineral pool, which is a bit rustic, yet clean and chemical-free. This is a Montana landmark with a welcoming bar, restaurant and lobby area for lounging. At the north end of the short main street, in an old white church, the **Buffalo Gal Hat Company & Gallery** (406-834-3236) is ready to outfit you with hats, gloves, photos, gift items, or just good conversation.

For the next 18 miles, you'll see enough Angus cattle to feed a small nation before you reach **Wisdom** (pop. 98). Turn left on MT 43 and head another 10 miles to the **Big Hole National Battlefield** (406-689-3155), one of the most poignant sites on the 1,170-mile **Nee-Me-Poo Trail**. It was here, on an eerily quiet August night in 1877, that the fate of more than 750 Nez Perce led by Chief Joseph was sealed (see sidebar). Be sure to ask to see the film when you go to the visitor center, which underwent repairs and restoration in 2011. If you're lucky, you might see a moose browsing on willows in the deep marshy river bottom below.

The visitor center remains open in winter, but you probably won't be able to access the battlefield trails unless you have snowshoes or skis. If you do have them, after exploring the historic site be sure to also continue west on MT 43 toward **Lost Trail Pass** (406-821-0025) for some of the best-groomed Nordic skiing in Montana at **Chief Joseph Cross-Country Ski Trails**—not to mention solid downhill skiing and a hot springs swimming pool at the pass to soothe tired muscles.

IN THE COLD, CLEAR WATER OF THE BIG HOLE RIVER, THE ARCTIC GRAYLING IS MAKING ITS LAST STAND IN THE LOWER 48 STATES

"I Shall Fight No More Forever"

Of all the Indian tribes encountered by settlers of the frontier, none earned more respect and admiration than the Nez Perce of Idaho, eastern Oregon and Washington, and western Montana. They helped Lewis and Clark cross the Bitterroot Range during a bitter winter, perhaps saving the expedition. They were as receptive to the white man's ways as any tribe. Many became Christians and changed their names to reflect their conversion.

Yet their cooperative and peaceful ways didn't prevent the Nez Perce from suffering the same shameful fate as the rest of their brethren in the late 1800s—banishment to reservations on a fraction of their ancestral lands.

For the Nez Perce, life amid their natural riches ended in 1877 after a remarkable three-month pursuit that covered five states and 1,170 miles. Many Nez Perce had already signed a treaty requiring the tribe to move to a small reservation in northern Idaho, but a handful of "nontreaty" members led by Chiefs Joseph, Whitebird, and Looking Glass refused to leave much larger homelands that were ceded to them in a previous treaty.

Ordered to move his people and livestock to the Idaho reservation, Joseph instead began a march eastward, hoping to find sanctuary with the Crows in south-central Montana—unaware that the tribe had aligned with the cavalry and had fought with Custer at Little Bighorn. For weeks, Joseph and his 700-plus Nez Perce—two-thirds women and children—outwitted General O. O. Howard and his 2,000 soldiers. They even handed the army a defeat at White Bird Canyon above Idaho's Salmon River in mid-June, shortly after leaving the sacred Wallowa country of northeastern Oregon.

After crisscrossing the Bitterroots between Idaho and Montana, the turning point came on August 9th at the Battle of the Big Hole west of present-day Wisdom. Until then, the Nez Perce had the upper hand in their skirmishes even as they fled, but the loss of 25 warriors at Big Hole left them on the defensive. They crossed the five-year-old Yellowstone National Park, where they killed two tourists, and ascended the Absaroka Mountains into the Clarks Fork of the Yellowstone River Valley. Once back into Montana southwest of Billings, they discovered the Crows wouldn't help because they feared retribution.

From there, the Nez Perce charted a course due north, hoping to find a new home in Canada with Sitting Bull and a band of Sioux. They fell 40 miles short. It was at the Bear's Paw Mountains, his tribe freezing and starving, that Chief Joseph uttered his famous surrender speech on October 6, 1877: "Hear me, my chiefs! I am tired; my heart is sick and sad. From where the sun now stands I will fight no more forever."

Today, the route the Nez Perce took is the federally designated Nee-Me-Poo Trail. It was added to the National Trails System in 1986.

Back in Wisdom, the place to grab a bite is Dennis and Diane Havig's, **Crossing Bar & Grill at Fetty's,** an upgrade from the former Fetty's Bar & Café. The restaurant is a combination platter of Fetty's and Big Hole Crossing Restaurant, which was destroyed in a fire on Memorial Day 2010. Nearby, what was once the creaky-floored Conover's Trading Post—a one-time hotel known for the alluring reclining "Indian lady" covering most of the building's classic western front—is now the **Hook and Horn** (406-689-3272, May–Nov.), which has upgraded to selling western fine art, artisan gifts, and trendy coffees, teas, and baked goods.

The brisk Big Hole River begins to gather some volume at Wisdom and becomes one of the state's most revered trout streams as it carves a horseshoe-shaped course north, east and then back southward on the east flank of the Pioneers. What makes this stretch truly one-of-a-kind is the

PRIMITIVE ELKHORN HOT SPRINGS OFFER A SECLUDED PLACE TO SOAK AWAY SORE MUSCLES AFTER A DAY ON THE SLOPES OR IN THE WOODS

LONG, LONELY STRETCHES OF HIGHWAY CHARACTERIZE TOURING THE GRASSHOPPER VALLEY

opportunity to catch six—count 'em—varieties of fish: the imported rainbow trout, brook trout, and brown trout as well as the native whitefish, cutthroat trout, and Arctic grayling. Farther downstream, the river's tea-colored waters are famed for their early summer salmonfly hatch and early fall caddis hatch, both of which lure fly anglers from the world over.

For the next 30 miles, MT 43 hugs the river and, after passing Country Road 569 headed to Anaconda, veers east into a pine-studded canyon with trophy homes and summer getaways. Eleven miles later, the Big Hole emerges into a modest valley at **Wise River** (pop. 323). Pick up a few necessities at the **Wise River Mercantile** (406-832-3271) and find out what the trout are rising to at the **Complete Fly Fisher** (866-832-3175). Just before the Wise River Club, look for an unmarked right turn on FS 484—here begins the **Pioneer Mountains Scenic Byway** portion of the route. The 49-mile north–south road, now fully paved, rises gently toward the headwaters of the tumbling Wise River and descends through the heart of the mountains along Grasshopper Creek, splitting the towering and rugged East Pioneers from the gentler West

Pioneers. This section has numerous campgrounds and trails north of the divide, including the federally designated **Pioneer Loop National Recreation Trail** (406-832-3178) near the upper reaches of the Wise River, **Browns Lake Trail** just before the divide, and the **Blue Creek Trail** near Elkhorn Hot Springs farther south. The 35-mile **Pioneer Loop Trail** isn't for the faint of heart, but this strenuous hike along the backbone of the West Pioneers provides dramatic vistas of the Big Hole Valley. It is reached from the main road by turning right on FS 90 about 20 miles south of Wise River. Browns Lake Trail is near the junction of FS 2465, which leads to **Coolidge** ghost town. Drive about 5 miles to the trailhead and hike another quarter mile to the abandoned Elkhorn Mine and town, which is remarkably well-preserved, due largely to its isolation.

Atop the gentle divide, the road levels and provides regular views of the jagged East Pioneers, which some compare to the Swiss Alps. There are several scenic turnouts, most notably **Mono Park** and **Moose Park**, where interpretive signs explain why the East and West Pioneers are so different. The **Lupine Picnic Area** has a small warming hut amid lodgepole pines that's amply stocked with firewood. Also near here is **Crystal Park** (406-683-3900), a day-use area where the Butte Mineral & Gem Club and Forest Service provide a summer opportunity to dig for quartz crystals. The 30-acre site has water, picnic tables, and trails to the digging sites, which look a little like minefields. A $5 fee is charged, but you get to keep any crystals you find.

Over the divide and in the tall timber, accommodations at **Elkhorn Hot Springs** (406-834-3434) are as primitive as Forest Service cabins, but the pool is a delightful respite of gravity-flow, sulfur-free warm water. Many of Elkhorn's visitors come after marking turns at **Maverick Mountain Ski Area** (406-834-3454), an intimate and out-of-the-way ski hill with 22 runs and 2,000 vertical feet. At $36 per lift ticket (2015–16), you can get your money's worth "Riding the White Thunder" on a credible variety of terrain.

Polaris (pop. 107), named by miners for the polar star, has a fitting moniker for this area, as it's a popular location for snowmobiles. From Polaris, it's another 6 miles back to MT 278 and the end of your loop. Look for a few more of the beaverslide haystackers that epitomize this region. Turn left on MT 278 for the drive back over Badger Pass to Dillon.

Best Places to Bunk

DILLON: The town has a handful of comfortable chain motels and a few small indies, but unique options simply don't exist. Probably your best bet is the **GuestHouse Inn & Suites** ($$, 406-683-3636). While in town, you'll surely notice the stately **Metlen Hotel & Saloon** on the corner of Railroad

Avenue and Bannack Street. Built in 1897 along the Union Pacific tracks, the highly haunted palace is the only remaining hotel from Dillon's prosperous railroad days. The Metlen, which has an attractive website, was for sale in 2015 and not yet available for lodging, dining, or imbibing—all of which could change quickly, promising a truly memorable stay.

JACKSON: Jackson Hot Springs Lodges ($$/$$$, 406-834-3151, Thurs.–Mon.) cabins and motels aren't for everyone, but they can be just the thing for those seeking a less-crowded stay with soaking privileges. The cabins are improving and many come with fireplaces. Their sleeping rooms are just that—barely big enough for a bed, and with walls so thin you can hear your neighbors think. There are about 30 tent spots, making it a popular stopover for cyclists, and there's a welcoming bar in the spacious lobby. Jackson Hot Springs seemingly changes ownership every few years, but now the same folks who own Quinn's near Missoula are in charge at Jackson, so brighter days might be ahead.

WISDOM: Brenda Huntley runs a neat and tidy place, all by herself, at the **Nez Perce Motel** ($, 406-689-3254). She's particular about the cleanliness of her rooms, and her rates are extremely reasonable. We like her place for a

DOWNTOWN WISDOM HAS UNDERGONE SOMETHING OF A MAKEOVER IN RECENT YEARS

WISE RIVER IS THE PLACE TO LEARN WHAT TYPES OF FLIES BIG HOLE TROUT ARE HITTING

winter ski getaway, when the crowds are thinner but the powder is thicker. The **Wisdom Cabin** ($, 406-689-3260), once a gathering place for women during World War I, today is a light, bright, cheery one-bedroom place to hang your rod or skis. The cabin sleeps two in its remodeled interior; the original log exterior remains. You can make arrangements through owners Diane and Dennis Havig at The Crossings Restaurant. In winter, a crisp and wondrous time in the Big Hole, they offer a stay-and-ski package (Lost Trail Powder Mountain is nearby, in Sula) for $60 per night.

POLARIS: A stunner of a log home and lodge, the **Montana High Country Guest Lodge** ($$, 406-834-3469), owned by sixth-generation Montanan Russ Kipp and his wife, Karen, caters to outdoor lovers of all types, but especially to hunters, anglers, and bicyclists. They have 12 comfy rooms that overlook gorgeous grounds with a centerpiece pond that's attractive to flora, fauna, and fowl alike. They also have bragging rights to some of the best views of the East and West Pioneer Mountains. One-night stays are welcome, but a minimum of four is required for fishing, winter sports, and cattle-drive packages.

Alternative Bunking

WISE RIVER: The two **Big Hole River Cabins** ($$$, 406-491-4841) 2 miles outside of town are hand-built for comfort and accompanied by private access to some fine fishing on the Big Hole. Each cabin sleeps four and has all the fixings for a self-sustained stay. **H Bar J Café** ($, 406-832-9292) opened three cabins in August 2015—two of them studio-style and a larger one-bedroom with full bath, kitchen, and deck. On the flip side of the fishing scale are the Orvis-endorsed and high-end **Big Hole Lodge** ($$$$, 406-832-3252) and the **Complete Fly Fisher** ($$$$, 480-485-4915), both with multi-day stays that include gourmet meals and guided fishing on the Big Hole and Beaverhead Rivers.

DILLON: On Cindy and Paul Peck's 22 acres on Horse Prairie Creek are their homier-than-home **Montana Guest Cabins** ($, 406-681-3127). They cater to anglers and hunters thanks to their location near prime fishing on the Beaverhead and Red Rock Rivers as well as some of the region's best public hunting lands. Bring your own groceries so you can enjoy your meals on the ample deck with expansive views.

CAMPING: The Dillon **KOA Campground** ($, 800-562-2751), west of I-15, is well-kept, quiet, and feels far from town even though it isn't. It has a secluded area for 30 tent campers along the Beaverhead River, with a fine trout fishery right alongside. You can stay connected with their free Wi-Fi and stay buzzed with free coffee, cappuccino, or hot chocolate. On the paved loops along the Pioneer portion of the route are five small first-come, first-served primitive Forest Service campgrounds. The two most appealing are **Lodgepole** and **Willow**, both sheltered in the pines on the banks of the Wise River. The **Mono Campground** has five tent sites and is on a couple acres in the woods near the Coolidge ghost town.

FOREST SERVICE CABINS/LOOKOUTS: (Reservations: 877-444-6777 or www.recreation.gov.) The **Birch Creek Cabin** (406-683-3900, $20/sleeps four) requires driving about 12 miles north of Dillon on I-15 and turning west at Apex for another 8 miles into the mountains, but it's the only Beaverhead-Deerlodge National Forest offering of its kind in the East Pioneers. The primitive cabin is isolated enough from the ubiquitous motor crowd that it's popular with hikers and cross-country skiers looking to explore the range's high lakes.

Best Eats

DILLON: For the best steak and fine-dining ambience in town, it's the **Blacktail Station** ($$, 406-683-6611, D). The western-themed restaurant, in the basement of an 1890 original and connected to **Mac's Last Cast Sports Bar**, has more than Rocky Mountain oysters and substantial steak (sirloin heaped with grilled onions) to boast about. Other selections include fresh seafood (Alaskan king crab legs), pasta (house-made lasagna), some of the best ribs anywhere, and four entrée-qualifying salads—go for the Blacktail with blue cheese, dried cranberries, sunflower seeds, and bacon. **Sparky's Garage** ($/$$, 406-683-2828, B/L/D), next to the University of Montana Western, is like a scene from the *Route 66* TV show, with the signage and décor to match. Consider the barbecue brisket, chili, and cornbread, or the catfish basket at a place that's popular among the college crowd. **La Fiesta Mexicana** ($, 406-660-0915, B/L), known simply among locals as "The Taco Bus," might be one of the more popular drive-by Mexican food stands anywhere in the Northern Rockies. Whether it's for the breakfast burritos or lunch tacos, the sizable portions and authentic taste keep bringing locals and tourists alike back for more. You can sit in the white converted school bus and watch the amiable cooks weave their magic in cozy confines, or sit outside on basic picnic tables.

JACKSON: The **Jackson Hot Springs** ($$, 406-834-3151 Thurs-Sun) dining room has been drive-worthy in the past, and all indications are that it will remain that way under the new ownership that took over in 2015. Expect to find traditional breakfasts in the morning, and dinner specials such as seafood and slow-roasted prime rib on Fridays, Saturdays and Sundays. Plan a stay around their special events.

WISDOM: The crowd-pleasing **Crossing Bar & Grill at Fetty's** ($/$$, 406-689-3260, B/L/D) has added a few gourmet touches to western-style comfort food. The resulting menu is heavy on the meat, yet not afraid to cross over to the green side with their salads and veggie sandwiches. Friday night is rib night, and the aroma alone coaxes people out of the hayfields. The Crossing took over the iconic Fetty's bar location after a disastrous fire. The new menu is a melding of the original Crossing and a few Fetty's favorites, like the Pioneer Burger and the Super Nachos. A bit of wisdom for these parts: the **Antler Saloon** ($, 406-689-9393) serves more than a good stiff drink or cold brew—they make a dynamite pizza as well. And if you just need a pick-me-up or shot of caffeine, the **Hook & Horn Trading Post** (406-689-3272) has

WISE RIVER CLUB SERVES UP GOOD EATS, BASIC LODGING, AND AN ADULT BEVERAGE CONCOCTION CALLED THE "GUIDE'S DRINK"

bona fide coffee, real western art, real good snacks, and is also the real deal for authentic western souvenirs.

WISE RIVER: H Bar J Café and Saloon ($$, 406-832-9292) has more than the standard Montana cuisine, with treats that aren't always easy to come by on road trips. The H Bar J builds true mixed-green salads with *fresh* veggies *and* fruit garnish. The homemade pizza is tasty, too, but served on Sundays only. The head cook takes pleasure in making and serving the fresh fare, which can be enjoyed in the refurbished dining room or adjacent saloon.

Best Bars

WISE RIVER: Like many Montana saloons, the **Wise River Club** ($, 406-832-3258, B/L/D) is a guides' hangout with burgers so big (6 to 8 ounces) they might require two people to reel 'em in. Go for any of their sides, like the green salads and hand-cut fries. Belly up to the bar and learn what the trout are hitting from local outfitters, who arrive soon after the last cast for a cold beer or Moscow mule in a copper mug. The club is divided between a small café and large bar. Mounted on the bar's ceiling are the impressive antlers of a single bull elk that lived a prosperous life for more than two decades in a corral across the highway. After an evening of good eats, pool or shuffleboard, you can retire upstairs to one of seven spartan rooms—each with double bed (communal bath and shower down the hall) for around $75 a night.

SIDE TRACK

Lemhi and Bannock Passes (65 miles)

Numerous passes cross the backbone of the Rocky Mountains, but only one was taken first by the Lewis & Clark Expedition: Lemhi. And four of the party, including Meriwether Lewis, did it twice.

The intrepid explorers reached this point after boating up the Missouri River, taking the Jefferson River at what is now Three Forks, and continuing up the Beaverhead River past contemporary Dillon to the confluence of Red Rock River and Horse Prairie Creek, where they hunkered down at what they called Camp Fortunate, now the site of Clark Canyon dam and reservoir. The expedition then continued up Horse Prairie Creek into the towering Beaverhead Mountains.

On August 12, 1805, Lewis and three members of the party, including Sacagawea, took an old Indian road over the Continental Divide into present-day Idaho in hopes of meeting the Shoshone Indians and trading for horses for the next phase of the journey to the Pacific. Lewis thus became the first US citizen to cross the Continental Divide. Once there, he saw what we see today: majestic mountain range after mountain range, running southeast to northwest. He assumed—erroneously, it turned out—that the trickle of cold water at the summit was the uppermost headwaters of the Missouri River. A day later, they met up with the Shoshone, ostensibly saving the expedition from a brutal winter. Two weeks later, the entire Corps of Discovery crossed the pass into Idaho.

Today this section is known as the Lewis & Clark Backcountry Byway and Adventure Road. To get a flavor of perhaps the most arduous part of the journey, travel south of Dillon on Interstate 15 to Clark Canyon Reservoir and MT 324. Stop at the **Lewis & Clark Camp Fortunate Overlook and Interpretive Site** along the lake shore about one mile into the drive.

Continue west on MT 324 through Grant about 20 miles through valley ranchlands until the turnoff for Lemhi Pass, at a picnic area called Shoshone Ridge. Turn right and begin the 9-mile ascent on gravel to the pass, where you'll be rewarded with magnificent views of Idaho's Lemhi and Lost River

(continued on next page)

Ranges along with the 480-acre Lemhi Pass National Historic Landmark. The final 4 miles are rugged, steep, and narrow, so high-clearance vehicles are advised. The 7,323-foot pass, named for a king in the Book of Mormon, has a stone monument and information kiosk, and from there the road descends on an even more rugged, steep, and narrow course to Tendoy, Idaho, along Agency Creek.

Less intriguing, and definitely less challenging for your vehicle, is 7,684-foot Bannock Pass, about 20 miles southeast of Lemhi, also on the Montana-Idaho border. Getting there from Dillon is similar to Lemhi, except continue on MT 324 at the Lemhi Pass Road turnoff and stay on the pavement another five miles until it becomes gravel at Donovan Ranch. It's a straight, well-maintained 10-mile shot along an old railroad grade to a strikingly arid summit that's more of a bump than a pass, where the road becomes paved again for the gradual descent through desert to Salmon, Idaho.

Note: This modest pass is not to be confused with Bannack Pass, which is about 35 miles southeast of Bannack and also crosses the Continental Divide separating Montana and Idaho.

DILLON: When Brett Maki grew up in the Beaverhead Valley, Dillon was a steak-and-whiskey cowboy town. It still is, of course, but the world is changing, and when Maki returned to town in 2011 after 10 years in Seattle, he saw a community ready to broaden its horizons. The result is **Beaverhead Brewing Company** ($, 406-988-0011), which is open 8 AM to 8 PM daily in a renovated building downtown. Beaverhead has six year-round brews on tap and four seasonals. Look for periodic music events.

DETOUR: ONE FOR THE ROAD

The Bitterroot Valley
Missoula to Lost Trail Pass

ESTIMATED LENGTH: 95 miles

HIGHLIGHTS: Historical Museum at Fort Missoula, Elk Country Visitor Center, Lee Metcalf National Wildlife Refuge, St. Mary's Mission, Fort Owen, Lake Como, Lost Trail Pass, Lost Trail Hot Springs Resort, Lost Trail Powder Mountain

GETTING THERE: Leave I-90 either on US 12 in downtown Missoula (Exit 105) or US 93 (Exit 101, Reserve Street) and head south along the Bitterroot River.

Long before outsiders discovered the aesthetic wonders of the Flathead and Whitefish, the Bitterroot Valley became synonymous with the Montana mystique. Though Missoula author William Kittredge's famous "Last Best Place" description was actually coined in a trailer house in the Paradise Valley south of Livingston, he drew much of his inspiration from the Bitterroot.

The Bitterroot is an exceptionally pretty north–south valley known for its moderate climate, prolific trout fishing, and high quality of life. One old timber town after another—Missoula, Lolo, Florence, Stevensville, Victor, Hamilton, Darby, and Conner—has become a bastion of 20-acre ranchettes and a jumping-off point for outdoor adventures in the wild Bitterroot Mountains.

At the north end of this route is progressive **Missoula** (pop. 69,122). Fueling the town's energy is the University of Montana, which has churned out enough conservation activists to rival any East or West Coast university. The atmosphere is like Berkeley and Madison, but with hiking boots, skis, and fly rods. Missoula still has a raw side reminiscent of the town's old Front Street honky-tonks, an image that only adds to an intrigue that has been tempered by the relatively recent arrival of strip malls, big box stores, and traffic.

Missoula has enough diversions to fill several days, but if time is short be sure to hike the switchback **Mount M Sentinel Trail** to the "M" above the university. The Rocky Mountain Elk Foundation's 22-acre **Elk Country Visitor Center** features terrific dioramas of elk in their natural environment and an outdoor hiking trail. The organization is largely responsible for restoring elk populations depleted by wanton hunting at the turn of the previous century. For an interesting look at Missoula's frontier legacy, the **Historical Museum at Fort Missoula** on the southwest edge of town looks at the area's military history, including exhibits about the Buffalo Soldiers bicycle corps—a group of black men who pedaled from Missoula to St. Louis, Missouri, as part of a U.S. Army experiment to see if bicycles could replace horses as the cavalry's primary mode of transportation.

Nine miles south of Missoula, after US 93/12 slips through a neck between the Bitterroot and Sapphire mountains, US 12 splits to the west at **Lolo** (pop. 3,892) and begins a 31-mile ascent to Lolo Pass and Idaho. This was Lewis and Clark's most famous crossing of the Rockies.

US 93 follows the Bitterroot past a series of river access points and through a procession of inviting communities, starting with the one-time sawmill town of **Florence** (pop. 765)—formerly called One Horse, for the creek that arrives in town from the flanks of the Bitterroots. Between Florence and Stevensville is the **Lee Metcalf National Wildlife Refuge**, named after a Montana senator from the Bitterroot who would become one of the state's great conservation champions. The watery refuge, created in 1963 as a safe stopover for migratory birds, has more than 2 miles of hiking trails and a gravel road that offers excellent waterfowl viewing.

Stevensville (pop. 1,881) was actually Montana's first Anglo community, begun as **St. Mary's Mission** in 1841 by the Jesuit priest Pierre DeSmet. The mission chapel has been restored and is a museum that features furniture belonging to the pioneering priest Anthony Ravalli, who built it. Nine years after DeSmet's arrival, Major John Owen built the trading and military post on the site he would call **Fort Owen**. The state's first gristmill, sawmill, and school for settlers were here. What remains is a barracks housing artifacts from Owen's day, plus some reconstructed buildings.

Next up on the road south is **Victor** (pop. 745), once a silver mining community. Named after a Flathead chief, Victor was the site of the lucrative Curlew Mine. The area's mining, timber, and railroad history is captured well in the **Victor Heritage Museum**, located in the old Northern Pacific depot.

South of Victor is **Hamilton** (pop. 4,556), after which the valley begins to narrow and takes on more of the characteristics of the "old Montana." Ranchettes and subdivisions, though creeping south, give way to a rural and ranching persona. Just past Como Bridge, Lake Como Road follows Little Rock Creek for about 3 miles to **Lake Como**, which was raised for irrigation purposes to be a full-fledged reservoir and features a Forest Service campground with 10 RV sites. This is the only handicapped-accessible equestrian campground in the western United States, revealing the popularity of pack trips into the Selway-Bitterroot Wilderness Area straddling the Montana-Idaho border.

Three miles south of Como Bridge is resilient **Darby** (pop. 726). Three times Main Street burned, and three times the town bounced back. Darby has ridden an economic rollercoaster: first fur trading, then mining, timber, apples, and ranching. As each has waned, tourism and the accompanying shops have become staples, and Darby is a popular base for pack trips and whitewater excursions into the Selway-Bitterroot. It also has another distinction: The all-inclusive and luxurious **Triple Creek Ranch** resort (with cabins starting at $1,400 per night!) was chosen as the Number 1 hotel in the world in 2015 by *Business Insider*, ranked third-best in the world by *Travel + Leisure*, and earned fifth place in *Condé Nast Traveler*'s 2014 Readers Choice Award.

Continuing south, the east and west forks of the Bitterroot join just north of the little logging wayside of **Conner** (pop. 250), which has three restaurants and a small motel. After Conner, US 93 begins its ascent along the East Fork Bitterroot River through woodsy **Sula** (pop. 37) toward **Lost Trail Pass** on the Montana-Idaho border. Four miles east of Sula on the East Fork Road is the **Broad Axe Lodge & Restaurant**, which features two rustic cabins and fine dining and is designated by the state as a wildlife-viewing area for its prolific number of critters. Back on US 93, the **Lost Trail Hot Springs Resort** at Sula has cabins, two lodges, and an RV park and is a great place to soak in the natural waters of the hot tub or swimming pool after a day on the runs at **Lost Trail Powder Mountain** ski area, a family-oriented operation open Thursday through Sunday from December until April.

THE 585-FOOT OLD SMELTER STACK ABOVE ANACONDA IS THE TALLEST MAN-MADE STRUCTURE IN MONTANA

5

MONTANA'S GOLD, SILVER, AND COPPER STANDARD

The Anaconda–Pintler Scenic Route

BUTTE TO DRUMMOND

ESTIMATED LENGTH: 88 miles

ESTIMATED TIME: 3 hours to 2 days

HIGHLIGHTS: Museums, hot springs, Berkeley Pit, Old Works Golf Club, George-town Lake, Philipsburg, Discovery Ski Basin, Ohrmann Museum & Gallery, Grant-Kohrs Ranch

GETTING THERE: The Anaconda-Pintler Scenic Route begins and ends at I-90 in southwest Montana. From the east, leave the freeway at the Anaconda-Opportunity turnoff (Exit 208) about 15 miles west of Butte and continue for another 6 miles to Anaconda. From the west, take Exit 155 off I-90 at the little ranch and railroad town of Drummond and head south along Flint Creek.

OVERVIEW

Montana's prolific mining past comes to life along much of this drive through thick conifer forests around one of the state's most rugged mountain ranges. The forests are so dense here that it's hard to imagine you're surrounded by the wild shoulders of the Flint Creek Range, which rises to nearly 11,000 feet. Just as prominent as the mountain range is the mining history, which fills your windshield the moment you turn off I-90 at Anaconda. A ghostly smelter stack—the tallest man-made structure in Montana—rises from the mouth of Dutchman Creek. In its heyday, Anaconda was a gritty town of rugged Irish-Catholics whose fortunes ebbed and flowed with the produc-tion of copper and gold from the cavernous mines at nearby Butte. This area once produced more copper than any place in the world.

The mines having played out three decades ago, today the communities along the Anaconda-Pintler route are reinventing themselves as tourist towns exploiting their unique histories. The same holds true for Philipsburg,

Donna Mitchell

TELLTALE TAILINGS AT THE BERKELEY PIT IN BUTTE POINT TO THE TOWN'S MINING GLORY DAYS

which has become an enclave of museums and theaters celebrating a lively past. Midway through the journey is Georgetown Lake, popular for fishing, snowmobiling, and summer cabins.

Once upon a time, Butte was a collection of ethnic communities—Italians, Austrians, Finns, Slavs, Mexicans, and, of course, Irish—where grimy workers poked underground for gold and silver in a mile-high bowl west of the Continental Divide. With the advent of electricity came the need for copper, and large quantities were excavated in the late 1800s. By the early 1900s, the population had swelled to more than 100,000 hard-working, hard-drinking, hard-brawling residents who spent their paychecks on booze and brothels in an area of town called "The Line." The landscape literally changed in the mid-1950s, when the Anaconda Copper Mining Company dug the massive Berkeley Pit for which Butte is renowned—or perhaps infamous. Entire communities vanished under the toxic slag.

Mining in the giant hole lasted for about three decades, until the 1980s, when operations ceased. Since then, the Berkeley Pit has been filling with toxic water. For a time it appeared that not even Our Lady of the Rockies, a bleached 90-foot-high lighted statue that stands guard over Butte from a high mountain atop East Ridge, could save a declining city. Yet Butte somehow endures and perseveres. Today it's capitalizing on its past with popular uptown tours. It's now one of the largest National Historic Landmark Districts in the nation—and it even makes money charging tourists to look into its giant hole filling with water.

HITTING THE ROAD

This scenic route starts in Anaconda in the state's eyes, but we suggest you begin in **Butte** (pop. 33,892)—a town so proud of its mining origins, ethnicity, and grit that it has its own license plates that state, immodestly, "Butte America." Once the butt of old FBI jokes and derided as the ugliest city this side of Gary, Indiana, today this brick-and-mortar town, rising to the lip of the gaping Berkeley Pit and sprinkled with classic mining head frames, emits a certain raw character and rock-ribbed charm.

Places to see while in Butte: The **Copper King Mansion** (406-782-7580, May–Sept.) with guided tour, the **World Museum of Mining** (406-723-7211), and the **Mineral Museum** (406-496-4172). For a glimpse of Butte's rambunctious past, don green garb and be there on St. Patrick's Day, when 30,000 residents and visitors take to the streets. After yet another year of scratching out a living and surviving the cold of winter, the city unleashes its pent-up inhibitions with a party as wild as Mardi Gras or Carnivale, but with a certain

OUR LADY OF THE ROCKIES STANDS GUARD IN THE MOUNTAINS HIGH ABOVE BUTTE

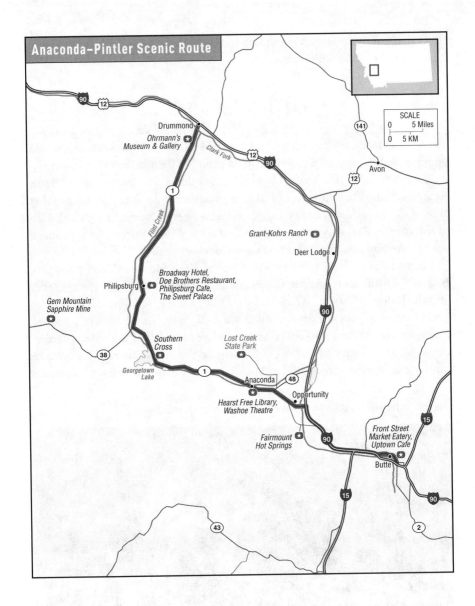

Anaconda–Pintler Scenic Route

SCALE
0   5 Miles
0   5 KM

Drummond

Ohrmann's
Museum & Gallery

Clark Fork

Avon

Grant-Kohrs Ranch

Deer Lodge

Flint Creek

Broadway Hotel,
Doe Brothers Restaurant,
Philipsburg Cafe,
The Sweet Palace

Philipsburg

Gem Mountain
Sapphire Mine

Southern
Cross

Lost Creek
State Park

Georgetown
Lake

Anaconda

Opportunity

Hearst Free Library,
Washoe Theatre

Front Street
Market Eatery,
Uptown Cafe

Fairmount
Hot Springs

Butte

Montanan flair. Don't be surprised to see brawling patrons come tumbling out of any number of imbibing establishments. And unlike in many modern frontier towns, these fights aren't staged. Another rowdy annual event is **Knievel Days**, named for one of Butte's favorite sons and a magnet for up to 50,000 bikers each July. Another one to mark on your calendar: The **Montana Folk Festival** in early July. Wander from venue to venue and from food vendor to food vendor for a rollicking good time against a backdrop of mountains and headframes twinkling with red lights.

Just over the hill off I-90, tucked into a gap in the mountains south of the freeway, is the former company town of **Anaconda** (pop. 9,329). It's easily recognized from a distance by the 585-foot smelter stack on the edge of town, the world's largest freestanding structure when built in 1919. The Stack, as it's known by locals, is now a state park, but not open to visitors. This was where the ore mined in Butte was processed, and until Anaconda Copper's purchase of mines in Mexico and Chile, no smelter in the world produced more copper.

If you've got kids in tow, consider taking a side trip between Butte and Anaconda to the **Fairmont Hot Springs** ($$$, 406-797-3241/800-332-3272), a large hotel and golf complex in the country with two mineral hot pools and two Olympic-sized swimming pools. Don't go expecting peace and quiet, though: Fairmont is full of kids squealing with delight. Take Exit 211 from I-90, drive about 3 miles to the resort, then go north on County Road 441 to the junction of MT 1 at Opportunity. The hot springs are at the foot of the state-owned, 56,000-acre **Mount Haggin Wildlife Management Area**, the state's largest wildlife area and ideal habitat for pronghorn, white-tailed and mule deer, elk, moose, and an occasional black bear. Another off-the-beaten-byway option worth the 10-mile drive is **Lost Creek State Park** (406-542-5500), featuring the 50-foot Lost Creek Falls and 1,200-foot limestone cliffs. The park is known for its mountain goats and bighorn sheep, which have bounced back from a lethal pneumonia epidemic in 2010. To get there, turn north on County Road 273 near the junction of MT 1 and MT 48, go left 2 miles later on Forest Service Road 683, and drive about 7 miles.

Anaconda is a long, narrow community, called An-da-CON-ta by residents. Back in the heyday, copper king Marcus Daly built an amusement park here; what's left is the simple **Super Copper Chute** in Charlotte Yeoman Martin Park, a free 140-foot slide the kids might enjoy. The town's fortunes fluctuated wildly with the copper industry, and when the smelter was shut down in 1980, the community was devastated. The weariness still shows, though as the cleanup of mining messes forges ahead there are efforts to reinvent Anaconda, à la Butte. The **Old Works Golf Club** (406-563-5989), marked by rusted mining equipment, was designed by Jack Nicklaus and is considered one of the outstanding courses in the country. It was built on the site of a dismantled smelter, and some of the ruins are visible from the course. The stately **Hearst Free Library** (406-563-6932) is another masterful example of century-old architecture. The library was created and then packed with books and art by infamous newspaperman William Randolph Hearst's mother, Phoebe, who developed an abiding affection for Anaconda during visits to Montana. The library has been a community gathering spot since 1898. If you're here in the evening, take in a movie at the ornate **Washoe Theater** (406-563-6161), an art deco palace built in 1931 and once chosen as the fifth most beautiful theater in the nation by the Smithsonian Institute.

Anaconda's motto is "Where Main Street Meets the Mountains," and that's just what happens as you head west on the officially designated Anaconda-Pintler Scenic Route. MT 1 weaves upstream along Silver Creek for about 15 miles before reaching Silver Lake, and then goes over a small divide to **Georgetown Lake**, a popular 3,000-acre summer and winter playground squeezed between the Flint Creek and Pintler ranges. Boaters ply these waters, usually in pursuit of landlocked kokanee salmon or football-shaped rainbow trout. The lake has a marina, four boat ramps, three national forest campgrounds, and numerous vacation cabins tucked into the pines. This is a snowmobiler's paradise, and 5 miles to the north is **Discovery Ski Basin** (406-563-2184). The small ski area geared to locals is unique in that the green, blue, and black diamond runs are generally segregated instead of

THE LEGACY OF SOUTHERN CROSS

Also on a south-facing hill above Georgetown Lake are the remnants of one of the numerous ghost towns in the region and the one with perhaps the most extraordinary story: Southern Cross. The community, which sits at 7,000 feet above sea level, was born during the gold rush days of the Civil War and was a busy place for the first half of the 20th century. It had a store, schoolhouse, dance hall, saunas, post office and even had passenger rail service from Butte into the 1930s. Once the region's gold- and silver-mining heyday ended in the early 1950s, many families, mostly Swedish and Finnish, remained at Southern Cross. One by one they passed away until, in 1991, the last of the old-time miners, a fellow named "Little John" Huttala, died. By then, though, a steady stream of eclectic newcomers had begun arriving, drawn by the lake and the isolation, eager to escape mainstream culture. They moved into the decaying, ramshackle homes scattered across the pine and aspen hillsides, and lovingly renovated them. They paid little or no rent to the long-departed Anaconda Mining Company, which even built a stunning wood and stone church, St. Timothy Memorial Chapel, for the hardy holdovers.

The new residents were basically squatters, so when a new company bought the rights to the leases in 1988, the owners initially wanted them all evicted. But few departed. In a happy ending to the story, after three years of wrangling, Magellan Resources allowed the residents to lease the homes for $150 per year. Today, the number of year-round residents at Southern Cross is estimated to range from three to five, and many of the old homes are boarded. But the handiwork of those who restored the community is evident, and, thanks to Georgetown Lake, the community is a busy curiosity revolving around events at St. Timothy. There's even a St. Timothy Summer Music Festival held for five Sundays every summer beginning in late June and ending in early August.

PHILIPSBURG, A BRIGHTLY PAINTED OLD MINING TOWN, HAS GEM SHOPS, A FABULOUS CANDY STORE AND A BREWERY FROTHING WITH HISTORY

interspersed. Philipsburg skiers are thrilled at plans for a road to be punched directly from town to the ski area.

From Georgetown Lake's outlet, MT 1 dives precipitously into a canyon carved by Flint Creek as it plunges toward the Philipsburg Valley. A worthwhile side trip after emerging from the canyon is a drive up MT 38 to the **Gem Mountain Sapphire Mine** (406-859-6463/866-459-4367) about 12 miles west of the junction. For about $15 a bucket, you can wash gravel over a trough while looking for sapphires—with a certainty you'll find at least a dozen small gems and perhaps even land a whopper. The mine is usually open Memorial Day Weekend through September, weather permitting.

Back in the valley, the highlight of the Anaconda-Pintler journey unquestionably is the old sapphire, ruby, and corundum mining community of **Philipsburg** (pop. 850)—or, once you've mingled with the 900-plus friendly locals for a few hours, simply "P-Burg." The town was built on the side of a hill and enjoyed boom times in the late 1800s. Today, it has been colorfully restored. Scanning Broadway Avenue, you'll quickly understand why Philipsburg has twice been a finalist for "Prettiest Painted Place in America."

It's easy to spend an entire day wandering the streets of P-Burg, given the plethora of shops related to the town's history. The aforementioned **Gem Mountain** is one of three purveyors of uniquely clear and colorful sapphires, discovered in Rock Creek in 1892. Other places to shop for loose stones and/or finished jewelry: **Mountain Gems of Philipsburg** (406-560-7469) and **The Sapphire Gallery** (406-859-3236), which will evaluate other stones or gems you own. And for a genuine step back in time, the **Granite Ghost Town State Park** (406-542-5500, May–Sept.) 4 miles outside Philipsburg offers walking tours of what's left of a community built around the richest silver mine in the world.

After leaving Philipsburg, MT 1 heads north along Flint Creek into a broad valley of ranches and Angus cattle. The one-blip communities of Maxville and Hall have some history worth noting, but definitely save time for a visit to the **Ohrmann Museum & Gallery** (406-288-3319), which is less than 3 miles south of **Drummond** (pop. 329). The gallery and yard-art menagerie features the one-of-a-kind works of the late Bill Ohrmann, who painted almost up to the time of his death at age 95 in 2014. Ohrmann, a lifelong area rancher, pulled no punches with art depicting society's social ills, especially as they related to our treatment of the environment and animals. One of his shows was aptly named "Something to Offend Everyone". The route ends where Flint Creek meets the Clark Fork and MT 1 meets I-90. Drummond has a close-knit populace with the usual handful of taverns, gas stations, and cafés, but the main attraction takes place on Friday nights in the fall when the powerhouse 8-Man football team plays.

If your tour takes you back to Butte on I-90, stop at Deer Lodge to visit the **Grant-Kohrs Ranch National Historic Site** (406-846-2070), once the hub of a 1-million-acre cattle operation and now 1,600 acres of trails, artifacts, historic buildings, museum collections, and other interesting remnants from Montana's open-range era. The self-sustaining ranch features all of its original livestock breeds and still uses old-time equipment. Operated by the National Park Service, the ranch is open daily except on Thanksgiving, Christmas Day, and New Year's Day, and is less than 2 miles from I-90 on the north end of Deer Lodge.

Best Places to Bunk

BUTTE: Toad Hall Manor ($$/$$$, 406-494-2625), a B&B in a five-story brick mansion, makes the world a better place with its tea and scones alone. Toad and Mole would have thought they'd died and gone to the high willows after a sleepover and breakfast at the Manor. And for less than a king's ransom, you can sleep at the appropriately appointed **Copper King Mansion** ($$/$$$, 406-782-7580). Run by the brother and sister team of John Thompson and Karen Sigl, the three-room Victorian built for US Senator William A. Clark was (and continues to be) a fixer-upper when their grandmother bought it in 1953. Even if you're not staying, take a tour and find out the secrets of a copper czar who was once one of the most powerful men in the West.

ANACONDA: The **Hickory House Inn** ($$, 406-563-5481) on East Park Avenue downtown is a five-bedroom B&B created from the former rectory of St. Paul's Church. The bright and cheerful colors include the outdoor gardens and thematic rooms, and the gourmet breakfast is a cut above.

PHILIPSBURG: The historic nine-room **Broadway Hotel** ($$/$$$, 406-859-8000) is P-Burg's best-known lodging; a continental breakfast is included. **The Kaiser House** ($$, 406-859-2004) has been a favored gift shop for many years, and now has four rooms upstairs renovated for lodging. Each room is dedicated to pertinent town history, and the mural room painted by local artist Liz Silliman is a tribute to local characters and color. An added enticement is the basement wine cellar, where you can find an outstanding bottle selection for purchase. The **Quigley Cottage B&B** has four English country style guest rooms ($$, 406-859-3812); two are private with their own bath and the other two share a bathroom. Davee Letford begins every breakfast with Scottish oatmeal served with ice cream, followed by a full traditional meal. If you're looking for out-of-the-norm, **The Sanctuary, A Unique Inn** ($$, 406-859-1003) is a shrine to Harleys and their two-wheeled brethren. Rooms and cabins (next door) are for two adults only.

Alternative Bunking

PHILIPSBURG: Off Broadway Avenue is the **McDonald Opera House** ($/$$, 406-859-0013) a 350-seat classic western stage with comedy and vaudeville performances June through Labor Day. During the theatre off-season, after Labor Day and before Memorial Day, you can bunk in one of two units—a two-bedroom that sleeps four and a one-bedroom that sleeps two. There's no additional charge for the occasional visit by a ghost who reputedly has been recorded saying "hello." Stay off the beaten path at the **Flint Creek Home** ($$$, 406-539-5912), a three-bedroom, one-bath rental on the banks of Flint Creek and tucked away on 42 acres. Fish for trout, explore the remains of the neighboring 1907 hydroelectric powerhouse, and walk to a ridge that provides splendid views of the valley.

CAMPING: Lost Creek State Park (406-542-5500) is a frequently full spot with 25 primitive first-come, first-served sites and no fee. The Beaverhead-Deerlodge National Forest has eight campgrounds along the Pintler Scenic Route. Coming from Anaconda, 14-site Spring Hill campground is on the right just past the junction of FS 170 and Warm Springs Creek, about 2 miles before Silver Lake. Georgetown Lake has three Forest Service campgrounds: **Piney** (47 sites), **Lodgepole** (thirty sites), and the popular **Philipsburg Bay** (67 sites). Piney and Philipsburg Bay have lakeside sites, while

Lodgepole is across MT 1 from the lake. If you like ATVs and dirt bikes, the **Cable** campground above the lake on Forest Service Road 65 is for you; the 11 sites offer instant access to old logging and mining roads. For those who prefer to stretch out streamside, **Flint Creek** campground offers 16 spots at the bottom of the precipitous descent on MT 1, including two walk-in sites for tenters.

FOREST SERVICE CABINS/LOOKOUTS: (Reservations: 877-444-6777 or www.recreation.gov.) The Butte and Pintler ranger districts offer many primitive cabins for nightly rental, including four close to the route: They are **High Rye Cabin** ($20/sleeps four), **Douglas Creek Cabin** ($20/sleeps six), **Moose Lake Guard Station** ($20/sleeps four), and **Stony Cabin** ($20/sleeps four). High Rye is in a retired mining area called German Gulch and popular with the motorized set. Douglas Creek, about 10 miles northwest of Philipsburg, is accessible by car for much of the year. Moose Lake Guard Station, about 25 miles southwest of P-Burg, also can be reached by car virtually year-round. Stony Cabin is favored by anglers pursuing trout in Rock Creek.

Best Eats

BUTTE: For quieter moments, sit down to a civilized, artful meal and well-chosen wine list at the **Uptown Cafe** ($$, 406-723-4735, L[weekdays]/D), where owners Barb Kornet and Guy Graham have cuisine that rivals big-city dining. Specials are just that: "special" (think duck, or ancho-rubbed pork tenderloin, or herb-crusted sole) and their sublime four-course dinners—which include soup, salad, two baked clams and an entrée—run less than $25. Cheryl Madison's **Broadway Café** ($, 406 723-8711, L/D Mon.-Sat.) is a mainstay for locals for several reasons: its comfortable bistro feel, warm colors and seating in the sunroom, her attention to fresh, healthy gourmet ingredients, daily lunch specials (handmade steak pasties), and a large menu. But what brings folks back is the perfect-crusted, more-than-pepperoni pizza pie. At lunch, a slice of pizza, leafy green salad and drink can be had for less than a 10-spot.

If you lean toward vegetarian fare and, say, aren't afraid of tofu, try the **Hummingbird Café** ($$, 406-723-2044, B/L), which calls itself an "organic coffee house" but is so much more. Organic local veggies go into their breakfasts and heart-healthy soups and sandwiches so you can feel good about eating well while supporting local purveyors. Plans to open for dinner were in the works in 2015.

Grab some homemade goodness to go, or stay, from Jim and Marla's Italian-style **Marla Mia's Front Street Market & Deli** ($, 406-782-2614, L). The market is literally packed from floor to ceiling with specialty foods and has one of the largest and best selections of wines and craft beer in the state. Front Street's busy crew makes their deli salads, sandwiches, and soups on site, and does catering off-site. They make a gorgonzola dip that's positively addictive—so recognizable in its cold case that it doesn't need a label.

ANACONDA: The **Classic Cafe** ($/$$, 406-563-5558, B [weekends]/L/D Tues.—Sun.) has family fun painted all over its white-and-black checkered exterior and a kid-friendly menu of pizzas, salads, and wraps. Dinner highlights include hand-battered fresh halibut with chips, calzones, and pasta plates. But the best reason to stop in is to see the authentic Herbie the Love Bug (and his girlfriend, Millie) parked in the dining room and converted into table seating. Grownups will appreciate the huge selection of microbrews.

PHILIPSBURG: The **Silver Mill** ($$/$$$, 406-859-7000 D, Wed.—Sun.), formerly Antlers, is a cozy, family-friendly establishment specializing in excellent Italian, steaks and seafood. Local owners Tim & Claudette Tringle and Anne Filmore found the mother lode in chef Tony Crittela. Reservations are required for groups of five or more. **Up 'N Smokin BBQ** ($, 406-240-1616, L/D), a relative newcomer to town, is garnering raves for authentic, world-class smoked BBQ chicken, pork, and ribs. Long, wood-plank tables made for the joint by a local woodcrafter create atmosphere. It's first-come, first served; no reservations or phone orders taken. Stepping into **Doe Brothers Soda Fountain and Restaurant** ($$, 406-859-6676, L, Wed.–Sun.) is like revisiting the 1920s. It's a local lunch hangout popular for burgers, though their Jimmy chicken-salad sandwich with secret ingredients earns kudos as well. Tourists come for the soda fountain, where they dish up Montana-made Wilcoxson's and Oregon's Glacier Cascade ice cream treats. You can put on five pounds just browsing in **The Sweet Palace** (406-859-3353,Sun.–Fri.), a sweet tooth magnet with a staggering assortment of fudge, saltwater taffy, truffles, and caramels, most made on-site. And, if you can't find your favorite jellybean here, it simply doesn't exist.

DRUMMOND: The healthy variety of fresh choices at **Parkers' Restaurant** ($/$$, 406-288-2333, B/L/D) is a welcome diversion from the litany of burger joints across Montana, but in the end you can't really talk about Parkers' without talking about . . . burgers. Gourmet chef Brent Parker and his wife, Jennifer, opened the restaurant in 2011 with 72 different styles of handmade burgers, and four years later they were up to 135 and counting. That means a lot of experimentation. Some examples: a burger with peanut butter and bacon (the Elvis), another with Mozzarella cheese sticks, pepperoni, and pizza sauce (the Ba-Da-Bing), and the seemingly football-size Monster-In-Law made with the works. Even with such creativity, it's short-selling Parkers' to stop at burgers. Locally grown produce, homemade chowders, 99-cent crunchy tacos with homemade salsa, and farm-to-table meats are just a few more reasons to finish your route with a meal here. The Coca-Cola memorabilia on the walls provides authentic diner flair, too.

Best Bars

ANACONDA: For a snapshot of what club life was like in the 1930s, look no farther than **Club Moderne** (406-563-7593) on East Park Avenue. The club does more than wink at an era of suit coats, fedoras, pink ladies, and sidecars. One look at the neon exterior sign, curved corner building, and rounded door window help explain why it's listed on the National Register of Historic Places. Step into the long backroom to find red tuck-and-roll vinyl seats, speckled Formica-topped tables, and wood inlay all integral to the Moderne style. Skinny Francesco opened the club in 1937, and it was the swinging-est place for miles. Black-and-white photos on the walls will dial you back to a time of snappy Sinatra songs, highballs, polished shoes, and bouffant 'dos. Owned by John and Steph Hekkel since 1999, it's now an any-age bar—a place to relax, watch a game, throw some darts, or chat up the bartender.

BUTTE: It's Butte, with a colorful Irish-Catholic mining history, so you just know there's no shortage of lively places to imbibe at any given time. Among the growing number of distilleries in Montana, all with distinctive personality, one with a terrific vibe is

THE NIGHTLIFE IN "BUTTE AMERICA" IS UNLIKE ANYWHERE ELSE IN THE STATE

Headframe Spirits (406-299-2886), which has great micro-distilled spirits and a cool logo that captures the city's essence. Stop by the always-busy tasting room for a wide assortment of offerings, ranging from fruity Moscow mules to their award-winning Neversweat Whiskey. Headframe opened in 2010 in uptown Butte, and in 2013 owners John and Courtney McKee were deservedly honored as Montana Entrepreneurs of the Year. The name Headframe comes from the distinct old mining towers that rise above Butte, all brightly lit in red at night.

PHILIPSBURG: You can see, hear, and smell the fine art of brewing at the **Phillipsburg Brewing Company** (406-859-2739), where the atmosphere is vibrant and there are always six to nine beers on tap. Cathy and Nolan Smith, along with Rob Jarvis, opened the brewery in 2012 and decided against erecting the common glass barriers between the hot and cold sides of the operation. So while you sip—and they actually encourage you to bring your own food—you can watch the brewmaster at work while savoring the aromas of his labor. Adding to the flavor is the location in an 1888 bank building that's in the heart of the Philipsburg National Historic District. Bits of old banking paraphernalia and mining equipment are prominently displayed, including a Jackleg drill and wooden water pipe. On Friday nights a mobile pizza unit lingers outside. Look for Pint Nights, when $1 per pint is given to a local charity.

DETOUR: ONE FOR THE ROAD

The Skalkaho Highway
Porters Corner to Hamilton

ESTIMATED LENGTH: 71 miles

HIGHLIGHTS: Skalkaho Pass, Sapphire Mountains, Gem Mountain Sapphire Mine, Rock Creek, Skalkaho Game Preserve, Skalkaho Falls, Daly Mansion

GETTING THERE: Exit I-90 either at Anaconda (Exit 208) or Drummond (Exit 163) to reach the highway from the east side; each approach is on MT 1, the Anaconda-Pintler Scenic Route. From the west, take US 93 at Missoula and head south through the Bitterroot Valley to Grantsdale, about 3 miles south of Hamilton. For an extra-adventurous approach—especially if you're a fly angler—take the Rock Creek turnoff on I-90 (Exit 126) and drive south along the creek, one of Montana's blue-ribbon trout streams, to the road's meeting with MT 38 about 12 miles west of Porters Corner.

D on't be fooled by the state-highway designation. For at least one-third of its length, MT 38 between the Flint Creek and Bitterroot valleys is anything but a highway. It's a narrow, twisting gravel road through some of southwest Montana's prettiest scenery.

Skalkaho comes from the Salish words *skalen* (beaver) and *kalalko* (green woods), the literal translation being "beavers of the green woods" and the direct reference being to Skalkaho Creek. For generations, the Salish used this route over the Sapphire Range, and then in 1924, the state and the Forest Service built the current road to facilitate access to the mines. The highlight—literally and figuratively—is 7,260-foot **Skalkaho Pass** at the crest of the north–south Sapphire Mountains, so-named for their abundant minerals. This drive is purely about scenery and wildlife viewing; there are no services or any other commercial endeavors except for the **Gem Mountain Sapphire Mine** about 13 miles into the route along **Rock Creek**. The road rises gently to the pass from the east side along the East Fork Rock Creek, through a variety of forest lands, then descends more noticeably in the west to the Bitterroot Valley.

SIDE TRACK

Rock Creek Road: Philipsburg to Clinton (65 miles)

Rule No. 1 for this dusty, bumpy, twisting drive: bring your fly rod. As any angler worth his 9-weight knows, **Rock Creek** is one of the state's blue ribbon trout-fishing treasures, albeit often crowded on weekends. It helps that the road charts the stream's course, making it easily accessible, and that more than half of the creek's journey to the Clark Fork River at Clinton flows through national forest lands. The creek—which has the size and power of a river—cuts a shaded ribbon between the steep hills of the John Long and Sapphire

A LITTLE FIXER-UPPER ON THE BACKROAD BETWEEN PHILIPSBURG AND ROCK CREEK

mountains. From Philipsburg, take paved MT 348 west across a low pass in the John Long Mountains to its meeting with Rock Creek at Bohrnsen Memorial Bridge. Continue straight on gravel, headed downstream. Aside from its famous concentrations of trout, Rock Creek is also known for a smattering of well-preserved old homesteads, most notably Morgan Case and Hogback. Also noteworthy is the **Rock Creek Microburst Site**, where an interpretive sign explains how a tornado-esque convergence of nature's forces in 1989 conspired to mow down hundreds of ponderosa pines on the mountainside across the creek. The road also has several campsites, the upscale Morgan–Case Homestead Forest Service rental cabin, and several trailheads that lead into the surrounding mountains, including the Welcome Creek Wilderness Area. Though the road mostly serpentines with the creek, there are a couple steep spots, so don't take your motorhomes or trailers on this one.

Porters Corner is at the junction of MT 1 and MT 38, about 6 miles south of Philipsburg. As you turn west on MT 38, look for moose in the willows on Flint Creek. In about 9 miles the paved road reaches East Fork Rock Creek, the headwaters of one of western Montana's premier trout fishing destinations. The upper stretches get less pressure because of the distance from Missoula, so there's a good chance you'll have the creek to yourself.

After following East Fork Rock Creek for about 5 miles, the West Fork joins to form the main branch of Rock Creek. The "highway" follows the West Fork Rock Creek on paved road for about 4 miles before turning into a glorified Forest Service Road that's closed for all but summer and early fall to automobile traffic (the groomed trails are popular among snowmobilers). A few miles before reaching the summit is the primitive **Crystal Creek Campground**, with three sites. At

Donna Mitchell

SKALKAHO FALLS BETWEEN PHILIPSBURG AND HAMILTON IS A HIGHLIGHT OF THE DRIVE

the pass, FS 1352 veers to the north toward the **Skalkaho Game Preserve**, a 23,000-acre forest and meadow area known for its birds, elk, deer, and occasional black bear. Three twisting miles below the pass is the route's primary attraction: the oft-photographed **Skalkaho Falls**, which lie in a popular day hiking and picnicking area. The falls tumble 150 feet over rocks just off the road.

From the falls, the road bends to the southwest and follows Daly Creek to a Darby Ranger District station and **Black Bear Campground**, another primitive Forest Service site with six camp spots. **Hamilton** (pop. 3,705), where the notorious Calamity Jane once operated a café, was a timber town but is now recasting itself as a tourist destination. Attractions include the **Daly Mansion**, built by former copper magnate and town founder Marcus Daly, and Rocky Mountain Laboratories, which was created to combat Rocky Mountain spotted fever but has since gone on to study some of the world's most dangerous diseases.

6

SOLITUDE AT ALTITUDE
The Centennial Valley

WEST YELLOWSTONE TO MONIDA

ESTIMATED LENGTH: 74 miles

ESTIMATED TIME: 3 to 5 hours

HIGHLIGHTS: Wildlife viewing, exceptional birding, hiking, Red Rock Pass, Fountain of the Missouri, Red Rock Lakes National Wildlife Refuge, Elk Lake Resort, Lakeview

GETTING THERE: From I-90, there are several ways to reach the Centennial Valley—all of them scenic. Coming from Butte on I-15, make any necessary stops for gas, food, or lodging in Dillon, Lima, or Dell before leaving the freeway at Monida, the last exit before Idaho and little more than a dilapidated collection of empty buildings. Drive through the remnants of this former railroad town and follow the signs for Lakeview and the Red Rock Lakes National Wildlife Refuge, both 28 gravel miles ahead. This is the west end of the valley and the road less traveled.

To begin at the east end, take US 191 from Bozeman through the scenic Gallatin Canyon and northwest corner of Yellowstone National Park to the community of West Yellowstone. Continue west on US 20 over the Continental Divide into Idaho. At the junction of US 20 and ID 87, turn right and drive along the north shore of Henrys Lake. Turn left on FS 055 around the west end of the lake, then veer right on Red Rock Pass Road. In West Yellowstone, stock up on any necessary goodies and fuel up because you won't see a single backcountry store until you're on I-15.

If you're coming down US 287 from Three Forks, you can shave a few miles by turning right on MT 87 across the Madison River and heading over Raynolds Pass into Idaho, where the road becomes ID 87. You'll quickly see Henrys Lake; turn right on FS 055. The entire Centennial Valley route is on gravel and dirt, and the shaded east side of Red Rock Pass can get especially soupy after spring runoff or a hard rainstorm. A high-clearance and/or four-wheel-drive vehicle is recommended, though unnecessary when conditions are dry.

SHIRAS MOOSE ARE FREQUENTLY SEEN FORAGING ON WILLOWS ALONG RED ROCK RIVER

OVERVIEW

Ask most Montana residents with an appreciation for wild country where they go to see and feel the open range of 150 years ago, and chances are good they'll take a reverent breath and utter, "the Centennial Valley." It's so remote, even for Montana, that you must leave the state to get there from the east end. Upon the second of two ascents to the Continental Divide, including a brief foray past log vacation homes on Idaho's Henrys Lake, visitors soon realize why Montanans have such high regard for this place.

The Centennial is a broad, largely unscarred and level plain with lakes, marshes, sagebrush, a handful of sprawling cattle ranches, one tiny unincorporated community (Lakeview, no services), and the Red Rock River meandering through its heart. It is buffered by the burly shoulders of the Centennial Mountains to the south and the southern tips of the rugged

THREE PIONEER CEMETERIES ARE WITHIN CLOSE PROXIMITY TO THE MAIN ROAD THROUGH THE CENTENNIAL VALLEY

A HANDFUL OF MULTI-GENERATIONAL RANCH FAMILIES LIVE IN THE CENTENNIAL VALLEY, WHICH LOOKS MUCH LIKE IT DID 150 YEARS AGO. THE 385,000-ACRE VALLEY ALSO HAS A WILDLIFE REFUGE

Snowcrests, Blacktails, and Gravellys to the north. It's a place where winged creatures outnumber bipeds by about 10,000 to one. Depending on your mindset, an aura of serenity or loneliness exists here, and there is a palpable separation from the modern world. Also making the Centennial extraordinary: The 385,000-acre valley and mountain range of the same name run east–west, an oddity in the Northern Rockies. It is thus a critical wildlife corridor between Greater Yellowstone—which is essentially an ecological island amid a sea of increasing development—and the wilds of central Idaho and Montana's Glacier region. Birders will be in avian heaven in the 44,963-acre Red Rock Lakes National Wildlife Refuge, which features more than 240 species. The refuge was created in 1935 because of its importance as a stopover for migratory waterfowl such as the endangered trumpeter swan and prehistoric-sounding sandhill crane. Almost all the native wildlife from 200 years ago still roam the valley—the notable exception being bison.

It's difficult to imagine, especially if you enter from the east side, that the Centennial was once relatively heavily traveled and occupied. Before E. H. Harriman of the Union Pacific Railroad punched his Oregon Short Line through the mountains from Ashton, Idaho, to West Yellowstone in 1908, one of the primary routes to Yellowstone National Park was through the Centennial. Passengers on the Northern Pacific Railroad disembarked at Monida and took the Centennial Stage to West Yellowstone, exchanging horses every 15 miles. Former president Teddy Roosevelt, perhaps the father of American conservation, reportedly took the journey once. Another ex-president, Harry S. Truman, shook the hands of locals at a train stop in Monida, now a virtual ghost town. Lakeview was a base for Utah & Northern Railroad workers who commuted to where the main Northern Pacific line crosses Monida Pass—which draws its name from the first three letters of both states.

The Centennial Valley, named by early cattle rancher Rachael Orr, who first saw the valley during America's centennial in 1876, has been preserved for many reasons, foremost among them its remoteness and an unforgiving climate. The valley also has been spared mineral exploration and rapacious logging for similar reasons. And the fifteen multigenerational ranch families that own 90 percent of the 100,000 acres of private land in the Centennial have cultivated a conservation ethic. The ranchers, the federal Bureau of Land Management, and The Nature Conservancy—which owns much of the remaining 10 percent of private land—have forged a partnership dedicated to preserving the Centennial's wide-open spaces and ranching legacy. Their shared vision has fostered a balance between utilitarian use of the land and preservation of wildlife habitat, so future generations can drive the bumpy 51 miles and see some of our most iconic critters, including grizzly bears, wolves, Shiras moose, bighorn sheep, eagles, snipe, and trumpeter swans.

HITTING THE ROAD

To fully appreciate the lack of intrusion into this wonderland, start your journey at **West Yellowstone** (pop. 1,321), a crowded metropolis compared to the rest of the route. Once a getaway for Las Vegas hoteliers and a few of their sordid friends—which explains the oddly named Desert Inn Motel, for example—this outpost enveloped by lodgepole pines and hard on the western boundary of Yellowstone National Park is working to transform its rubber-tomahawk souvenir-shop image into one of more sophistication and diversity. For nearly five decades, its winter existence has revolved around snowmobiling, and its summer season has been dominated by families in station wagons and minivans, all eager to see Old Faithful. If you're looking for activities other than what the natural world has to offer, the **IMAX Theater** (406-646-4100) and **Grizzly & Wolf Discovery Center** (406-646-7001/800-257-2570), adjacent to each other near the edge of town, will fill the bill. If you miss seeing some of the wildlife in the park, catch them in living

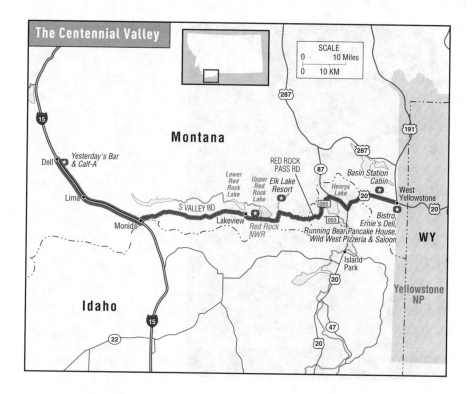

The Centennial Valley

SCALE
0   10 Miles
0   10 KM

Montana

Idaho

WY

Yellowstone NP

color at the Discovery Center, where the bears don't hibernate because they have a year-round source of food. West Yellowstone has plenty of lodging and dining during the summer, but many businesses close during the winter and shoulder seasons.

As you head west from West, look closely at the mountain range in full view straight ahead. With a little imagination, it's easy to see why the 10,080-foot peak along the Continental Divide is called Lionhead. You'll soon be over Targhee Pass into Idaho. Though this is a book about Montana, we suggest spending a day on **Henrys Lake** trolling for legendary trophy trout. The sweeping valley before you is the key wildlife connector between Yellowstone and the Centennial. To the southwest, you'll see what looks like a giant golf ball on top of a peak. This is a radio tower atop Sawtelle Mountain, the eastern terminus of the Centennials. If you turn right on ID 87, you'll meet up with FS 055 in about 6 miles.

If you continue south on US 20 toward **Island Park, Idaho**, you can turn right on FS 053 in 6 miles. Either way, the two gravel Forest Service roads meet just off the southwest corner of Henrys Lake, about 3.5 miles shy of **Red Rock Pass**. After passing a few log homes, the road ascends through aspens to the modest pass—and a welcome step back in time.

Red Rock Pass is more of a long and gradual bump in the road than an

THE CONTINENTAL DIVIDE TRAIL
CROSSES THE CENTENNIAL RANGE
ALONG THE MONTANA-IDAHO BORDER

actual pass. After a brief descent through fir and pine, the Centennial's wide world of wonder begins to unfurl, with an endless horizon between five mountain ranges. There are no homes and few power lines to mar the view—only a few fence lines and an occasional mailbox marking a hidden ranch house. Immediately to the south are the towering Centennials. Tucked deep into the forest, **Brower Spring**, aka the Fountain of the Missouri, trickles from the flanks of Mount Jefferson at 9,030 feet in elevation, and its waters begin a 2,530-mile journey to their meeting with the Mississippi River in St. Louis. No waters anywhere in the United States travel farther. It's a strenuous hike into wild country, but if you're fit and determined, you'll be one of few Americans to say they have sipped from the uppermost Missouri headwaters, which are marked by a pile of rocks; an easier trail comes from Sawtelle Peak. Park at the Hell Roaring Creek Trailhead, give yourself a good half day to cover the territory, and bring bear spray. If you're not comfortable going on your own, **Hellroaring Powder Guides** (208-360-0385) and **Centennial Outfitters** (406-276-3463) offer backcountry pack trips, the former to a yurt in the winter and the latter on half-day, full-day or overnight horseback trips to cabins in the summer.

Back on Red Rock Pass Road, you'll follow the south shore of Upper Red

Rock Lake. Look for trumpeter swans and ducks on the lake, sandhill cranes and white-faced ibis in the grasses, and Shiras moose browsing on the willows. On the other side of the road, look for pronghorn in the sagebrush and elk moving in and out of the tree line—and you might even spot a wolf or bear. If you have your fly rod, these clean, cold waters offer great fishing, including the chance to catch (and release) westslope cutthroat trout.

Welcome to the **Red Rock Lakes National Wildlife Refuge** (406-276-3536), literally the country's last best place for trumpeter swans. Some 30 to 50 can be seen at any given time (in pairs and family groups), with that figure bumping up to 100 cygnets and mature birds in the summer. The northeast corner is federally protected wilderness, one of the few marshes in the country given a designation that strictly prohibits development, mechanized vehicles, and even chainsaws for cutting firewood. There are no established human trails. Any noticeably trafficked route across the grasslands was created by wildlife. The refuge is also a National Natural Landmark.

Much of the area's human activity begins at the refuge's headquarters in **Lakeview** (pop. 86). A drive-through kiosk provides maps and an overview, and a cabin houses U.S. Fish & Wildlife Service staffers who happily offer more detailed insights and information. Though abundant bird life is every-

COMMONLY SEEN IN THE SAGEBRUSH, PRONGHORN IS THE FASTEST LAND MAMMAL IN NORTH AMERICA

THIS REFUGE POINT ABOVE THE MADISON RIVER, WHERE CAMPERS SPENT A TERRIFYING NIGHT IN AUGUST 1959, IS NOW A POPULAR NORDIC SKIING SPOT

where, you'll be thankful for bringing a spotting scope. Access to both **Upper and Lower Red Rock Lakes** is limited. Hiking is allowed anywhere, but it can be dicey. Wander off a game trail, and you could find yourself thigh deep in a bog. The best time to see the widest variety of wildlife here is in the fall, before snowdrifts close Red Rock Pass to autos.

Lakeview is mostly a collection of small cabins. Aside from the refuge, it's also the home of the **International Center for Earth Concerns**, a non-profit that preserves and protects habitat in the United States and as far away as Kenya. Headquarters are located in a renovated historic structure that's hard to miss. The center has also been restoring and preserving settler homes in the valley, and has plans for a museum.

Heading west, you'll notice Lakeview's connection to the outside world: telephone poles stretching to the horizon. The valley broadens even more, and thousands of black dots appear amid the grass and sage. These are Angus cattle tended by ranching families that have braved long, fierce winters and isolation for more than a century. Most of those same cattle will spend their winters in milder climes to the north. These sweeping views remain much the same for the next 28 miles, with only the mountains to the north changing—from the southern tip of the Gravellys to the southern edge of the even more secluded Snowcrests. The more adventurous and freeway-averse might consider turning north on FS 202, an improved gravel road that slices between the Snowcrest and Blacktail ranges en route to a meeting with I-15 at Dillon.

If you continue on to I-15 at Monida, the first services are still another 15 miles to the northwest at Lima. For more conventional lodging and dining, continue past Lima to Dillon. **Clark Canyon Reservoir** is a well-used recreation site, and the Beaverhead River downstream from the dam is a favorite of trout fishermen, especially in the spring and early summer when other rivers are largely unfishable due to spring runoff. See the Big Hole Loop for more on Dillon.

Best Places to Bunk

WEST YELLOWSTONE: Lodging is pretty homogenous in this theme-park-like town, ranging from clean and well-kept mom-and-pops to standard chain motels. It's difficult to distinguish between the 30-plus properties, including chains such as the two Best Westerns, a Days Inn, and an upscale Holiday Inn, many of which sprang up when West Yellowstone had unrestricted snowmobile access to Yellowstone National Park during the winters. A few to which we're partial begin with the year-round **Brandin' Iron Inn** ($$, 406-646-9411). It's a basic motel, but the 80 affordable rooms were recently renovated and the owners are engaged in the community. Another is the year-round **Hibernation Station** ($$, 406-646-4200), an intimately grouped collection of log cabins with bright interiors. The 1931 **Evergreen Motel** ($$, 406-646-7655, April–Oct.) is a pleasant motor-court motel—in fact, its original name was Evergreen Auto Court—with pretty hanging flower baskets outside of tastefully decorated rooms. For a taste of the town's earliest history, **The Historic Madison Hotel** ($$, 406-646-7745, May–Oct.) is a hotel, motel, and youth hostel rolled into one. The two-story 1912 building, which is on the National Register of Historic Places, has much of the original architecture, and many of the rooms feature original antique furnishings and clawfoot tubs. Lodging options include upstairs hotel rooms that sleep up to four, cabin-themed motel rooms in back and male/female dormitory-style hostel accommodations for less than $45 per night.

CENTENNIAL VALLEY: The **J Bar L Ranch** ($$$$, 406-684-5927) is an innovative working cattle ranch that raises grass-fed beef in a valley that time forgot. Rockefeller heir Peggy Dulany bought the ranch in the early 2000s and restored four decaying pioneer buildings for vacationers who'll truly appreciate the regenerative values of being in the middle of nowhere. The two-story Anderson House and three-story Smith House were originally homes. The log-built Stibal Barn once housed livestock, and the most luxurious, the Brundage Cabins, are actually three rustically elegant off-road cabins overlooking the meandering Red Rock River. For anyone wanting another original Centennial Valley experience, **Elk Lake Resort** ($$/$$$, 406-276-3282) is a throwback to dude ranch camps. The resort, which likes to say it's on the "backside of nowhere," is open seasonally and only accessible by snowmobile in the winter. The modest collection of seven cabins plus ranch house can be rented nightly with breakfast buffet included, or as multi-day packages with or without three meals. Due to the effort required to secure food elsewhere, you'll be glad you opted for the meals.

LIMA: The **Mountain View Motel & RV Park** ($, 406-276-3535) just off the I-15 exit has clean, serviceable lodging for "bucks and does," and a made-in-Montana gift shop. **Jan's Café** ($$, 406-276-3484) has two gussied-up cabins (next to the diner) that sleep up to six in each. Beware: no Wi-Fi.

DELL: Off the interstate and just down the road from the Calf-A is the **Stockyard Inn** ($$, 406-276-3501), providing seasonal lodging (closed Dec. 15–April 15) in six upscale western-themed rooms, including one suite with a *pink* Jacuzzi tub. Ellen and Mark O'Brien's reasonable rates ($85/night) include a continental breakfast with homemade muffins. High-end dinners are planned entirely around guests' wishes—Ellen went to culinary school—and average around $20 per person. Many returning guests request the pork medallions in apricot brandy sauce or stuffed shrimp.

Alternative Bunking

WEST YELLOWSTONE: Six miles west of town on US 20 is the 200-acre **Bar N Ranch** ($$$, 406-646-0300, May–Oct.), which has upscale lodge rooms and cabins, and a chef-prepared breakfast that can be included in your package deal. Besides the distinctions of personal hot tubs (cabins), wood-burning fireplaces, and a full-service bar, guests have access to a secluded section of the Madison River for blue-ribbon trout fishing. Six lodge rooms share a hot tub and heated pool. For "glampers," now located behind the ranch are tents that range from $90 to $400 per night (May–Sept.). Several styles are available, including a family tent with an adjacent teepee for the kids. When the lodge is open, the restaurant is open to the public. For what you get, the prices aren't out of line.

CAMPING: In the Red Rock Lakes National Wildlife Refuge, the **Upper and Lower Red Rock Lake Campgrounds** are open year-round. They are accessible in winter only by snow machine and seldom filled—perfect for solitude and wildlife viewing. A bit primitive, you'll find Port-a-Potties, potable water in the spring, fire rings (no chainsaws permitted), and picnic tables.

FOREST SERVICE CABINS/LOOKOUTS: (Reservations: 877-444-6777 or www.recreation.gov.) The **Basin Station Cabin** (406-823-6961, $30/sleeps four) on the Gallatin National Forest is 2 miles off US 20 and along Denny Creek Road about 7 miles west of West Yellowstone, so it isn't the primitive experience one thinks of in terms of cabins and lookouts, but its accessibility is a bonus. For a serious sense of solitude, try the remote **West Fork Cabin** (406-682-4253, $35/sleeps three) on the West Fork of the Madison River on the Beaverhead-Deerlodge National Forest. As the crow flies, it's less than 10 miles due north of the North Side Road just east of Eureka Basin, but get a map from the Madison Ranger District when making reservations. Another great primitive experience is the **Antone Cabin** (406-682-4253, $35/sleeps two) at the end of a gravel road in the southern end of the Snowcrests. Though Antone has a nearby spring, it's unreliable, and potable water should be brought to all these cabins, which feature propane cooking stoves and outhouses. Antone Cabin can be reached from the Centennial Valley via the Blacktail Creek Road (FS 202), which is an exceptional off-the-beaten-byway gravel route back to Dillon.

Best Eats

WEST YELLOWSTONE: The Pulitzer Prize–winning novelist J. R. Moehringer once said that "history is the narrative of people searching for a place to go." The **Madison River Crossing** ($$, 406-646-7621, D) fits the narrative for people searching for *that* place to go . . .a low-key place away from West's tourist energy. American food staples and neon arrows point "this way" to a well-stirred cocktail or fine glass of wine and some delectably delicious dinners served by a professional yet friendly staff. **Bullwinkle's Saloon & Eatery** ($$, 406-646-9664/406-646-7974, L/D), and **Ernie's Deli** ($, 406-646-9467, B/L/D) are also open year-round. Bullwinkle's is the place to get messy with baby-back ribs but also offers some not-so-standard specialty salads, pan-fried trout, and pasta along with the ubiquitous beef and bison steaks. They also own a conveniently located liquor/wine/beer store where you are welcome to purchase a bottle to accompany your meal. Ernie's has eye-opening morning coffee, sandwiches, salads, and plenty of vegetarian options. Check out the latest area earthquake activity on Ernie's Web site; it will awaken you to the shaky ground beneath your feet. If you're a big breakfast fan but not in a big hurry, head over to **Running Bear Pancake House** ($/$$, 406-646-7703, B/L), open summer and winter but not during the shoulder seasons. For an

Gravelly Range Road (72 miles)

For those who have traversed it, the Gravelly Range Road evokes a certain reverence. What makes this adventure on gravel unusual even for Montana is that about half of the route rides the spine of a mountain range—the Gravellys.

The Gravellys aren't the most dramatic mountains in Montana, but the ability to drive along their backbone yields extraordinary views of the Snowcrest, Madison, Tobacco Root, and Greenhorn ranges in addition to the Gravellys, plus the Madison and Ruby River valleys, and the Madison River—all from a road that seems to unwind just beneath the clouds, and all with an incomparable sense of isolation. What makes this adventure possible are the relatively sedate contours of the Gravellys, though don't be fooled: some peaks rise above 10,000 feet, and much of the route is above 8,000 feet.

Especially spectacular are the 38 miles from Ennis southwest to Black Butte Cabin. But we encourage taking an entire day and covering all 72 miles at a leisurely pace. And the beauty of this drive is that it's comfortable in a typical sedan; no high-clearance or 4-wheel-drive needed, unless you encounter rain and subsequent gumbo where the roads are dirt instead of gravel.

The Gravellys got their name from the coarse pebbles that comprise much of the range. In some of the lower reaches, over time these pebbles have been ground to a fine dust called talc. The range is one of the largest producers of talc in the world, though you won't see any evidence of it on this adventure. The Gravelly Range is so wild—with the grizzly bears and wolves to prove it—that conservation groups have worked (unsuccessfully thus far) to protect parts of it and the Snowcrest Range to the west as wilderness. These mountains serve as stepping-stones for geographically isolated Greater Yellowstone wildlife going to and from the wilds of central Idaho and northwest Montana. Elk and deer are everywhere.

Don't come on the Gravelly Range Road thinking you'll find an ice cream stand or souvenir shop for a break. The closest thing to services is **Black Butte Cabin**, a primitive one-room building at 8,900 feet in elevation that's in the Forest Service's recreational rental program. The cabin is B.Y.O.E.— Bring Your Own Everything, except mattress pads, cooking utensils, and firewood. It does offer unobstructed views of 10,546-foot Black Butte Mountain (the highest in the range) and incomparable stargazing.

In short, this drive is all about scenery and seclusion at the top of the world. Much of the route is rolling from sub-alpine mountain meadow to sub-alpine mountain meadow, punctuated by forested draws and ravines. Spectacular expanses of wildflowers linger here deep into July, long after they've succumbed to the heat of summer elsewhere. About 20 miles past the junction at Black Butte, which offers the opportunity to escape westward to the Ruby River Valley or east to the more populated Madison at West Fork, the road begins its gradual descent into the remote Centennial Valley.

There are several ways to come at the Gravelly Range Road: Starting in Ennis in the Madison River Valley and finishing in the Centennial, starting in the Centennial and concluding in Ennis, or a shorter compromise. Most folks start in Ennis, but that means after 72 miles you've still got another hour or more of driving on dirt and gravel in the Centennial before eventually arriving in West Yellowstone. Starting in the Centennial means you'll have dining, lodging, and fuel options awaiting you're arrival in Ennis, where you can drop your bags in a motel and head for the Madison River with a fly rod. If you don't want to commit an entire day, start in Ennis, drive to the Black Butte junction, and return to US 287 on the gravel Standard Creek Road to West Fork.

As with many of Montana's dirt backroads, it isn't advisable to drive this route during or immediately after a rainstorm. Parts of the road turn to muck or become rutted, especially in the southern reaches. Also, the road typically isn't entirely accessible until late June; earlier in the spring, it isn't unusual to be able to drive for miles on a dry, sunny day, only to be abruptly halted by a snowdrift.

ultra-fine dining experience Memorial Day through September, **Bar N Ranch** ($$$, 406-646-0300) will tantalize your taste buds with seared salmon, pasta prima, hazelnut trout, and bison ribeye. If a full dinner is more than you want, select from their bistro menu offerings that include well-dressed burgers, roasted chicken tacos, and Cajun shrimp salad.

LIMA: Jan's Café ($$, 406-276-3484, B/L/D) has been around since the 1960s and is known locally for a filling pork-sausage cowboy burger and delicious deep-dish fruit and cream pies.

DELL: Bring your hunger to one of the more renowned rural restaurants in Montana—and not just among I-15 truckers. **Yesterday's Calf-A** ($$, 406-276-3308, B/L/D) is 8 miles northwest of Lima on the interstate, seemingly in the middle of nowhere. They still believe in old-fashioned service, real home cooking, and huge helpings. The Calf-A, housed in an 1890s red-brick schoolhouse, bell and belfry still intact, has school furniture, real chalk boards, and pleasing aromas. Tender beef pot roast alongside a mountain of mashed potatoes and thick brown gravy is a staple, as are the homemade pies, cinnamon rolls, and other sweet treats. Outside seating in summer gets an A-plus for views of the towering Tendoy Mountains.

YESTERDAY'S CALF-A IN DELL, ONCE A PIONEER SCHOOLHOUSE, IS A FAVORITE OF I-15 TRAVELERS FOR ITS HOMESTYLE COOKING

Best Bar

WEST YELLOWSTONE: Not only does the **Wild West Pizzeria & Saloon** (406-646-4400) have the best pizza in Greater Yellowstone, it also has the best hangout factor. The pizzas—hand-tossed, made from Wheat Montana brand flour, and topped with freshly grated Wisconsin mozzarella cheese—take some time to get to your table. But they are definitely worth the wait. Meanwhile, big-screen TVs in the handsome, expanded digs make the wait tolerable as well. The bar has a pool table and can get loud, so just take your beverage back to the pine tables and benches for cordial conversation about Yellowstone National Park and other elements of the Wild West. Another bonus: it's open year-round.

DETOUR: ONE FOR THE ROAD

The Gallatin Canyon
Gallatin Gateway to West Yellowstone

ESTIMATED LENGTH: 76 miles
HIGHLIGHTS: Scenic vistas, wildlife viewing, Big Sky, Yellowstone National Park

Some of the most beautiful images from *A River Runs Through It* were filmed in this picturesque canyon. For about 65 miles, twisting US 191 separates the Gallatin and Madison ranges, hugging the Gallatin River from the mouth of the canyon just south of Bozeman to within a few miles of the river's genesis in Yellowstone National Park.

The highlight is clearly the scenery, with realistic chances of seeing bear, moose, elk, deer, and bison. In fact, from March to May, when bison are migrating from the park to greener pastures west of US 191, it's imperative to keep a close eye out for the shaggy beasts—especially at night. Most of the drive features steep canyon slopes blanketed in Douglas fir and lodgepole pine, but midway you'll reach the congestion of **Big Sky** (pop. 2,308), a destination resort that sprang from a mountain meadow almost overnight in the mid-1970s. Along the way are periodic guest ranches and steakhouses, all adding to the vibe.

A note of caution: The Gallatin Canyon is also one of Montana's most dangerous drives, a sobering reality marked by the steady parade of white crosses flanking the road. Many locals headed to West Yellowstone opt for the broad Madison Valley just to the west instead of negotiating the S-turns in the canyon. The traffic eased some in the down economy, when fewer construction workers were making the twice-daily pilgrimages to build trophy homes for the rich in Big Sky and the ultra-rich at the Yellowstone Club. But a building boom was underway again in 2015 and traffic has picked up, especially in the early morning and late afternoon.

US 191 leaves I-90 at Bozeman, but you can also continue to the Belgrade exit 8 miles to the northwest and take Jackrabbit Road south to Four Corners. Continue south toward the mountains and the mouth of the Gallatin Canyon. The most striking feature before the canyon is the **Gallatin Gateway Inn**, an extravagant 42,000-square-foot Spanish-style building constructed in 1927 as a terminus for the Chicago, Milwaukee & St. Paul Railway spur that brought Yellowstone visitors to the area. The inn has had lodging and dining, even recently, but as of late 2015 neither was offered, and the stately building was for sale.

A few miles later, you'll enter the canyon, and the Gallatin immediately changes from a braided, meandering cottonwood-lined stream to a swift emerald river with solid whitewater stretches. Just past Spanish Creek, look upstream to Storm Castle, a jutting rock formation. Farther along on the left is a fast-paced straight stretch of river known as "The Mad Mile," a favorite of rafters and kayakers when water levels are accommodating in the spring and early summer. The highlight is a giant boulder midstream called House Rock. A wide pullout allows drivers to watch rafts and kayaks navigate the frothy run.

Thirty-six miles south of Gallatin Gateway is the only stoplight between Four Corners and West Yellowstone: The junction of MT 64. Two miles up that road is the town of Big Sky, and a few miles past that are **Big Sky Ski Resort** and **Lone Mountain Ranch**, both popular ski destinations. This area was a picturesque ranch when the late NBC newscaster Chet Huntley, a Montana native, rode in with friends on horseback in the early 1970s, envisioning a golf resort. When he saw Lone Mountain rising on the western skyline, the vision abruptly changed to deep powder and chairlifts. Big Sky still has plenty for golfers, most notably the courses designed by former professional stars Arnold Palmer and Tom Weiskopf, a Bozeman resident.

South of Big Sky, the terrain gets wilder and less populated. Aside from an occasional restaurant (**The Corral** is a great beer and burger stop) and a few historic guest ranches (the **Cinnamon Lodge** has an above-average restaurant, bar, and cabins on the Gallatin River), there aren't as many people on this stretch, though you'll have company in the form of fly fishermen casting to rainbow and cutthroat trout. After Sage Creek, Taylor Fork, and the rustic all-inclusive **Elkhorn Ranch**, the road enters Yellowstone National Park, where the speed limit drops to 55 mph for 25 miles; there is no park fee to drive this stretch. Several trailheads are along US 191 here, including the popular Bighorn and Fawn Pass trails, which join to form a loop in the mountains to the east. If you do hike, bring bear spray, make noise, and, if possible, travel in groups of four or more.

Eventually US 191 leaves the park, crests a hill, and brings into view the broad Madison Valley, carpeted by lodgepole pine. In the winter and spring, chances are good you'll see a bison ambling alongside the road. They are allowed to remain outside the park until mid-May, when Montana's Department of Livestock chases them back. Long, pine-lined straightaways subsequently lead into the town of West Yellowstone.

REMNANTS OF PARROT CASTLE, AN OLD MINING FACILITY, RISE ABOVE THE JEFFERSON RIVER

7

GHOST TOWNS AND LIVING HISTORY

The Vigilante Trail

THREE FORKS TO CARDWELL

ESTIMATED LENGTH: 118 miles

ESTIMATED TIME: 3 hours to 2 days

HIGHLIGHTS: Missouri Headwaters State Park, Norris Hot Springs, Madison River, Virginia City, Nevada City, garnet mines, Parrot Castle, Renova Hot Springs, Lewis and Clark Caverns State Park

GETTING THERE: Because a small section of this loop parallels I-90, there are several options: Leave the interstate at Whitehall and head south on MT 55 toward Twin Bridges; get off at Cardwell and drive toward Whitehall or La Hood, then exit at US 287 just west of Three Forks; or, start your tour at the Three Forks exit with a visit to Missouri Headwaters State Park. Coming from the east, you might even leave I-90 at Bozeman and follow US 191 down Main Street through Four Corners to Norris. Regardless, leave plenty of time because few routes pack more unique adventures into 120 miles than this one.

OVERVIEW

Think Montana mining history, and the yawning holes in the earth around Butte and Anaconda may come to mind. To reach farther back into Montana mining lore, back to the pick-and-shovel days, ply the Vigilante Trail, which has no fewer than six ghost towns within its circumference. The drive surrounds the stately Tobacco Root Mountains, which are littered with rusting mining equipment easily rediscovered by hikers ascending to the range's sparkling alpine lakes. The ghost towns of Pony (which is still active) and Mammoth (which isn't) are tucked into this deceptively burly mountain range.

The fulcrum of this route is colorful Virginia City, the Colonial Williamsburg of the West. Once a rootin'-tootin' territorial capital that was the largest city in the Inland Northwest after the Civil War, today "VC" boasts the oldest functioning county courthouse in Montana amid authentic buildings still doing business—albeit mostly for tourists. Virginia City is at the eastern and uppermost end of what 150 years ago was dubbed "Fourteen-Mile City" because the community stretched for 14 miles along Alder Gulch to present-day Alder. As you drive between Virginia City and Alder on MT 287, you'll notice mile after mile and pile after pile of rounded river rock along Alder Creek, almost as if a backhoe were breaking ground for a long strip mall. These are the remnants of placer mining, which entails collecting gold nuggets and flakes on the surface—as opposed to hard-rock mining, where shafts or open pits are dug to reach veins underground. The mounds are a result of using hydraulic jets to separate gold from dirt and rocks, a high-tech form of mining that replaced the less intrusive but less effective gold pans. The Alder Gulch placer mines produced more gold than any other region in the Northwest. Because of this prosperity, in its heyday Virginia City had 1,200 buildings, as well as the first school and newspaper in the territory.

The area wasn't just about mining, though. Before railroad spurs were built to West Yellowstone and Gallatin Gateway, Virginia City was the hub of traffic to Yellowstone National Park. By 1875, as the mines began playing out and settlers migrated, the state capital was moved to Helena. The town rapidly began losing population and fell into disrepair until the 1940s, when a family named Bovey bought much of what remained and began restoration. The entire city became a National Historic Landmark in 1961 and has a multitude of street-side plaques to prove it.

After spending an afternoon or longer walking the wood planks of Virginia City and absorbing all the activities, you might be inclined to take a passing nod at what appears to be little more than a collection of dilapidated frontier buildings and speed right through the blinking yellow light in Nevada City. We advise against it. In many ways, Nevada City captures the essence of Montana's frontier mining legacy even more than Virginia City, and it is a museum unto itself. There are fourteen original buildings here. The remainder, thanks in great measure to the Boveys, were rescued from just about every corner of the state, including a saddlery from the Indian agency in Fort Benton frequented by celebrated Western artist C. M. Russell.

But there's much, much more to this route. The Madison River at fly-fishing-centric Ennis is a world-famous trout stream, and the four rivers converging near the bicycle-friendly community of Twin Bridges aren't far behind in their angling prowess. Lewis and Clark Caverns State Park features the most extensive and accessible labyrinth of limestone caves in the Northern Rockies. Two hot springs, Norris and Renova, offer contrasting experiences: one primitively developed, the other just primitive. And then there's Three Forks, with its white and pillared Sacajawea Hotel, a choice spot to unwind after a day exploring the site where the mighty Missouri River begins its journey to St. Louis after collecting the waters of the Madison, Jefferson, and Gallatin rivers.

HITTING THE ROAD

Where to begin? We suggest **Three Forks** (pop. 1,904), a mostly blue-collar community whose economy is tied to agriculture and a talc plant. The most impressive landmark is **The Sacajawea Hotel**, which had its first heyday around the turn of the previous century. That's when passengers were dropped at the Milwaukee Road railway station across the street and then rested at the hotel while awaiting a carriage ride to Yellowstone. Three Forks' fate changed when the railroad extended a spur farther south to Gallatin Gateway, and now the old station is a Chinese restaurant. But the 100-year-old hotel, owned and carefully refurbished by the Folkvord family of Wheat Montana renown, is breathing living history into the community.

Before leaving Three Forks, wander the trails and read the interpretive signs at the 532-acre **Missouri Headwaters State Park** (406-285-3610). Each summer evening features speakers who recount stories, including tales of Lewis and Clark camping at the confluence of the three rivers and the Shoshone woman Sacagawea's capture by Hidatsa Indians when she was 13 years old. Heading southwest of Three Forks on US 287/MT 2 west of the Jefferson River, the sod-roofed **Parker Homestead**, formerly a part of Montana's state parks system, is still standing on the west side of the highway, though now on private property and blocked from any exploration by a barbed-wire fence.

Where MT 2 and US 287 split near Sappington Bridge over the Jefferson, veer south on 287 toward **Harrison** (pop. 162). Agricultural lands begin to give way to sagebrush steppe as you continue another 12 miles south to **Norris** (pop. 131), which is little more than a wide junction in the road with little more than a gas station and the friendly **Norris Bar**, with a trinket shop in back. Most people hurry through from Bozeman to Ennis, but 1 mile east on MT 84 is a rejuvenated and family-friendly **Norris Hot Springs** (406-685-3303), aka "Water of the Gods." Norris lures locals and tourists in the know for a soak, good eats from a predominantly locally sourced menu, and live music played from a geodome stage on weekends. The intimate pool is emptied and filled daily, but closed on Mondays and Tuesdays for a thorough scrubbing.

South of Norris, US 287 climbs over a modest pass, revealing majestic views of the Tobacco Root, Gravelly, and Madison ranges above Ennis Lake and the famous Madison Valley. Although the Madison River is a fisherman's paradise from source to mouth, the brisk stretch above **Ennis** (pop. 852), reverently called the 50-Mile Riffle, is famous for its lunker rainbow and

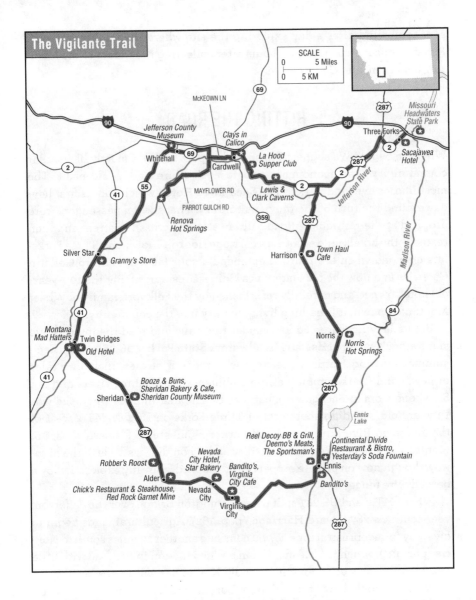

The Vigilante Trail

SCALE
0   5 Miles
0   5 KM

McKEOWN LN

69

287

Missouri
Headwaters
State Park

90

Jefferson County
Museum

Clays in
Calico

Three Forks

Whitehall

69

Cardwell

La Hood
Supper Club

Sacajawea
Hotel

2

MAYFLOWER RD

Lewis &
Clark Caverns

287

41

55

PARROT GULCH RD

2

2

Jefferson River

Renova
Hot Springs

359

287

Silver Star

Granny's Store

Harrison

Town Haul
Cafe

Madison River

41

84

Montana
Mad Hatters

Twin Bridges

Old Hotel

Norris

Norris
Hot Springs

41

Booze & Buns,
Sheridan Bakery & Cafe,
Sheridan County Museum

287

Sheridan

Ennis
Lake

Reel Decoy BB & Grill,
Deemo's Meats,
The Sportsman's

Continental Divide
Restaurant & Bistro,
Yesterday's Soda Fountain

287

Robber's Roost

Nevada
City Hotel,
Star Bakery

Bandito's,
Virginia
City Cafe

Ennis

Alder

Bandito's

Chick's Restaurant & Steakhouse,
Red Rock Garnet Mine

Nevada
City

Virginia
City

287

brown trout. That Ennis caters to these anglers is obvious from the large
sculpture of a fly fisherman in a small plaza at the junction of US 287 and
MT 287. For some tasty Montana treats, **Deemo's Meats** (406-682-7306),
formerly Restvedt & Son Meat Market, is renowned for its jerky and smoked
meats but also has baked goods, sweet treats, and fresh vegetables. From
Ennis, head right on MT 287, which curls south and begins rising to a divide
between the Tobacco Roots on the north and Gravellys to the south. After
driving past clusters of ranchettes, stop at one of the overlooks and take
a sweeping last look at the Madison Valley, with the Madison Range as a
dramatic backdrop. Looking due east, you'll see the treeless Blaze and Lone

Mountains, and to the south is a square-jawed buttress called Sphinx Mountain. Once at the summit, you'll immediately begin the winding drop toward **Virginia City** (pop. 195). Most of the historic buildings are on the main drag, Wallace Street, west of Broadway. Virginia City and **Nevada City** both provide informative tabloid-shaped handouts during tourist season for walking tours. Park in Virginia City and get a different view of both towns by taking the narrow-gauge **Alder Gulch Short Line Railroad** (406-843-5247) to Nevada City and back. The train operates Memorial Day Weekend through mid-September and leaves on the hour.

A requisite stop while visiting Virginia City is to take in one—or both—of the town's lively entertainment offerings. The **Opera House** (406-843-5314, May–Sept.) is home to the state's oldest professional acting company, the Virginia City Players, who perform classic family-oriented vaudeville Tuesdays through Sundays. In the original Gilbert Brewery building is the more tawdry **Brewery Follies** (406-843-5218/800-829-2969, May–Sept.), which offers blue humor that can turn any ghost's face red. Speaking of ghosts, tours of the town's many haunted buildings are offered at 9 PM each night in the summer.

Unlike its neighboring city, where folks still work and play amid living history, Nevada City is a sprawling open-air museum. Rusted mining equipment is scattered about crumbling railroad cars on the south side of MT 287. On the north side, the Boveys have put together an entire community of wooden structures, accessed between the Music Hall and Dry Goods Store. If some of the buildings look vaguely familiar, perhaps it's because of the scenes from *Little Big Man, The Missouri Breaks,* and other Western movies filmed here. The town features daily living-history reenactments during the summer, with locals dressed in 1860s garb and engaging in period-appropriate conversations. Try to see the two-story outhouse, the gallows barn where a triple hanging took place, and China Town—a tribute to an often-exploited but nevertheless invaluable Asian culture and its contributions to the American West.

After departing Nevada City to the west on MT 287, the placer mounds along the creek become more pronounced as you get closer to a blip on the blacktop called **Alder** (pop. 116), the railroad terminus for all the mining equipment transported to the gulch. Right before you enter town you'll find **Red Rock Garnet Mine** (406-842-5760), where you can pan for gold or try your luck digging for gems. You're now in the mistakenly named **Ruby Valley**, so dubbed because when garnets were first discovered here they were confused for rubies. If trout fishing is your gig, the Ruby River below Ruby Dam is great for wading or bank fishing. Much of the Ruby flows through private land, but there are four fishing access sites south of town, and you're allowed to ply any stretch of a Montana river as long as you stay below the normal high-water mark. At Alder, MT 287 bends north through **Laurin** (La-Ray),

THE ALDER GULCH SHORTLINE NARROW-GAUGE RAILROAD CONNECTS VIRGINIA CITY WITH NEVADA CITY, A MILE AND A HALF AWAY

a ghost town of sorts that has a **Hangman's Tree,** the stately limestone **St. Mary of the Assumption** gothic-style church, and the abandoned two-story **Robber's Roost** roadhouse on the left side of the highway. At Robber's Roost, read the story of stagecoach travelers between Virginia City and Bannack who were robbed and terrorized by so-called road agents.

This is the heart of the Garnet, er, Ruby Valley, with **Sheridan** (pop. 659) as its peaceful hub on the Ruby River. From Sheridan, the valley broadens to accommodate the convergence of the Ruby, Beaverhead, and Big Hole rivers at **Twin Bridges** (pop. 381), where Lewis and Clark camped two centuries ago. Bicycle-friendly Twin Bridges, which bills itself as "The Town That Cares," has a lot going on for a community with one blinking-light intersection. This is the home of the world-famous **R.L. Winston Rod Co.** (406-684-5674), which has produced coveted bamboo and graphite fly rods since the company moved here from San Francisco in the mid-1970s; tours are offered at 11 AM weekdays and there's a casting lawn for testing their rods. On the western edge of town is a curiosity: a group of weathered brick buildings that looks like an abandoned small college campus. It was once the state orphanage, and is begging for someone like Oregon's McMenamin Brothers to come along and create a destination resort.

MT 287 ends in Twin Bridges. Go straight through the intersection on MT 41, which follows the Jefferson River north between the Tobacco Roots on the east and Highland Mountains on the west. Ten miles up the road is little **Silver Star** (pop. 98), marked by a highway sign and a fenced collection of privately owned railroad cabooses and retired mining equipment—including five giant wheel-shaped pieces hauled out of a defunct mine at Butte. Across the highway is **Granny's Country Store** (406-287-3605), which has the usual sundries complemented by an extraordinary collection of mostly regional books. Four miles north of Silver Star, veer right onto MT 55 toward **Whitehall** (pop. 1,077), whose primary industry is evident in the gaping mountainside gash straight ahead—the Golden Sunlight gold mine. Although our route takes you around Whitehall, one reason to pass through is to see 10 brightly colored **Lewis & Clark Murals** generally near the intersection of First Avenue and Division Street. Local artist Kit Mather has put journal entries from the expedition into a detailed picture format. On the south side of town is the free **Jefferson Valley Museum** (406-287-7813, summers), located in a bright red barn and featuring exhibits honoring the former NBC newsman Chet Huntley, who was born in nearby Cardwell and lived as a child in Whitehall.

Heading through Whitehall, just before reaching I-90, turn east on MT 2/69 toward **Cardwell** (pop. 40). About halfway between the towns, turn on Mayflower Road. Cross the Jefferson River and backtrack to the west on Parrot Gulch Road. After several miles, a mysterious round brick structure rises to the west of the gravel road. A few feet beyond, the remains of **Parrot Castle**, once part of an old mining community and now a river access point, open up at your feet. A few hundred yards up the road, the Tobacco Roots foothills meet the river at Point of Rocks. In a side channel of the river is a geothermal hot spot known as **Renova Hot Springs**. It's about 10 feet below the road and one of the few undeveloped thermal areas in Montana suitable for soaking. There are two pools identified by the sulfur odor and rock rings built by soakers. The best times to take in nature's hot tub are summer and fall, when river levels are down and water temperatures are ideal. From the springs, reverse course, recross the Mayflower Bridge, and turn west on MT 2 toward Cardwell. At the T junction one mile south of Cardwell, stop at **Clays in Calico** (406-287-3498), which calls itself the oldest pottery house in the state and crafts all of its vessels from Montana clay.

Before reaching the interstate in Cardwell, turn east on MT 2. The highway follows a railroad past a wide spot in the road called **La Hood** and into a short serpentine canyon carved by the Jefferson. Once out of the canyon, you'll arrive at the entrance for **Lewis and Clark Caverns State Park** (406-287-3541/406-287-3032), a must on any itinerary unless claustrophobia is an issue. Montana's first state park offers camping, picnicking, and hiking year-round. But the primary attraction—the largest collection of limestone caves in the Northwest—is only available by guided tour May 1 through September 30. Park at the visitor center and hike the 3 miles from the dusty sage into the pines to the gift shop and information center, or drive to the top parking lot where there is also a small snack and souvenir stand. The tours take two hours and are a window into a fantastic world of stalagmites, stalactites, bats, and other underground curiosities. There are some tight quarters, including the Beaver Slide, where you must either waddle, limbo, or slide on your derriere through a narrow gap, but the experience is too good to pass up. The park also offers Friday night campfire programs and naturalist talks during summers.

After leaving the caverns on MT 2, you'll pass a large area on the left that looks like an F Troop stockade with an old railroad bridge out front. This is the site of the **Rockin' the Rivers Festival**, a wildly popular outdoor concert held every August that has featured the likes of Alice Cooper, Foreigner, REO Speedwagon, and Steppenwolf, among other famed rock bands. You'll shortly rejoin US 287 about 10 miles southwest of Three Forks, where you can close the day where it began—at the Sacajawea Hotel.

Best Places to Bunk

THREE FORKS: To begin the Vigilante Trail fully refreshed, spend at least one night in **The Sacajawea Hotel** ($$/$$$, 406-285-6515). The Folkvord family, with a respectful eye to the explorers, homesteaders, and ranchers before them, fronted a multimillion-dollar facelift to the historic inn that now provides first-class sleeping comfort. The décor, attentive service, and special touches (a glass of bubbly at check-in) will intrigue and entice. **The Lewis & Clark Motel of Three Forks** ($$, 406-285-3474), owned by the same folks who renovated and rejuvenated the iconic Lewis & Clark in downtown Bozeman, is every bit the "charming little inn" it likes to call itself.

ENNIS: Many Yellowstone National Park visitors who want to avoid the hustle and bustle of West Yellowstone like to stay at the legendary and immaculately landscaped **El Western Motel** ($$, 406-682-4217) south of Ennis on the east bank of the Madison River. The El Western is a family favorite, with its setting and collection of cabins and lodges befitting a picture postcard from the 1950s. Fishermen like to park their Orvis rods and Simms waders at **The Rainbow Valley Lodge** ($$ 406-682-4264), another attractive motor court that harkens to an earlier era. **The Fan Mountain Inn** ($, 406-682-7835) in town is a traditional-looking motel that has prideful owners who provide clean rooms at reasonable rates.

VIRGINIA CITY: To feel the true grit of the old West, book a room at the creaky **Fairweather Inn** ($$, 800-829-2969, May–Sept.). The amenities in its fifteen rooms only slightly surpass those of a prosperous yesteryear, but you'll have close access to the plank-board sidewalks that lead everywhere in town. A little fancier is **The Gingerbread House B&B and Cabins** ($$$, 208-727-7101, May–Sept.). With the cabins, a continental breakfast is included; at the B&B, it's a delicious sit-down meal. "Rest, Relax, and Enjoy" is the theme at the **Elling House Inn** ($$, 406-843-5454). Toni James owns Henry & Mary Elling's 4,000-square-foot stone mansion on the corner of Idaho & Fairweather. Henry, a banker and dry-goods merchant, needed a big home for his wife and their nine children. Henry wasn't much for socializing but his wife was, so after he died Mary added a ballroom, library, and a few more bedrooms for guests of all social standings. Mary loved to entertain and began doing so in 1876—a practice that continues today at the house, which doubles as a nonprofit arts and humanities center. Check for rental availability after October through May—it takes some effort to heat that large home.

NEVADA CITY: The **Nevada City Hotel** ($$, 800-829-2969, May–Sept.) is owned by John and Linda Hamilton, who are also the proprietors of the Fairweather Inn. Parts of the hotel were carted over from Twin Bridges and other parts were reclaimed from an old employee dorm in Yellowstone National Park. Its uneven floors and creaky doors provide an element of authenticity. Behind the hotel are seventeen actual pioneer cabins—numbered 1 to 18, superstitiously skipping number 13—gathered from around Montana, including two from the original Nevada City. If you stay here, you'll have close encounters with the living historians who patrol the cluster of buildings that make up the living-history museum. Just before you reach Nevada City is **Just An Experience B&B** ($$, 406-843-5402), which offers lodge

LIVING HISTORY ACTORS AT NEVADA CITY WILL TAKE YOU ON A TIME-TRAVEL JOURNEY TO THE 1870S AND THE ERA OF THE NOTORIOUS VIGILANTES

rooms with private or shared bath, two private cabins, and even a mining museum to boot. It's also one of few choices open during the winter.

ALDER: Chick's Motel & RV Park ($, 406-842-5366) is one of those all-in-one places with a bar, a bed, and a bite to eat. A clean, drive-to-your-door room at an economy rate might hit the spot after a bite to eat and bit of time in the bar.

LAURIN: Vigilante and road agent history notwithstanding, you'll feel perfectly safe and comfortable at **Elijah's Rest** ($$, 406-842-7295). Tom and Sheri Luksha have three externally similar but internally unique log cabins from which to choose your place of rest. Included in the deal is a full breakfast highlighted by Elijah's biscuits & gravy. Lunches are available for a nominal fee. The addition of a commercial kitchen means you can rent the cabins and the Mantle (gathering room) for your event.

SHERIDAN: Two miles southeast of Sheridan is where you'll step back into the 1880s at the Victorian **Ruby Valley Inn B&B** ($$, 406-842-7111). This charmer on 10 acres with mountain views is comprised of four suites geared to ladies and gentrified anglers wanting to cast a day or two away in one of the nearby streams.

Alternative Bunking

ENNIS: Usually full in the summer are both the **Camper Corner** (406-682-4514) in the heart of town and **Ennis RV Village** (406-682-1463) north of town. Both have full hookups and sites for tenters. For a country lake experience, the **Lake Shore Cabins & Campground** (406-682-4424, May–Nov.) on the north side of Ennis Lake has RV and tent sites, as well as a studio apartment, a four-bedroom house, and a marina; three-night minimum applies.

VIRGINIA CITY: The **Carriage House** ($$, 406-843-5211), a studio apartment with a queen bed and kitchenette, and the **Cozy Cabin** ($$, 406-843-5211), a one-bedroom with full kitchen and bath, are both typically open year-round, but it's best to check with Christine Stadler (406-580-7881) for availability in winter. The Carriage House is a more modern construction above a two-car garage; the cabin, while cozier, has contemporary upgrades while still retaining its mining-days feel. For campers, there's **Virginia City RV Park** (406-843-5493) on the left just as you enter the east end of town. They have Wi-Fi, showers, a free RV dump station for guests, and they're pet-friendly.

ALDER: Ruby Valley Campground ($, 406-842-5677 March–Nov.), formerly a KOA site, now under new management, has pull-through RV sites, cute cabins, and many tent sites. New owner Jim Sibert was retired and not even looking for a job when he stopped in for a stay on his way back to Canada. A deal was struck, and Jim and his son have some lofty plans. It's cleaner and prettier than it was. Six sites have been winterized and the flawed canvas cook tent that catered to hunters will be replaced by a more modern wood structure.

SILVER STAR: About 2 miles south of town, fishing is the focus at the 75-acre **Jefferson River Camp** (406-684-5225), which has 14 RV sites and eight places for tenters. The camp has a half-mile of private river access and features guided fishing trips from the Four Rivers Fly Shop. There's also a cabin and an apartment.

CARDWELL: Lewis & Clark Caverns State Park (406-287-3541/www.reserveAmerica.com, May–Oct.) has thirty-nine campsites, three basic camping cabins that sleep up to four, and one teepee. The cabins are similar to those at KOA campgrounds, so bring your own bedding.

CAMPING: The Beaverhead-Deerlodge National Forest has four primitive but free campgrounds in the Tobacco Root Mountains—three in the Mill Creek drainage accessible from Sheridan on the west side and one on South Willow Creek on the east side near the head of the Potosi Trail, a popular way to access the mountains' many glistening alpine lakes. **Potosi** has 15 sites and two water pumps on 80 acres. The three on the west side are **Mill Creek** (nine sites), **Balanced Rock** (two sites), and **Branham Lakes** (13 sites); Branham is the highest in elevation and has potable water, as does Mill Creek.

Best Eats

THREE FORKS: The elegant **Pompey's Grill** ($$/$$$, 406-285-6515, D) and the more casual downstairs **Sacajawea Bar** ($, 406-285-6515, L[Sat.–Sun.]/D) are both in the Sacajawea Hotel and worth any drive. Pompey's has set the bar high for gourmet dining with the help of energetic Chef Matt, who brings a big-city flair to a small town. The dining room has more continental listings (roasted chicken, seafood, steaks, braised bison short ribs) and they are all a cut above the rest. Additional small plates are available for sampling, for those who can't decide. Favored items on the bar menu, which also changes seasonally, showcase the best of ultimate comfort food—three-cheese macaroni loaded with smoked bacon and chicken, pulled pork sandwich, bison burger, and huge green salads accompanied by house-made dressings. Wherever or whatever you eat, save room for their coconut cream pie. You won't soon forget it.

HARRISON: The **Town Haul Café** ($/$$, 406-685-3207, B/L/D, Thurs.–Sat.) not only uses local beef, they raise it. Also locally sourced are the potatoes and sometimes the salad greens as well. There's a haul of good ol' homemade goodness in every meal, which is also evident in their soups, pies, and classic cinnamon rolls. The clever name is a nod to the truckers who have the cafe dialed in during their US 287 long hauls.

ENNIS: This fly-fishing mecca enjoys a plethora of solid eating establishments befitting a tourist destination, though most are only open seasonally. Even the well-stocked local supermarket, **Madison Foods** ($, 406-682-4306), packs an angler lunch to go. Another super choice for a sack lunch is **The Pic-A-Nic Basket** ($, 406-682-7900, B/L, closed Wed. & Sun.), which is best known for bakery items. Ennis has two coffee-shop-style diners worth mentioning: **Yesterday's Soda Fountain** ($, 406-682-4246, B/L) and **Summit Coffee & Café** ($, 406-682-4442, B/L). Yesterday's does indeed have the soda fountain amid a working pharmacy and is popular for malts and shakes. Summit is less old-fashioned, but with the same friendly food fare. Get your hungry Mexican on at **Nacho Mama's Burritos** ($, 406-682-4006, Mon.–Sat.), where the burritos and quesadillas are *muy bueno*, and the daily $5 lunch deal (11 AM–2 PM) is *muy especial*. Fridays are nacho days, but be forewarned: they usually sell out. Dinner choices are many, but we find ourselves gravitating to the **Gravel Bar** ($, 406-682-5553) and **Banditos** ($$, 406-682-5552, Tues.–Sat., summers). Scott & Amy Kelley moved over from Virginia City and brought their flair for gourmet food and fun with them. The G-Bar serves pub grub, but you can also order from Banditos' menu (the dining room is right next door) when they're operating. Another one of our picks, **The Sportsman** ($$/$$$, 406-682-4242, B/L/D), suffered a devastating fire in January 2015, but has rebuilt with a commitment to bring back the local favorites and preserve their reputation for fine dining at affordable prices. **The Alley Bistro** (406-682-5695, D, Tues.–Sat.) is next door to a small bowling alley (three lanes) and has a little something for everybody with a surprisingly well-thought-out menu. It's so popular among locals you might want to make a reservation. If you're in the mood for a high-end gourmet meal paired with exceptional wine, the trendy and spendy **Continental Divide Restaurant** ($$$, 406-682-7600, D, Thurs.–Mon.) will fit the bill as long as you're there between May and mid-October.

VIRGINIA CITY: Housed in the old Wells Fargo building, the **Virginia City Café** ($/$$, 406-843-5311, L/D, May–Sept.) adjoins the town's favorite watering hole, the **Pioneer Bar** (See Best Bars). The "VC" is a personal favorite for its "scratch" cooking and perfectly grilled elk-bison burger served with a pile of kitchen-made fries.

NEVADA CITY: Star Bakery & Restaurant ($, 406-843-5777, B/L/D, May–Sept.) is in one of Nevada City's fourteen original buildings (circa 1863) and a weekend destination during the summer season. Burgers, reuben sandwiches, homemade pies and cinnamon rolls—it's all good. The fried pickles, fresh-cut potato chips, and extraordinarily friendly service make it a worthy destination.

ALDER: Chick's Restaurant & Steakhouse ($, 406-842-7366, B/L/D) really is the "all-in-one" place: a hangout bar with good eats *and* a place to hang your hat at the end of the evening. (See Best Bunking). The steakhouse has the usual suspects, including chicken-fried steak, sirloin, and prime rib. But new owner Laurie Stiffler has added a few touches of her own. Try the porkies sandwich, which consists of marinated and slow-roasted pork loin, sliced and then panko-coated before it's plopped into a thick bun. The hand-cut sirloin finger steaks aren't bad, either. Every day brings a homemade dish that that goes well with an upgraded salad bar. Favorites include creamy chicken and mushroom, black bean and steak, and corn chowder. You can order dinner at the bar, but the restaurant is in back and has outside access.

3-7-77 Instilled Fear in Lawless Montanans

Look closely and you'll see the numbers 3-7-77 in some interesting places: on the shoulder patches of Montana Highway Patrol officers, on the jumpsuits of Montana Air National Guard pilots, and, most revealing, above the front entrance to the historic Robber's Roost roadhouse outside Laurin. The origin of these numbers has always been a mystery, but in the late 1870s and early 1880s everyone in Montana's gold country knew what they represented: vigilante justice.

The numbers were a reference to an 1860s gang who hunted down thieving road agents and hanged them without trials. As the vigilante legend has grown over the years, the story goes that if the numbers appeared in the middle of the night on a man's cabin, he knew he had precious little time to get out of Dodge: precisely 3 hours, 7 minutes, and 77 seconds, according to local lore. Officially, this method of law enforcement was frowned upon, but it's understandable why lawmen looked the other way. After all, for a time, the rowdy Alder Gulch area was as crime-free as anyplace in Montana.

Thing is, history and legend don't quite align. The vigilantes' heyday was in 1864, when within five weeks they rode through a number of mining camps and hanged twenty-one ne'er-do-wells, one being a local sheriff. Such thirst for this unique brand of frontier justice continued until about 1870, when a combination of the arrival of new residents via train and the departure of miners for the gold in the Black Hills briefly led to a kinder, gentler society.

It wasn't until 1879, though, after the unexplained murder of a Helena businessman led the town's newspaper editor to call for vengeance and the rebirth of 1864 vigilante justice, that the numbers 3-7-77 first appeared, all in conspicuous locations around the capital city.

Though careful study has shown the numbers have no relation to the actual vigilantes of the 1860s, the two are inextricably linked in history, and today the numbers are a symbol of Montana law enforcement. The word *vigilante* remains popular in Montana, where it appears on a sports stadium, a rodeo's name, and a popular theater group's marquis.

Speculation about the meaning of the numbers remains a subject of debate, though we're inclined to believe the period actors at Nevada City, who say with conviction that 3 hours, 7 minutes, and 77 seconds was the time rascals had to leave town before justice was served. A solid, shiver-inducing runner-up: 3-7-77 refers to the width, length, and depth (the latter in inches) of a thief's grave.

SHERIDAN: Booze & Buns ($, 406-842-5790 Tues.–Sat.) has more than 380 wine labels, well-stocked liquor shelves, a fine selection of coffee, and tasty pastries that includes the ultimate "sticky bun." It's the place in Sheridan to get your giddy-up goin'.

TWIN BRIDGES: The Old Hotel ($$$, 406-684-5959, D, Tues.–Sat.) has a Pacific island flair to its ever-changing menu complemented by a well-chosen wine list that would fit any foodie city's menu. The soups (apple walnut, if you're lucky) and kitchen-made sorbet are just two of many extraordinary touches. Owners Bill and Paula Kinoshita celebrated their 10-year anniversary in 2015 and plan to stay open year-round, but with limited winter hours. Extended summer hours include a Sunday brunch. For casual dining, **The Shack** ($/$$, 406-684-5050, B[Sat.–Sun.]/L/D), with its hand-tossed pizzas, true-greens salad, stacked sandwiches, cold brews on tap, and down-home service, gets the job done. The Shack recently added a breakfast buffet on Sundays that's quite popular with townies. Since **The Wagon Wheel** ($/$$, 406-684-5099) has new owners, we optimistically include it in our recommendations. If you're lucky, their smoked prime rib will be on the menu.

LA HOOD The historic **La Hood Park Supper Club** ($$/$$$, 406-287-3281, L/D, Wed.—Mon.) has credible hand-cut steaks, seafood, and baby-back ribs served against a backdrop of local western paintings. Summer floaters on the Jefferson River know the best reason to stop is for a margarita and to hang in the well-worn bar or on the splintery back deck overlooking the river. Sad to say, owner Steve Darnell has passed, but his wife, Mary, is still cooking up the same home-style goodness while searching for a buyer for a business she's owned since 1993.

Best Bars

THREE FORKS: The Sacajawea Bar (406-285-6515) is a classic Montana bar, only with polished boots. There are a few slot machines along the perimeter, a card room for live poker, several flat-screen TVs affording views for everyone, a glossy wooden bar, and an attractive back bar. For imbibers, there are pub tables, lower four-tops, and a place for the band to set up on Friday and Saturday nights. They even have enough floor space for some cowboy two-steppin' and line dancin'. High-end cocktails or shots, low-end domestic beer or fine wine, martinis or trendy cocktails . . . whatever you're looking for, they'll pour it. The Sac's food selection should make everyone happy, too. If not, most nights you can order from the dining room menu. Life is simply sweeter at the Sac.

VIRGINIA CITY: The dark and musty Pioneer Bar (406-843-5550) doesn't do much dressing up, but it isn't necessary. And maybe that's why this is where the locals hang, including the actors from the raunchy Brewery Follies after they've left another crowd howling and blushing. The walls are cluttered with historical artifacts, including a bison wall mount with a plaque telling the sad saga of the shaggy beast that once roamed the prairies by the tens of millions. Consider yourself fortunate if you happen by on Bloody Mary Day. During the summer you can order food from the Virginia City Café's menu next door. The rest of the year, it's pizza at Bob's Place or bust—not a bad consolation prize, actually.

NORRIS: Don't let the slightly worn biker bar façade scare you away. You'll be glad you stopped at the Norris Bar, (406-685-3304) at the junction of US 287 and MT 84. We admit, we drove past more than a few times because it seemed a bit uninviting. Boy, were we surprised when we finally stopped. The amiable proprietor with an attitude, Carmen, is quick with a welcoming smile and laugh that usually turns into a snort. She makes and sells mouth-watering barbecue sauces, marinades, and salad dressings, and she weaves some magic in her smaller-than-a-breadbox kitchen, which is really just a nook in the wall. There is an outside grill, only open in summer, that expands her food selection beyond the meatball sandwich, homemade soup, and nightly sandwich special. What will surprise you after the welcoming aura is the genuine goodness going on in this bar. Old-timers are ready to talk to newcomers, fly fishermen are at ease talking with hook-and-bullet types, and all are there to see what Carmen comes up with next. One night, she paid a young couple drifting through in need of gas money to play a (very) short set for her patrons. Carmen and her husband, Steve, have dreams of selling the bar and doing something different, but we hope they hang on, at least for a while. Oh, and about her reported "attitude"? She only uses it on people who need it.

DETOUR: ONE FOR THE ROAD

The Madison Valley
Ennis to West Yellowstone

ESTIMATED LENGTH: 91 miles
HIGHLIGHTS: Madison River, Ennis Lake, Quake Lake, Hebgen Lake
GETTING THERE: Leave I-90 at Three Forks and take US 287 south to Ennis, or exit in Bozeman, drive south on US 191 to Four Corners, head west on MT 84 to Norris, and turn south on US 287 over the pass through McAllister to Ennis.

THE MADISON RIVER FLOWS THROUGH BEAR TRAP CANYON AND THE LEE METCALF WILDERNESS WEST OF BOZEMAN

Want to see a fly fisherman genuflect? Just mention the Madison River. As American trout streams go, none has more cachet among anglers. And although the entire 100-plus miles of the Madison provide excellent fishing, it's the 50-Mile Riffle above Ennis that graces the covers of fly-fishing brochures and fills with drift boats for eight months of the year.

The Madison Valley is broad and sweeping, with US 287 roughly paralleling the river, though usually from a distance. The route has numerous river-access points. And if you don't have a driftboat or raft, there are sections above and below the riffle suited for wading. At McAllister, just north of Ennis, a dirt road goes east to the dam backing up Ennis Lake; below the dam is terrific brown and rainbow trout water. Just below Quake Lake, at the upper end of the valley, is a wading-friendly stretch marked by Three Dollar Bridge, so named for the toll once charged to cross there.

There are other reasons to be in the Madison Valley, of course—most of them related to outdoor activities and scenery. At Cameron, a road goes east toward the Madison Range and a trailhead that leads to 10,876-foot Sphinx Mountain, the prominent peak whose name requires no explanation.

The farther up the valley you go, the narrower it gets, and the sparkling river comes into view. Off to the left is 11,292-foot Hilgard Peak, second only to Lone Mountain as the tallest in the Madison Range. Eventually the highway begins to bend toward the east. Look for the turnoff across Three Dollar Bridge to Cliff and Wade lakes, part of a string of jewels just over the hill that feature outstanding fishing and the rustic **Wade Lake Resort** cabins (one of our favorite getaways).

Back on US 287, you'll pass MT 87 and drive past an attractive collection of summer homes into Madison Canyon. Immediately coming into view is one of the most unique geologic features in southwest Montana: **Quake Lake**. Looking up to the south, you'll see where, on August 17, 1959, an earthquake registering 7.3 on the Richter scale sent 80 million tons of rock and debris into the river and up the other side of the valley. Twenty-eight people died—many remain buried in the rubble to this day—and the slide created a natural dam that formed Quake Lake. The eerie bleached spires of drowned pine

SIDE TRACK

Pony and South Fork Boulder (32miles)

This worthwhile drive explores the hidden world of the Tobacco Root Mountains, a burly range that's relatively unappreciated compared to the nearby Madison, Pioneer, and Pintler Mountains, despite its raw beauty and 43 peaks towering above 10,000 feet—many of them still unnamed.

Few remote areas offer a better glimpse of Montana's mining past than the Tobacco Roots, which are littered with rusting equipment from the pick-and-shovel days. **Pony** is an old gold-mining town of about 100 families clinging to the Tobacco Roots' northeastern foothills, and the South Boulder Road pierces the heart of the range, providing trail access to sparkling lakes, cirques and other high-mountain gems.

From the Vigilante Trail, leave US 287 at Harrison and head southwest on MT 283 about 6 miles to Pony, which boasts a great bar, a vacant bank building that bustled when the town's population topped 5,000, a century-old church popular for weddings, and 10,604-foot Hollowtop Mountain—highest in the Tobacco Roots—rising like a sentinel in the background.

After quenching your thirst in Pony, turn north past the church and brick school to the graveled Johnson Road for an undulating drive through ranchlands. Weathered old homesteads with little sound but the wind and startled pigeons leave stories of a bygone era to your imagination. At a pronounced dip in the route, head west on Carmichael Road toward the mountains. You'll come across little more than cows, deer, and wildflowers until you reach the Judson Mead Geologic Field Station of Indiana University on the pretty little

VESTIGES OF THE HOMESTEAD ERA IN SOUTHWEST MONTANA DOT THE LANDSCAPE NEAR THE OLD MINING TOWN OF PONY

South Fork of the Boulder River. Cross the stream and go left on the gravel South Boulder Road. The road soon provides grand views of the inner workings of the Tobacco Roots and is easily navigated here, but after **Mammoth**, a one-time mining community that's mostly summer homes for Jefferson Valley residents today, it deteriorates noticeably. Eventually you'll arrive at a fork in the road that requires one of three decisions: take the right fork about 4 more rugged miles to the Brannan Lakes area, the left fork about 2 even-bouncier miles to the Louise Lake Trailhead, or head back down the road toward meetings with the Vigilante Trail at Cardwell.

Fishing for brook and cutthroat trout in the upper South Boulder is entertaining, though holes holding fish more than 8 inches long are scarce.

trees still poke through the lake's surface. You can walk to the site of the natural dam, which was breached not long after the quake to avoid a future dam breach that might imperil residents and fishermen downstream. Stop at the **Earthquake Lake Visitor Center**, where you can read more about the events.

Upstream is man-made **Hebgen Lake**, a boating and fishing favorite. Along the north shore of the lake, the **Hebgen Lake Mountain Inn** is a comfortable place to put your feet up for the night, and the **Happy Hour Bar & Restaurant** has deceptively good dining for a place with a well-earned, raunchy reputation. In a few miles, US 287 meets up with US 191 for the 9-mile drive into the town of West Yellowstone.

BREATHTAKING BEAUTY GREETS DRIVERS AT EVERY TWISTY TURN ON THE BEARTOOTH HIGHWAY

8

HIGHWAY TO THE SKY

The Beartooth Pass

COLUMBUS TO SILVER GATE

ESTIMATED LENGTH: 131 miles

ESTIMATED TIME: 4 hours to 2 days (open June–Oct.)

HIGHLIGHTS: Scenic vistas, wildlife viewing, hiking, skiing, Top of the World Store, Yellowstone National Park's northeast entrance, mining history in Cooke City and Red Lodge

GETTING THERE: The Beartooth All-American Road typically is either the kickoff or exclamation mark for a Yellowstone National Park trip. For the kickoff, exit I-90 at Columbus. For the exclamation mark, folks leave Yellowstone through the northeast entrance after driving through the wildlife-rich Lamar Valley. The closest airports served by major airlines are in Bozeman and Billings, Montana, and Cody, Wyoming. To come through Yellowstone, leave I-90 at Livingston and drive 50 miles south through the aptly named Paradise Valley on US 89 to Yellowstone's north entrance at Gardiner. From there, it's 51 memorable miles through the park to Silver Gate. If you do happen to come from Cody, the drive over Chief Joseph Pass through Sunlight Basin on WY 296 to the junction of US 212 is one of the best-kept semi-secrets in Greater Yellowstone.

OVERVIEW

It has been several decades since the Beartooth was dubbed America's most beautiful drive. You'll quickly see the justification as you follow a twisting ribbon of pavement that has the distinction of being the highest road in the Northern Rockies. The Beartooth All-American Road quickly rises from the vibrant old mining town of Red Lodge to almost 11,000 feet—less than 2,000 feet below the summit of nearby Granite Peak, the highest point in Montana.

Montana Dept of Transportation

AN AERIAL VIEW OF THE BEARTOOTH HIGHWAY'S SWITCHBACKS SOUTH OF RED LODGE

For context, the apex of the breathtaking Going-to-the-Sun Road in Glacier National Park is a paltry 6,646 feet.

Once on top, US 212 levels onto a broad alpine-tundra plateau known as the Beartooth Corridor, where the clouds seem close enough to pluck from the sky. Some 20 peaks of more than 12,000 feet are nearby, and the landscape is littered with glacial lakes that shimmer like jewels. Mountain goats and elk are common, and an occasional grizzly bear is spotted in the distance—a good reason to bring binoculars or a spotting scope. The elevation is so high that the road is typically only open from the Friday before Memorial Day to the Tuesday after Columbus Day; the remainder of the year it's covered in snow. Frequent avalanches make winter plowing a proposition too futile or dangerous, and it takes weeks of work by skilled drivers to prepare the highway for its annual opening.

At first glance, you might wonder what would move anyone to undertake such a daunting construction project. The short answer is that the road was seen as a way to boost Red Lodge's economy in the Great Depression and create access to the potentially lucrative New World Mining District just northeast of Cooke City. The gold mining never panned out, but the road has been a boon to Red Lodge. The town has effectively marketed itself as a destination reminiscent of a younger Park City, Utah, and is a vibrant stopover for Harley riders, skiers, and anyone who appreciates combining a day in the great outdoors with an energetic nightlife.

A portion of this route is in Wyoming. But Montana has never been shy about claiming Yellowstone as its own even though only 3 percent of the park is within the state's boundaries, so why not all of the Beartooth All-American Highway as well? Furthermore, the only way to reach Cooke City and Silver Gate in Montana is by passing in and out of Wyoming from either direction. The drive ends amid the spruce and firs of Silver Gate, a mile outside the northeast—and least-traveled—entrance to Yellowstone.

Even so, there is much more to this drive than the dramatic mountain vistas. The rolling pine, sage, and grass country between Columbus and Red Lodge is beautiful in its own right, and the Beartooths are always there with their spectacular and ever-closer backdrop. The communities along the way—Absarokee, Fishtail, Roscoe, and Red Lodge—are as inviting as any back-to-back collection of rural towns in Montana.

HITTING THE ROAD

Columbus (pop. 1,990) sits in pretty pine and cottonwood bottoms along the Yellowstone River, a working-class town along the railroad and interstate dominated by a smelter and refinery. One stop to make is the free **Museum of the Beartooths** (406-322-4588, May–Sept.), which peeks into the region's mining and homesteading history. **Montana Silversmiths** (800-634-4830) has been the manufacturing home of finely crafted jewelry for women, glossy western belt buckles for real and wannabe cowboys, and watches for forty years.

As you leave Columbus on MT 78 and follow the Stillwater River toward the Beartooths, look for some of the region's prettier barns and an occasional glimpse of colorful flotillas of rafts plying the frothy river during spring and summer. The Stillwater is one of southwest Montana's favorite whitewater streams because of a relatively lengthy season. Guided full- and half-day raft trips along with fly-fishing excursions—the fishing is excellent, too—can be arranged with **Absarokee River Adventures** (800-334-7238), which also rents rafts and inflatable kayaks for do-it-yourselfers. To see the country on a mount, call Wanda at **Paintbrush Adventures** (406-328-4158) and arrange a one-hour or full-day ride, or a weeklong pack trip into Beartooth country. The Paintbrush hosts also provide guided day hikes and fishing trips, and for a true taste of western life, you can sign up for a working vacation on the ranch.

Twelve miles into the hill country is the cheerful community of **Absarokee** (pop. 1,150), pronounced ab-SOHR-kee. It's a cute little town that ought to have more for tourists, but it lost two of its biggest draws when an art gallery and an unusual rug business both closed.

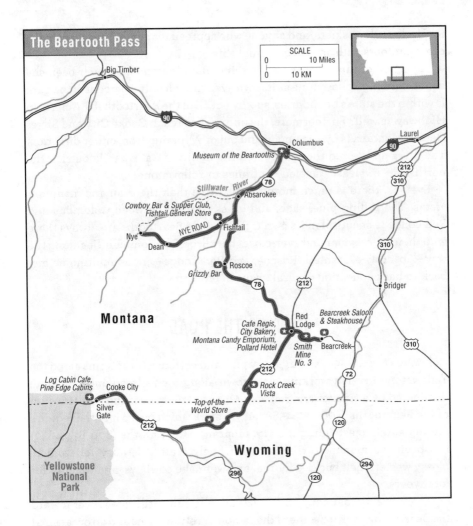

SCALE
0   10 Miles
0   10 KM

Big Timber

90

Columbus

Laurel

Museum of the Beartooths

212

310

Stillwater River

78

Absarokee

Cowboy Bar & Supper Club,
Fishtail General Store

Nye

NYE ROAD

Fishtail

Dean

310

Roscoe

Grizzly Bar

78

212

Bridger

Montana

Cafe Regis,
City Bakery,
Montana Candy Emporium,
Pollard Hotel

Red
Lodge

Bearcreek Saloon
& Steakhouse

Smith
Mine
No. 3

Bearcreek

310

212

Log Cabin Cafe,
Pine Edge Cabins

Cooke City

Rock Creek
Vista

72

Silver
Gate

212

Top-of-the-
World Store

120

Wyoming

Yellowstone
National
Park

296

120

294

The next stop over a small divide and just off the highway is **Roscoe** (pop. 14), another leafy oasis—this one along East Rosebud Creek. An early postmistress renamed the town after one of her horses. You can't drive anywhere south of I-90 without eventually seeing a bumper sticker asking "Where the hell is Roscoe Montana?"—a successful marketing campaign driven by the popular **Grizzly Bar** (406-328-6789). Along the way to Roscoe, look for two historical points: one marking the site of what had been the Crow Nation capital until the U.S. government reneged on a treaty, the other noting a challenging descent on the famed Bozeman Trail. Past Roscoe, MT 78 undulates toward the Beartooths, signaling your arrival in **Red Lodge** (pop. 2,199).

Save at least a day and perhaps two to explore the museums, galleries, and bountiful boutiques of this energetic foothills town, which is rapidly losing its distinction as the least-discovered gateway to Yellowstone. Once a raucous coal-mining center with more than 20 saloons and nearly as many ethnic neighborhoods, Red Lodge is decidedly tamer but still abuzz. Possibly named for a breakaway band of Crow who erected a red teepee, the town is squeezed between grassy benches along Rock Creek, hard against the broad eastern shoulder of the Beartooths. Even when the Beartooth Highway is closed, Red Lodge remains a popular winter destination for skiing and snow-mobiling. The town also stages numerous unique events during its shoulder seasons to bolster a year-round economy.

The main drag is great for hours of people watching and shopping, but carve out time to spin off the beaten byway onto MT 308 and drive over a small but steep divide to **Smith Mine No. 3**. You can park and walk amid the remnants of the worst coal mine disaster in Montana history (71 killed). Another 7 arid miles east on MT 308 is **Bearcreek** (pop. 83) and a less somber attraction: the famed Bear Creek Downs pig races at **Bear Creek Saloon &**

ATTRACTIVE COUNTRY BARNS ARE PART OF THE BUCOLIC LANDSCAPE IN THE STILLWATER VALLEY

AND THEY'RE OFF! PIGS TROT THEIR WAY AROUND THE TRACK BEHIND BEAR CREEK SALOON

Steakhouse (406-446-3481). Yes, pig races. These little piggies go round and round a dirt track, cheered on by bettors, every Thursday through Sunday in the summer. The unconventional entertainment began in 1988 as a way to spark business after the infamous fires that burned up one-third of Yellowstone took a bite out of tourism.

Back in Red Lodge, you might want to grab some essential snacks for the journey to the pass. Stock up on a staggering array of candy—including many hard-to-find varieties—at the **Montana Candy Emporium** (406-446-1119), open every day except Christmas. You can also sit a spell, sample local brews at the transformed **Red Lodge Ale Brewing Company** (406-446-0243), and wait for a panini or baked sandwich for the road. Once literally a hole in the wall of a brewery, the taproom has an updated, yuppified look, but draws the same outstanding drafts.

Shortly after leaving Red Lodge, US 212 enters a broad U-shaped valley and begins zigging and zagging up the face of a pine-studded granite mountain. Be prepared with a jacket or fleece because the temperatures can drop as much as 30 degrees in the next 20 miles. Up, up, and up—the road seems to rise forever. Pines and firs give way to the prehistoric whitebark pine, which is making a last stand in these mountains. Enjoy the trees while you can. Armies of pine bark beetles, thanks to the warming climate that has enabled them to survive once-brutal winters, are killing conifers by the millions in all but the highest elevations—most notably the Beartooth. Prolific snows linger into July here and create a unique opportunity for skiers who want to avoid buying a lift ticket at **Red Lodge Mountain** (406-255-6973). Many schuss through the trees to lower portions of the highway, where they hitch a lift back to their car—or even higher—for more runs.

Just before the East Summit is the impressive **Rock Creek Vista Site**, with its sweeping views of the canyon far below. The highway has now nearly reached the alpine tundra, almost a mile higher in elevation than Red Lodge. Early visitors are usually treated to a blaze of wildflowers such as columbine and Indian paintbrush, which emerge after the long, harsh winter to make a colorful splash during their brief bloom window. A string of alpine lakes gleam in the sunlight. Pull off the road and hike one of the dozens of Forest Service trails toward glacial lakes and other spectacular scenery in the Absaroka-Beartooth Wilderness. The area looks much the way it did when General Phillip Sheridan made the first documented crossing of the plateau on horseback in 1882. The 14-mile roundtrip **Black Canyon Lake** hike captures the essence of the mighty Beartooths and can be completed in one day. Crossing the Montana-Wyoming border, a favorite shorter hike is the **Beartooth Loop**, a National Recreation Trail that includes the oft-photographed Gardner Lake. At the East Summit, a chairlift seems to disappear into the invisible. This is the **Twin Lakes Headwall**, and skiing camps are conducted here in June and July, after snowmelt allows access but while enough powder remains on the shaded north face to allow top-flight training opportunities for Olympic hopefuls.

After traversing the tundra on the plateau for several miles and beginning a lengthy descent below the West Summit, you'll eventually arrive at the no-place-like-it **Top of the World Store** (307-587-5368). You are now a little past the midway point to Cooke City. At 9,400 feet in elevation, you'll find intermittent phone service at the store—they ask that you not call for weather conditions—and limited electricity, but a world of warmth from the folks who welcome you into their high-elevation harbor. The store was built along Beartooth Lake while the highway was under construction in 1934, then moved to its current site in 1964. If you want to wet a line in a Wyoming lake or stream, Cowboy State licenses are sold here—along with gas, snacks, maps, books, souvenirs, and just about anything else an outdoor person needs. Rentals for a wide variety of outdoor activities also are available.

From the Top of the World, the Beartooth Highway's complexion changes but remains attractive. One of the most photographed sites on the way down to Cooke City is the **Index Overlook**. It's an unobstructed view into the North Absaroka Wilderness and of the pointy 11,708-foot Pilot Peak and its sister mountain, the 10,709-foot Index Peak, both carved by glaciers. A short distance later is **Clay Butte Lookout**, one of the few fire lookouts easily accessible from a paved highway. It's a 2-mile drive or hike to the lookout, which has marvelous panoramic views and interpretive information about the scars of the 1988 fires that nearly left Cooke City in ashes. After the junction of WY 296, the road follows the meandering Clarks Fork of the Yellowstone River, an angler's paradise. The highway soon crosses back into Montana and descends gently through towering pine and spruce into **Cooke City** (pop. 140), the end of the road coming from the other direction in winter. Like Red Lodge, Cooke City had its genesis as a mining town; unlike Red Lodge, its economy is narrow—Yellowstone visitors in summer, snowmobilers and wolf watchers in winter. The lodging and dining befits such uniformity. The **Cooke City Store** (406-838-2234), built in 1886, still has some of its original hardware and is worth a stop for ice cream, souvenirs, and history. For more charm but fewer lodging and dining opportunities, continue along Soda Butte Creek toward the park's northeast entrance another 3 miles to **Silver Gate** (pop. 15), where year-round non-motorized peace is the antithesis of its motor-friendly neighbor. On the way, look for the inconspicuous sign on the right for **Hartman Gallery** (406-838-2296), an extension of Dan and Cindy Hartman's house in a conifer thicket. You can view or purchase paintings of stunning landscapes and/or wildlife—and may catch a glimpse of a resident pine marten, if you're lucky.

Silver Gate also has its roots in mining and has an equally breathtaking Absaroka backdrop, but the similarities stop there. The entire population, a dozen or so year-rounders, has made a conscientious effort to be the quiet alternative to neighboring Cooke City, with an emphasis on sustainable, human-powered recreation. Also here is the stately and reputedly haunted **Range Rider Lodge**, once one of the two largest freestanding log structures in the nation (behind Old Faithful Inn in Yellowstone National Park). The former bordello rooms upstairs are available for large group bookings, and the lodge frequently hosts musical events and other activities during the high season. For your hiking, skiing, and climbing needs, the **Silvertip Mountain Center** (800-863-0807) gears its retail and rental inventory to the season. **Stop the Car Trading Post** (406-838-2130) is a year-round place to stock up on convenience items and made-in-Montana gifts.

Silver Gate and Cooke City are along Soda Butte Creek, which meanders through some of the best grizzly bear habitat in America. Locals have grown accustomed to living with bears in their midst and take all the proper precautions. Whenever in grizzly country, it's mandatory to bring bear spray, make noise, store food properly, and travel in parties of at least four if possible.

From Silver Gate, it's a mere mile to the park. You can continue your journey by taking the only year-round road in Yellowstone through the Lamar Valley. But that's a trip described in our *Great Destinations: Yellowstone and Grand Teton National Parks and Jackson Hole* from Countryman Press.

Best Places to Bunk

ABSAROKEE: For the economy-minded, the country kitschy **Stillwater Lodge** ($/$$, 406-328-4899) has six cute and tightly quartered rooms on the main drag of town. It makes a good base camp for all the outdoor adventures popular in the area.

RED LODGE: The historic landmark and literally the cornerstone of downtown Red Lodge is the red brick **Pollard Hotel** ($$$$, 406-446-0001). The Pollard has accommodated the likes of Buffalo Bill, Jeremiah "Liver-Eating" Johnston, and Martha Jane Cannary Burke, a.k.a. Calamity Jane, among other frontier celebrities. The building fell into disrepair, then was renovated and reopened in the early 1990s as a fully modern hotel and dining room that retains much of its former charm. It even has a racquetball court in the basement. Plus, breakfast off the menu is included in your rate. For upscale-plus B&B lodging, the **Rocky Fork Inn Bed & Breakfast** ($$$, 406-446-296, June–Sept.) has six suites in a sprawling log structure overlooking Rock Creek and serves a small breakfast. **Gallagher's Irish Rose B&B** ($$, 406-446-0303, closed April/May and Oct./Nov.), is a century-old home with three themed rooms that reflect the town's Irish miner roots. Original artwork from Leah Gallagher and others adorns the walls of the 1910 home. The **Yodeler** ($/$$, 406-446-1435) is our pick for a motor-style inn. We love its throwback Euro ski-lodge ambience, old-style Jacuzzi tubs (in some rooms), and covered outdoor hot tub. The stylish **Rock Creek Resort** ($$$/$$$$, 406-446-1111) is an invitingly understated collection of townhouses, condos, and standard rooms in a variety of decors ranging from Guatemalan to Montanan. You'll be surprised to learn that rooms start at $130, and it all includes a continental breakfast served at the Old Piney Dell Restaurant. The **Beartooth Hideaway**

Inn & Cabins ($$/$$$$, 406-446-2488), formerly a Super 8, has standard motel rooms but also new detached log cabins. Their indoor swimming pool is the largest in town and always a draw. What's a Wyoming motel doing in a Montana book? Well, the out-of-the-ordinary **Top of the World Resort Motel** ($, 307-587-5368) is on the route and open year-round. Although it's quite a stretch to call it a resort, Top of the World does have RV and camp spots as

Beartooth Highway Softened Depression in Red Lodge

By the turn of the previous century, Yellowstone National Park was becoming an international tourist destination. Such gateway communities as West Yellowstone, Gardiner, and Cody were riding a tidal wave of economic success since automobiles were legally allowed into the park for the first time in 1915. Though separated from Yellowstone by some of the region's most rugged terrain, Red Lodge nevertheless wanted a piece of the action—especially after the nearby coal mine closed in 1924.

A road over the rocky Beartooth Plateau, city fathers surmised, would give tourists direct access to the park's northeast entrance and enable businesses in Cooke City to tap a mother lode of gold in the New World Mining District about 3 miles from Yellowstone's boundary. They weren't the first to consider travel over the Beartooth—Indians had been doing it for thousands of years—but the task was daunting nonetheless. The grandiose vision was to punch a road into Rock Creek Canyon, carve switchbacks out of the side of a 4,000-foot mountain, lay pavement across the plateau's fragile tundra and 3-billion-year-old rocks, and then etch a serpentine route down the backside into Wyoming and back to Montana at Cooke City. It took years of planning.

But in 1931, as the darkness of the Great Depression enveloped a nation, construction began. Remarkably, it would take only five years, opening to great fanfare in 1936. It has been a bucket-list drive ever since. Answering a letter in the 1970s from a fan inquiring about the most beautiful drives in America, the late CBS newsman Charles Kuralt, renowned for his regular "On the Road" features, responded "US 212."

Not surprisingly, keeping the Beartooth All-American Highway open and maintained is a chore. Wicked weather and extreme temperatures cause the road to heave and hiccup, resulting in constant repairs that require patience from drivers. In 2005, a mudslide ruined 13 sections of road and kept it closed all summer, to the detriment of Red Lodge businesses.

The road officially opens on Memorial Day and closes on Labor Day, though it's often possible to drive the route well into October. Don't be surprised if you run into patches of snow—terrific for summer photo-ops—at any time of year, or if your summer plans to reach the plateau are waylaid by a snowstorm.

well as four standard motel rooms. It might not look like much, but the prime location just below the Beartooth plateau and access to spectacular country make it so popular that reservations are recommended months in advance—especially since road work companies like to use it for construction projects here that never seem to end.

SILVER GATE: A personal favorite is the woodsy **Pine Edge Cabins** ($$/$$$, 406-838-2371), the only year-round lodging in this one-block village. The remodeled units are part of a collection that includes the **Silver Gate** and **Whispering Pines** cabins, which are open during the summer. The view from the Pine Edge Cabins is of towering Mount Republic, and during winter months, guests often see a menagerie of wildlife that includes silver fox, moose, and a lone bull bison affectionately named Jackson who arrives from the park annually. Through Pine Edge, groups can also rent the sprawling **Range Rider Lodge**, once a lively brothel and bar. The tight quarters with twin and bunk beds feature the names of the girls that plied the world's oldest profession there during the mining era of the 1930s. Ask the managers at Pine Edge about the female ghost who reputedly haunts the site.

Alternative Bunking

ABSAROKEE: Paintbrush Adventures ($$$$, 406-328-4158) has a cushy cabin on the Stillwater River—you can literally fish right off your deck—that sleeps eight for $250 per night, with weekly and monthly discounts negotiable. Dividing the rate among eight makes this a steal. Located on the Barron Ranch, the home and apartment above the garage are part of Montana Bunkhouses Working Ranch Vacations, a group that is trying to bolster local economies by offering authentic Montana experiences.

BELFRY: Another Montana Bunkhouses offering is the **Beartooth River Ranch** ($/$$, 406-664-3181), just over the hill from Red Lodge south of Belfry. The lodge, located on the Clarks Fork of the Yellowstone River, has 12 guest rooms—including eight suites—starting at an affordable $60 per night even during the summer high season.

SILVER GATE: Laurie Hinck, a full-time resident who was born in a log building in Silver Gate, has two traditional log cabins for rent at the **Log Cabin B&B** ($$, 800-863-0807, May—Sept.), each with two double beds. The best part of the $99/night rate is that a full cooked-to-order breakfast at the neighboring café is included.

CAMPING: Campers and picnickers might like the shade of the towering cottonwoods drinking from the Yellowstone River at the **Itch-Kep-Pe Park** ($, 406-322-533) in Columbus, which has 13 campsites. The Custer National Forest in Montana and Shoshone National Forest across the border in Wyoming combine for 14 campgrounds with 226 campsites, most within close proximity to the highway. There are six on the Montana side before US 212 begins its precipitous switchback rise out of Rock Creek Canyon, two on the plateau, one each at Island and Beartooth lakes, three along the Clarks Fork of the Yellowstone, and three just outside Cooke City. Expect chilly nights any time of year—and the higher the elevation, the chillier it'll be. In Fishtail, another appealing choice is camping with quick and easy fishing access at Rosebud Isle along the banks of the West Rosebud Creek.

Best Eats

COLUMBUS: Once dubbed "The Bloody Bucket" for its frequent brawls, the **307 Bar, Grill & Casino** ($$, 406-322-4511, B[Sun.]/L/D) is now a family-friendly joint where log furniture and art on the walls sets the stage for wine and beer drinkers to imbibe side by side. The 307 serves good-enough-to-brake-for burgers; most favored is their mountain man burger steak smothered in gravy, mushrooms, and onions. Understated **Whitlock's Stillwater Steakhouse** ($$, 406-322-8677, B/L/D) is a meat, potatoes, and fried-food kinda place that serves up everything from rib eye to walleye.

ABSAROKEE: The unpretentious **Rosebud Cafe** ($, 406-328-6969, B/L, Fri.–Tues.) does everything right, from rancher-sized portions of steak, eggs, hash browns, and piles of buttermilk pancakes to chicken fried steak and sack lunches to go. Roger and Sylvia are known for their "small town America" hospitality and generosity.

FISHTAIL: Wrap your hands around a half-pound burger, halibut sandwich, or any number of appealing dinner choices at the **Cowboy Bar & Supper Club** ($$, 406-328-4288, B[Fri.–Sun./L/D; see Best Bars). If you're in more of a hurry—or even if you aren't—the **Fishtail General Store** ($, 406-328-4260) always has fresh made-to-order deli sandwiches, a pot of soup, slices of pizza, and gigantic chocolate-chip cookies.

ROSCOE: The **Grizzly Bar** ($$, 406-328-6789, L/D) is one of Montana's most iconic steakhouses, where sizzling steaks, prime rib, Alaskan king crab, and king-sized burgers make folks "growl with hunger". The large patio is idyllic for outdoor dining in this little oasis of trees along East Rosebud Creek. Every so often on the Backroads, you'll spy a bumper sticker that asks, "Where the

EVERYTHING FROM SOUP TO NUTS—PISTACHIOS ARE LOCALLY SOURCED—IS IN STOCK AT THE FISHTAIL GENERAL STORE

hell is Roscoe?" The Grizzly is where they're from. You can order from the lunch or dinner menu at any time.

RED LODGE: Plan your drive so that you can dine in Red Lodge more than once, because there are many outstanding choices. **The Pollard Hotel** ($$, 406-446-0001, B/D) has exquisite dining from a seasonal menu, an extensive wine list, and a full bar. Hours and days of operation also depend on the season; during the winter it's only open on weekends. The **Pub at the Pollard,** on the other side of the hotel, is open every day all year and has a diverse, aim-to-please menu. Representing more traditional Red Lodge is the **Carbon County Steakhouse** ($$/$$$, 406-446-4025, D), with its "cowboy cuisine" highlighted by hormone-free beef, bison, and elk, as well as fresh seafood and mussels flown in regularly from the Pacific Northwest. Tom Kuntz owns the steakhouse as well as **Red Lodge Pizza Company** ($$, 406-446-3333, L/D) and **Bogart's** ($$/$$$, 406-446-1784, L/D), both more casual places. With its robust back bar, Bogart's combines a rustic western feel with a Mexican menu and thirst-quenching margaritas. The **Cafe Regis** ($, 406-

John Baker

COME AS YOU ARE, GRIZZLED OR NOT, FOR A DINNER AND LIBATIONS AT THE GRIZZLY BAR IN ROSCOE

446-1941, B/L, Wed.–Sat.), located in a retro-esque grocery store, is a diner with a handful of healthy groceries, all co-owned by a vegetarian, Martha Young, who knows how to take care of her fellow greenies while pleasing the meat-eaters with many farm-to-fork foods. Breakfasts plates are memorable and lunches remarkable. Try to snag a table in the backyard, where she grows herbs and vegetables. To see where the old-timers hang out for coffee and conversation, stop at the historic **City Bakery** ($, 406-446-2100, B/L), best known for something called *schnecken*—a rich, doughy concoction of cinnamon, butter, cream cheese, and nuts. The bakery's fame started with its après ski French bread and slab of butter. Lucky for you they still bake the French bread. Breakfast or lunch at the **Red Lodge Café** ($$, 406-446-1619, B/L/D) is a lesson in history, with their practically life-sized murals on the walls, log furniture, and neon teepee sign. Locals come for beans and eggs smothered in green chili gravy, humongous pancakes, homemade chicken fried steak, and a veritable cornucopia of pies: cherry pumpkin, apple, black and blueberry, and peach, all served daily. Later on a summer day, cool off with a cone of soft-serve ice cream or fuel up with a burger creekside at Red Lodge's oldest drive-in, the **Red Box Car** ($, 406-446-2152, L/D, May–Sept.), housed in a 100-year-old—you guessed it—boxcar from the Northern Pacific's old Rocky Fork and Cooke City Railroad spur.

BEARCREEK: The **Bear Creek Saloon & Steakhouse** ($$, 406-446-3481, D, Thur.–Sun.; see Best Bars) is best known for the pig races out back, but the steaks rank a close second. It's nothing fancy—just heaping helpings of good food. The restaurant is open May through September and December through March. Just a note: You can't eat at the bar, so call ahead or be prepared to wait for a table.

COOKE CITY: Dining at the **Miner's Saloon** ($$, 406-838-2214, L/D, closed November and May) is a course in the unexpected, and that's how the owner, Raz, likes it. They still have their popular hand-tossed pizza, but with the new kitchen and revamped dining room comes fois gras, lamb sliders, poutine with pork belly, rack of lamb off the new smoker, and some delectable dinner specials from trained chefs. Come with low expectations, leave with great anticipation for a return. The seasonal **Beartooth Café** ($$, 406-838-2475, B/L/D, May–Sept.) is the place to sit on a breezy deck and listen to live music or to hear the latest on grizzly bear sightings while sipping on one of 130 beer choices and slicing into a hand-cut sirloin steak. For a seemingly out-of-place change of pace, you'll find fare with a French flair at **The Bistro** ($$/$$$, 406-838-2160, B/L/D, closed Oct.–Nov.), which warms the hearts of winter visitors by reopening in late December (post-Christmas) after a short hiatus. Their homemade soups and dinner specials are *très bon*. Another place we've grown to appreciate is **The Saloon** ($/$$, 406-838-2251, B/L/D) in the Soda Butte Lodge. You can order from the neighboring Prospector Restaurant's menu and either watch a game on TV or gaze into the woods outside their large picture windows. It's one of the places snowmobilers like to hang out after a day of high-marking.

SILVER GATE: Currently the only restaurant in town, **Log Cabin Café and B&B** ($$, 800-863-0807, B/L/D, May–Sept.), is favored for its lightly breaded and grilled Idaho trout, which you can get with eggs for breakfast or as an entrée for lunch or dinner. Another signature item is their flown-in Alaskan sockeye, which is either prepared lightly smoked or as a simple filet. They're also rightfully proud of their burgers, made from grass-fed beef from Belfry. Insiders' tip: Regardless of what you order, save room for their spoon-licking good pumpkin-bread drizzled with honey and served with a scoop of vanilla ice cream.

Best Bars

BEARCREEK: Grab a cold one, place your bet at the window, and get ready to cheer on your chosen porker at the **Bear Creek Saloon's** (406-446-3481) summer pig races. Folks come from as far away as Billings and Cody to help with a good cause: Proceeds help pay college tuition for Carbon County students. Although you can't eat at the bar, you can whet your appetite with $2.50 bottled beer or equally cheap, generously poured well drinks served in a plastic cup to take out to the track's viewing deck. Oh, and the food—emphasis on steaks—is pretty good too. No pork served, of course.

FISHTAIL: Like the general store, the well-used but well-kept and laid-back **Cowboy Bar & Supper Club** (406-328-4288) is a longtime icon for shooting the bull and imbibing. While enjoying an ice-cold beer or shaken cocktail, savor a cut-to-order steak, chicken, or—and this might seem redundant in Montana—a mighty impressive burger. Hunker down to dinner on the brands-on-the-wall, wooden-stools, everyone-knows-each-other's-business bar side, or opt for a different experience on the cheery-country-Italian-dining room side. During the rowdy annual Testy Festy, you get the rare privilege of sampling beer-battered calf testicles—locally produced, naturally. The business was for sale in late 2015, but it's such an area icon it's unlikely that it would shutter its doors.

RED LODGE: Like many good dive bars, the **Snow Creek Saloon** doesn't list a phone number. What it does have is live music Saturday nights, open-jam Tuesday nights, and enough floor space and table tops to squeeze in some dancing. We've experienced all of the above or just quietly nursed a (reasonably priced) drink while watching a game on the flat screen with friends, familiar and not, after hitting the trails or slopes. With its pressed tin ceiling, hard wooden stools, dollar bills pinned to a wall, and a few dusty animal mounts, it doesn't spiff up much. But that's part of the appeal. That and the fact you just never know who might show up to crank out some hot guitar or belt out the blues. "Live to your own beat," as they say at the Snowy.

DETOUR: ONE FOR THE ROAD

East River Road in the Paradise Valley
Livingston to Yankee Jim Canyon

ESTIMATED LENGTH: 47 miles
HIGHLIGHTS: Yellowstone River, Chico Hot Springs, Pine Creek Tavern
GETTING THERE: Take Exit 333 off I-90 in Livingston.

In many ways, the visually appealing drive along the **Yellowstone River** embodies the new Montana. Lured by the jagged peaks of the Absarokas, the trout-rich waters of the Yellowstone, and proximity to the world's first national park, both the well-heeled and off-the-grid sorts call the aptly named Paradise Valley home. In the beginning, the name came from the Crow Indians, who once thrived on the prolific wildlife drawn here in winter when ferocious winds scoured the grasslands of snow. The Crow, who call themselves the Absaroka ("children of the large beaked bird"), have been banished to a reservation farther to the east, but the name and the unparalleled beauty remain.

Livingston, immortalized in song by Jimmy Buffett with "Livingston Saturday Night," "Monday Monday," and, reputedly, "Cheeseburger in Paradise," is an old railroad town that has become an artist colony with more professional writers per capita than any town in the United States. From Livingston, drive south on US 89 through a skinny gap in the Absaroka and Gallatin ranges, and imagine for a moment a dam there instead; yes, flooding the Paradise Valley with a reservoir was actually proposed at one time. When the valley opens, look for a left turn on East River Road (Highway 540) and cross the Yellowstone River at Carter's Bridge.

Drive along the river and absorb the views of the Absarokas. For a down-home weekend evening in the summer, dance under the pines and stars to live music at the **Pine Creek Tavern**. Or take a break for a soak and five-star dinner at **Chico Hot Springs**, 30 miles south of Livingston. The walls of the historic main lodge at Chico are adorned with photos of one of the springs' biggest fans many years ago, the actor Warren Beatty. At **Pray**, a community you could've owned in its entirety for the tidy sum of $1.2 million in 2012, cross over the river to US 89 and the homespun **Wildflower Café & Bakery** for some baked goods, soup, and perhaps some live music before doubling back to East River Road.

East River Road reacquaints itself with US 89 after hugging the Yellowstone for about 8 miles. About 4 miles to the north on US 89, and then another 5 miles up Dry Creek Road, is the comfortably rustic **Mountain Sky Guest**

East Rosebud (18 miles)

If you're coming from Columbus and Absarokee, prepare yourself for a visual feast. As you leave MT 78 at the leafy little community of **Roscoe**, the landscape becomes increasingly undulating and the snow-capped Beartooth Mountains fill up your windshield with wonder and anticipation. Rosebud Lake Road follows tumbling East Rosebud Creek—protected in 2015 under the federal Wild & Scenic Rivers Act—through prime ranchlands into the mouth of the mountains. Look for moose in the willows along the creek. After passing **Sand Dune Picnic Area** and **Jimmy Joe Campground**, the shear walls of the Beartooths quickly envelop the view. You'll need to crane your neck to see the tops of granite walls that compare to Yosemite National Park's famed Half Dome.

The picture keeps evolving to the Swiss Alps-like grandeur at the little enclave of **Alpine** at shimmering East Rosebud Lake, where you're as likely to run across a moose as people. This community, which was tight-knit before a fire roared through a decade earlier and is even more so now, is composed of multiple generations of Montanans. Stop for an ice cream sandwich at the quaint little general store, where any fantasies about buying a cabin in this idyllic mountain setting will quickly be tempered. Land and cabins rarely become available, and when they do the neighbors have a lot to say about who gets invited into the circle of trust.

Park in the gravel area near the Forest Service campground and consider one of two trails leaving the area. We recommend following the east shore of the lake—being mindful of private property and moose—and traversing the rock-strewn trail along East Rosebud Creek, where you might see otters frolicking in the froth. The trail switchbacks from one lake to the next before eventually reaching Rainbow Lake, about 5 miles east of 12,799-foot Granite Peak—Montana's tallest.

West Rosebud (25 miles)

The road to West Rosebud isn't as dramatic as East Rosebud, but it does offer more diversity. Leave MT 78 at the junction of Nye Road, marked by a gas station/convenience store and signs for the cottonwood oasis of **Fishtail** (pop. 478), an L-shaped wide spot that hugs two briskly moving forks of West Rosebud Creek. Stop in Fishtail for lunch at the cuter-than-cute, white-and-red **Fishtail General Store**, a community gathering spot that has been "selling a little bit of everything since 1900"—making it the oldest continuously operating mercantile in Montana still in its original location. These days the bright and cheerful store has everything from soup to nuts to bolts. Made-in-Montana gifts, sundries, DVD rentals, and fishing and hunting gear make room for local honey, pistachios, made-to-order deli sandwiches, freshly

WESTERN TIGER SWALLOWTAIL BUTTERFLIES CONGREGATE ON BLOOMING LILAC BUSHES MIDSUMMER

crafted pizza, huge homemade cookies, sweet rolls, and divine cheesecakes. Owners Bill and Katy Martin bought the store as a retirement project and have been welcomed into the community. One visit and you'll soon see why.

Up the road, beyond a little roadside blip called **Dean**, is **Nye** (pop. 272), home to a buffalo jump, a three-room motel, and the country's only palladium mine, which sits, relatively unobtrusively and perhaps somewhat ironically, near the entrance to the Absaroka-Beartooth Wilderness. Wilderness trails traverse boulder-strewn valleys through old burns along the east and west forks of the tumbling Stillwater River.

Ranch, a gateway to the Gallatin Range's wild country. Mountain Sky and the lands surrounding it receive special affection from owner Arthur Blank, who co-founded Home Depot and also owns the Atlanta Falcons of the NFL. Equally spectacular, if not more so, is Maryanne Mott's eco-oriented **B Bar Ranch** about 10 miles up Tom Miner Road, almost to the Yellowstone National Park boundary. The B Bar is the ranch where the movie *Rancho Deluxe* was set, but today its lodge and cabins are a magnet for conservation groups and others who come in winter to ply the extensive cross country ski trails.

Just after the turnoff for Tom Miner Basin, US 89 squeezes through **Yankee Jim Canyon.** For a step back in time, cross the river on the old iron bridge at the Carbella Fishing Access site and follow the signs for the Yankee Jim historical site. Park and walk along the old railroad grade into the canyon

ADS FOR GARDINER BUSINESSES IN YANKEE JIM CANYON PREDATE THE RAILROAD AND CAR TRAFFIC

and note the rock walls from the Yankee Jim toll road, which pre-dates the railroad's arrival more than a century ago. Several rocks are still adorned with painted advertisements from a bygone era.

At the upper end of Yankee Jim on US 89, look to the right for a unique red rock formation called **Devil's Slide**. As you continue toward Gardiner, you'll see a string of four large high fence enclosures with ominous government "No Trespassing" signs and the handful of bison that are normally inside. These are quarantine pens where bison migrating out of Yellowstone National Park are tested for brucellosis and other diseases. The state has planned to release disease-free wild bison at wildlife refuges and on Indian reservations across the West, but thus far resistance from ranchers has stifled progress. Small herds were moved to the Fort Peck Indian Reservation in northeast Montana in 2012 and 2014, some animals were eventually trucked to the Fort Belknap Reservation in north-central Montana, and ten more went to a natural prairie area outside of Fort Collins, Colorado, in late 2015.

Gardiner (pop. 875) is an incorporated town with much of its frontier character and is home to many Yellowstone National Park employees. For eats, the **K Bar & Cafe** has average ambience but a surprisingly excellent pizza. The **Tumbleweed Bookstore & Café** is the place for a veggie sandwich, earthy soup, coffee or tea, and Internet access. **Helen's Corral Drive-In** (summers) was famed regionally for "Helen's hateful hamburger" until she passed away, but new owners have kept the tradition going, sans the grumpiness and precariously dangling cigarette for which crusty old Helen was famed. The **Cowboy Lodge & Grille** is a place to satisfy your hunger with southern-style BBQ pork, chicken, brisket, or ribs and then settle in for the night in one of the thoughtfully refurbished townhouse-style rooms. **Yellowstone Grill** is the latest new restaurant trying to provide some semblance of upscale dining, though the seasonal dining room at **Mammoth Hot Springs**, 5 miles up the hill in the park, has a creative menu. Before entering the park, stop at the classy **Yellowstone Association** headquarters near the Roosevelt Arch. The group, whose mission is to educate and inspire, refurbished the 1903 Reamer Building and has Yellowstone-related displays, books, gifts, helpful tips for sightseers, and a cool interactive map showing where wildlife have been seen.

The end of this route is at the park entrance, where road construction in 2015 significantly altered a familiar landscape, enabling visitors to bypass the arch and the frequent photo-op traffic jams. The arch, an impressive stone-basalt structure, was built in 1903—31 years after the creation of the park—to commemorate the arrival of the railroad, which brought wealthy tourists to Yellowstone's doorstep. President Theodore Roosevelt, a former mason, placed the first stone. Look for bison, elk, and pronghorn browsing or resting in the grassy meadows on both sides of the park entrance.

THE CRAZY MOUNTAINS ARE A SO-CALLED "ISLAND" RANGE. THEY RISE ABOVE 11,000 FEET AND EVEN HAVE A GLACIER

9

HEART OF MONTANA
Musselshell Country

LEWISTOWN LOOP

ESTIMATED LENGTH: 205 miles
ESTIMATED TIME: 6 hours to 2 days
HIGHLIGHTS: Charlie Russell Chew Choo, Upper Musselshell Museum, Train Park,
 Judith Gap wind farm, Yogo sapphires, Alberta Bair Museum, Gigantic Warm
 Springs, Big Spring Creek, Musselshell River
GETTING THERE: Lewistown is nearly in the geographic center of Montana, so
 in theory you can get there from anywhere. From I-90, take one of the two
 Big Timber exits and drive north on US 191. From Billings, exit US 87 for
 Roundup. And from Great Falls, go south on US 89 to MT 3 and continue to
 Lewistown.

OVERVIEW

Ask longtime residents where they'd choose to live if they could somehow
find the perfect blend of scenery, pace, and mix of past and present Montana,
and many will whisper "Lewistown." On the surface, Lewistown—with its
towering county courthouse rising above leafy streets—seems to embody a
Rockwellian ideal.

Lewistown sits in a valley and is just close enough to such mountains as
the Judith and Big Snowy Mountains (called "island ranges" because of their
isolation from other mountain ranges) to paint a classic Montana portrait,
right down to the trout stream that flows through town. Yet it's far enough
away from the stark ranges and cold-water fisheries of glossy magazines to
offer isolation and escape from the trophy home frenzy.

At first glance, it might seem this square-shaped central Montana route
doesn't offer much. Mesmerizing scenery isn't the calling card here. It's simply mile after mile of eye-pleasing, pastoral surroundings, with grasses—

THE FERGUS COUNTY COURTHOUSE IN LEWISTOWN IS ONE OF THE STATE'S MOST PICTURESQUE COUNTY COURTHOUSES

that's why they call them Wheatland and Golden Valley counties—swaying against a distant backdrop of snowcapped mountains in every direction: the burly Absarokas and Beartooths, the deceptively brawny Crazys, the timbered Castles and Little Belts, the captivating Big Snowys, the Judiths standing guard over Lewistown, and, in the shadowy distance, the Highwoods and Little Rockies. Along the way, you'll pass ranches and tractors, white-tailed deer and pronghorn, and get a glimpse of Montana's energy future at Judith Gap, where fields of spinning white wind turbines protrude from the range as far as the eye can see.

This region also factors heavily into Montana's railroad history. The Milwaukee Road's electrified line began in Harlowton and navigated rugged terrain for 252 miles into Idaho. You can still see the old grade snaking along the Musselshell River, along with a few weathered signals, and the periodic railroad building sporting peeling paint.

We recommend starting in Lewistown and heading east on US87/MT200 toward the little oasis of Grass Range. Continue south on US 87 through ranch country into the pine-studded environs of Roundup, an agricultural and coal-mining town that's been through a lot in recent years and is hoping for better days ahead.

HITTING THE ROAD

Start your journey in red, white, and blue **Lewistown** (pop. 5,813), which sits in a modest bowl bisected by Big Spring Creek—an anomaly in these parts in that it has the cool waters to support a healthy trout population. It's quickly obvious that Lewistown is the hub of a vast region. The community has all the standard services and some of the usual fast-food suspects.

Before heading out of town, check out the **Central Montana Museum** (406-535-9289), which chronicles the area's frontier history along with more recent events. Like seemingly every other museum in Montana, it also boasts a replica of a dinosaur (*Torosaurus*); this one was discovered about 65 miles northeast of town. Lewistown also is perhaps the best place in Montana to gain an understanding of the Hutterite culture whose colonies dot the region. The **King Colony Walking Tour** (406-350-2307) offers an inside look at the community's laundromat, slaughter house, upholstery shop, milking parlor, and more for $15. Hutterites, who are similar to the Amish and Mennonites, migrated to the Canadian prairies and the Dakotas beginning in the mid-1870s. The three colonies near Lewistown are among the 50 that dot the state.

Another fascination in the area is **Gigantic Warm Springs**, which, at 50,000 gallons per minute, is considered the largest warm spring in the world and is also said to be the third largest of any type. A dam forms a pool about the size of a football field, and the 68-degree waters are pleasant on a summer day. The springs are on a private ranch; a $3 donation is requested. To get there, drive about 10 miles north of Lewistown on US 191 and go west on MT 81 for about five miles until you reach the Gigantic Warm Springs sign.

Lewistown has one other must-do if you're not in a hurry: The **Charlie Russell Chew Choo** (406-535-5436) is a 56-mile round-trip nightly dinner train ride on a Milwaukee Road spur toward Great Falls. Highlights are two trestles, a tunnel, prime-rib dinner, no-host cash bar, and the obligatory train robbery by characters looking suspiciously like Butch and Sundance—all for anywhere from $100 to $135.

Leaving Lewistown, US 87/MT200 winds through a pretty countryside of pine and pastures past the Ayers Colony on the left to **Grass Range** (pop. 103). If you're feeling adventurous, backtrack west out of Grass Range a little more than 10 miles on gravel Forest Grove Road to a meeting with Fairview Road. Turn left until you reach the **Bear Gulch Pictographs** (406-428-2185) and the remarkably vivid pictures painted by ancient cultures on rock. The fact that they are on property owned by a single five-generation family, the Lundins, partially explains why they're so well-preserved. They're open from 10 AM to noon Wednesday through Sunday; remote tours are $15.

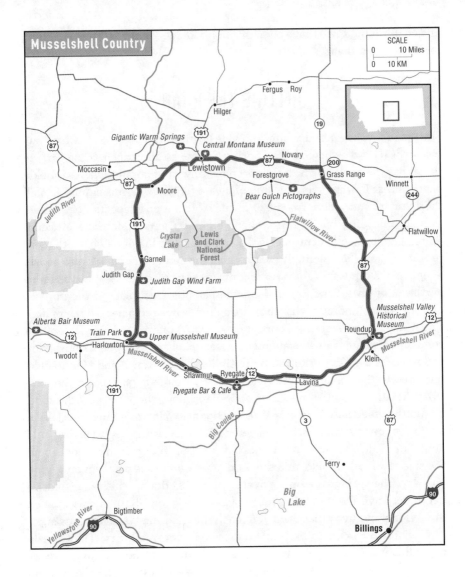

Musselshell Country

SCALE
0   10 Miles
0   10 KM

From Bear Gulch, consider heading southeast on the wonderfully named Surenough Creek Road and then Upper Flatwillow Road, both gravel, about 20 miles along Flatwillow Creek and back to US 87. You won't have missed much on the main highway, and that'll hold true until you reach **Roundup** (pop. 1,859) at the foot of the modest Bull Mountains. Its economy already tied to a struggling coal industry, Roundup has been battered by a flood (2011) and fires (2012) in recent years, leaving residents to wonder when Mother Nature's next shoe will drop. The **Musselshell Valley Historical Museum** (406-323-1525) is open every afternoon during the summer and features a "Clovis to Coal" exhibit that explores the 11,000-year evolution of the valley.

At the junction of US 12, venture west along the Musselshell toward Lavina, Ryegate, Shawmut and Harlowton. The Musselshell is a hard-working, pretty little riparian ribbon amid pastures and rangeland. There isn't much happening at **Lavina** (pop. 180), where the streets are eerily quiet at dusk. One reason to make the 1-mile detour on MT 3 at the **Cozy Corner Bar** and gas station is to snap photos of the white-chipped-paint Adams Hotel and the two-story brick Slayton Mercantile, both on the a National Register of Historic Places. The Adams is a large colonial-style structure that once was one of the most elegant hotels in the region but now is a private residence that has been getting some badly needed TLC. The Slayton also has weathered trying times. **Ryegate** (pop. 245) is more vibrant, with a little park across the street from the **Ryegate Bar & Café**. It also has fuel and a grocery store. The town's claim to historical fame is that Chief Joseph crossed the Musselshell River near here in 1877 when he took his Nez Perce on their valiant march from Oregon and Idaho through Wyoming and Montana to their final surrender near Canada. If you're passing through in June, make time for the annual Testicle Festival, where the showcase cuisine, for the uninitiated, is cattle cahones—otherwise known as Rocky Mountain oysters. Continuing west, you won't find any services or much of anything else at **Shawmut** (pop. 42), which saw better days before the Milwaukee Road rolled up its tracks—it had a hotel, restaurant, store, and lumber yard. Still, it's worth taking a few extra minutes to make a loop on the shaded streets to admire the ubiquitous rusting remains of headier times: the 1950s tractors and automobiles scattered throughout the yards, a vermillion school that looks as if it was plucked from Mexico, and a sweet little church.

Harlowton (pop. 1,062), an agricultural center mostly on a hill above the Musselshell, was just a small stage stop known as Merino until the Milwaukee Road came along and laid the longest stretch of electric railroad in North America. The state's last electric railway removed its tracks in 1974, but its legacy and other area history lives on in the **Upper Musselshell Museum** and in the electric Milwaukee Road locomotive that greets visitors in **Train Park**. "Harlow" is a friendly place that boasts of mild (relatively) winters.

Eighteen miles north of Harlowton on US 191 is **Judith Gap** (pop. 164), named for the slot the Musselshell River creates between the Big Snowy and Little Belt mountains. The gap creates a funnel, and the wind always blows, making the grassy landscape between Harlowton and Judith Gap an ideal place for Montana's first large-scale wind farm. The project went online in 2005, and the 90 rotating turbines rising more than 250 feet to the big sky produce about 7 percent of the state's electricity.

After passing the wind farm, you'll reach **Judith Gap**, which was founded in 1908. A mercantile regionally renowned for its milkshakes once drew travelers for miles around, but it has closed, leaving few reasons to stop. Five miles past Judith Gap is **Garneill**, notable only for a large granite rock that features the names of early pioneers and the dates they arrived in the valley etched in it. The **Ubet and Central Montana Pioneers Monument** sits on a concrete base made of Indian relics, ore, and petrified wood. For the trivia minded, Ubet was a nearby town whose name came from A. R. Barrows, an area resident. When asked if he could figure out what to call the new community, he responded, "You bet!"

In another 14 miles is Eddie's Corner, where you'll turn right at the large gas station at the junction of US 191/89 and MT 200. Drive amid fields of grass toward **Moore** (pop. 186) and another 19 miles to Lewistown. The Judith Basin to the west is the home of the all-natural, sparkling-blue Yogo sapphire, the state gem. The sapphires, prized because they are untreated,

AN ELECTRIC HISTORY: ALONG THE OLD MILWAUKEE ROAD

As you drive US 12 between Roundup and Harlowton, look carefully and you'll eventually identify an abandoned grade along the Musselshell River that represents a railroad history unlike any other in Montana. The Chicago, St. Paul, Milwaukee & Pacific Railroad—better known as the Milwaukee Road—operated trains along this stretch from the late 1800s until the mid-1970s. In the 212 miles between Harlowton and Avery, Idaho, the tracks were electrified beginning in 1914.

HARLOWTON IS THE HUB OF THE MILWAUKEE ROAD HISTORIC DISTRICT AND HOME OF E57B, ONE OF THE LAST TWO ELECTRIC LOCOMOTIVES TO OPERATE ON THE LINE

This history is on display in several parts of Montana, including Harlowton, which is part of the Milwaukee Road Historic District. Prominent downtown in this little agricultural community on the Musselshell is E57B, one of the last two electric locomotives to operate along the line. E57B hauled freight and passengers west through White Sulphur Springs and Ringling and then through mostly roadless Sixteen Mile Creek Canyon to Lombard, on the Missouri River near Townsend. Also worth visiting in Harlowton is the old train depot, which has walls and walls of fascinating Milwaukee Road memorabilia.

Equally enticing for railroad buffs are the active lines coming out of Lewistown, one of which hosts the Charlie Russell Chew Choo dinner train. The 157-mile line from Lewistown to Lombard was called the "Jawbone," not because of its rugged features but because of the Montana Railroad's consistently precarious financial status. The line going northwest out of Lewistown has two extraordinary trestles, over Big Spring Creek and the Judith River.

were found more than a century ago in Yogo Gulch between Utica and Windham west of Lewistown. *Yogo* is the Blackfeet word for "romance," and among the bearers was one Lady Diana Spencer of England, who was presented a nine-carat cornflower-blue sapphire set amid diamonds on a gold ring when Prince Charles asked for her hand in marriage. There's no doubt Lewistown has a love affair with the gem: There's the **Yogo Inn** and **Sapphire Café**, among another mineral-inspired names of businesses.

Best Places to Bunk

LEWISTOWN: If a slice of a community's history has meaning, you'll want to choose **The Historic Calvert Hotel** ($$/$$$, 406-535-5411). Though the two-story brick building doesn't necessarily meet the eyeball test for "historic," in part because new owners spent two years rehabilitating the decaying structure less than a decade ago, The Calvert actually was built in 1912 as a girls' dormitory. The 28 rooms, including some larger king suites with fireplaces, are tastefully decorated. Lewistown has numerous other lodging options, but standing out among the mom-and-pop motor-court variety is the economical **Sunset Motel** ($, 406-535-8471). It's a case of appearances deceiving—though it looks ordinary from the outside, the 16 rooms (four with kitchenettes) are updated, spacious, and comfortable.

GRASS RANGE: The **Elk Creek Lodge** ($$, 406-428-2160) is isolated in more ways than one—it has no website—but the five-room facility offers a nice snapshot of central Montana's rolling countryside. The lodge, which features a common area and has Wi-Fi, is perched on a sagebrush hill overlooking the tiny community.

ROUNDUP: If you're looking for a clean, hospitable, and affordable place to lay your head, the **Big Sky Motel** ($, 406-323-2303) on the main drag is as basic as they come but won't disappoint.

HARLOWTON: Of the two motels in town, the standout is the **Country Side Inn** ($/$$, 406-632-4119), a cute and clean little motor-court style structure with an older log section and a newer wing with private rooms and log accents.

Alternative Places to Bunk

LEWISTOWN: For a marvelous country experience with some privacy, three **Cottonwood Log Cabins** ($$, 406-538-8411) are 10 miles outside of town and have eye-pleasing views and access to some excellent hiking where you might stumble upon some gray quartz. All three log cabins have the basics, and one has satellite TV if you absolutely need a fix. All three sleep up to six and there's a shared hot tub.

FOREST SERVICE CABINS/LOOKOUTS: The **Crystal Lake Cabin** ($25/sleeps four) is about 20 miles south of Lewistown in the pretty Big Snowy Mountains. Don't expect privacy—the cabin is next to the Crystal Lake Campground—but you've got a roof over your head, you're close to decent fishing on Crystal Lake, and there are several worthy hiking trails in the area. The Big Snowy and Castle Mountains also have several campgrounds. (Reservations: 877-444-6777/www.recreation.gov.)

Best Eats

LEWISTOWN: The town has the plethora of options you'd expect from a regional agricultural hub. Lewistown lost some fine dining when the Onyx Bar & Grill in The Historic Calvert Hotel closed, but luckily they still have **Pourman's Southwestern Café** ($/$$, 406-535-4277, B/L) and its spicy breakfasts, **Harry's Place** ($/$$, 406-538-9520, B/L/D) with its sandwiches and seafood bisque, and the **Mint Bar & Grill** ($$, 406-535-9525, D, Tues–Sat.) for steak and potatoes. As of October 2015, the Mint's grill was closed due to an accident suffered by the owner/chef, but they were still serving on the bar side. Every little town has a popular burger joint, and in Lewistown it's **Ruby's 100 Percent Montana Burgers** ($, 406-535-7450, L/D). Yes, it's a bit spendy by fast-food standards, but Montana-sourced beef comes at a price and, besides, it's one of those iconic places where the burgers, fries, and chocolate shakes are too good to pass up.

ROUNDUP: You'll get a good flavor for the locals and for outstanding home-made pie—try the strawberry rhubarb—at the **Busy Bee Family Dining & Gift Shop** ($/$$, 406-323-2204, B/L/D), the favored stop for coal miners and ranchers alike for its friendly vibe and man-sized portions. The café has a little more spark since a remodel after the town's devastating 2014 flood. The place to go for a thick steak, burger, and peanuts is the **Grand Bar and Grill** ($/$$, 406-323-3104, L/D), which stays open until 2 AM.

RYEGATE: The **Ryegate Bar & Café** ($/$$, 406-568-2330, B/L/D) is another one of those friendly places that beckons because it provides a flavor of the town's surroundings. Farmers and ranchers gather here to talk weather, grain prices, and local politics. The food is what you'd expect: burgers, fries, steak, chicken strips, etc., but all made with pride.

Martinsdale (52 miles round-trip)

Take an extra couple hours—and maybe even a night—to continue west from Harlowton on US 12 to **Martinsdale**. For a community with all of 64 residents, it's a happening place. And before you even arrive, you'll be able to say you've been in famous **Two Dot**, home of the famous Two Dot Bar and geographic center of Montana.

To reach Martinsdale, turn left on MT 294 off US 12 and be sure to take a tour of the **Charles M. Bair Family Museum** just across the Musselshell River. The museum is actually the family ranch, and it positively sparkles with its bleach-white buildings and red roofs. Bair was an Ohio man who was said to have come west with "fourteen cents and seven green apples in his pockets." After making a fortune during the Alaska gold rush by investing in a ground-thawing device, he put his money into coal, oil, mining, and an assortment of other endeavors that made him even wealthier. Along the way he built friendships with Teddy Roosevelt, Charlie Russell, Chief Plenty Coups, Will Rogers, and a handful of U.S. presidents. A guided tour of the elegant home—with its eclectic collection of Native American, western and European art, along with a wide variety of antiques—is not to be missed. Hours vary from Memorial Day through the end of October; admission is $5 for adults.

After visiting the Bair complex, you'll want to have dinner at the **Crazy Mountain Inn**—and perhaps even spend the night. The frontier-style rooms are priced from $47–65. Bathrooms with shower and tub are in the hallway. The restaurant, open May through November, is renowned for its chicken-fried steak, thanks to kudos from both Esquire magazine and frequent visitor Jim Harrison, a part-time Livingston resident and author of *Legends of the Fall*. If you're a fisherman, **Martinsdale Reservoir** is a productive playground—unless the winds headed for Judith Gap are howling, in which case the lake is turned over to windsurfers.

HARLOWTON: You can't stay—yet—at the visually arresting Graves Hotel, but **Whistle Stop Café** ($/$$, 406-632-5798, B/L) is the place to go for a bite to eat if you're passing through "Harlow." In an old railroad town, naturally a menu highlight is the Engineer Burger. Breakfast and lunch already are served, and plans for a dinner menu were in the works in 2015. Four new owners opened the restaurant and have big dreams of restoring the 1909 three-story sandstone structure "to its former glory". The Graves was the fulcrum of the community until the Milwaukee Road left town four decades ago. **Snowy Mountain Coffee** ($, 406-632-6838, B/L/D Mon.–Sat.) is a breath-of-fresh-air spot for fresh-roasted coffees, muffins, scones, smoothies, soups, and sandwiches. And if you're passing through Thursday, Friday, or Saturday night don't miss their pizza.

Best Bar

HOBSON: You've got to venture just off the beaten backroad for this one, but **Tall Boys Tavern** merits veering left at Moore on US 87 for the short drive to this bright little street corner in Hobson, an agricultural community with twin grain elevators. Opened in the spring of 2015 in Hobson's 1910 brick Murray Block Building, Tall Boys isn't your classic Montana tavern. In fact, they toss around the words "gourmet" and "gluten-free" here when they talk about their versatile food menu. They also serve everything from traditional whiskeys, bourbons, beers, and wines to margaritas, Murray mules, cosmopolitans, and a concoction called the Icelandic Trashcan that tosses in everything sweet-ish but the kitchen sink. As expected with a new endeavor in a rural setting, their menu—which highlights chicken salad, Philly cheesesteak sandwiches, burgers, prime rib, and steaks—is a work in progress. Something must be working, though: Tall Boys has become a magnet for folks from Lewistown to Great Falls, and points between.

DETOUR: ONE FOR THE ROAD

Harlowton/Big Timber/McLeod

ESTIMATED LENGTH: 65 miles
HIGHLIGHTS: Crazy Mountain Museum, Greycliff Prairie Dog Town State Park, Natural Bridge and Falls, Melville Lutheran church, Judith Gap Wind Farm
GETTING THERE: This rural route bisects I-90 in Big Timber—head north on US 191 to reach Harlowton and south on the Main Boulder Road (MT 298) to reach McLeod.

The route starts in **Big Timber** (pop. 1,624), home of the Sheepherders and a site of a significant chapter in Lewis and Clark history. Having split with Meriwether Lewis upon the duo's return from the Pacific in 1806, William Clark camped at a spot where the Boulder River and Big Timber Creek joined the Yellowstone River on opposite banks. The creek sported especially large cottonwood trees—hence the name Big Timber. The expedition felled a cottonwood to build a flat-bottomed boat called a *pirogue*. Settled by Norwegians, Big Timber was one of the last great sheep-ranching areas in Montana. Today, it remains a quiet agricultural community with tree-lined streets, but it's gradually absorbing the spillover of solitude-seeking newcomers who find Bozeman and Livingston too urban for their tastes. The

THE PERKY AND PERSECUTED NATIVE PRAIRIE DOG HAS FOUND SANCTUARY AT PRAIRIE DOG TOWN STATE PARK AT GREYCLIFF

history is encapsulated well at the **Crazy Mountain Museum**, which features a remarkable 1907 replica of the town's 184 buildings. Montanans from as far away as Bozeman and Billings make the drive to Big Timber for dinner and an overnight at the historic **Grand Hotel**, and the **Thirsty Turtle** is a lively place to enjoy a brew and a burger.

Before heading north or south, take a detour from the Detour. It's a 7-mile drive east on I-90 to **Greycliff Prairie Dog Town State Park**, one of few places in Montana where you can see these persecuted critters in all their perky glory. Once back in Big Timber, turn south on MT 298 and drive at least 25 miles (we recommend more) through **McLeod** (pop. 199) and past the façade farmhouse along the tumbling Boulder River where scenes from *The Horse Whisperer* were filmed. Continue to **Natural Bridge and Falls** on the Boulder. The natural arch over the river collapsed in 1988, but the 105-foot falls remain. In lower water, some of the falls disappear and the river vanishes underground, emerging a short distance downstream. A trail system offers great views, and it isn't difficult to scramble into the canyon bed when it's dry.

Return the way you came back to Big Timber, taking US 191 north for 19 miles to **Melville** (pop. 142), where the state's first Lutheran church was built in 1914 in the foothills of the towering Crazy Mountains to the west. All but a few of the first services were performed in Norwegian. Beyond Melville, the landscape changes from grass to pine-studded hills off to the right—the sandstone Cayuse Hills—before dipping into Harlowton along the Mussel-shell River.

10
THE WARRIOR TRAIL
The Tongue River Loop

HARDIN/CROW AGENCY/BUSBY/BIRNEY/
ASHLAND/LAME DEER

ESTIMATED LENGTH: 147 miles

ESTIMATED TIME: 5 hours

HIGHLIGHTS: Little Bighorn Battlefield National Monument, Reno-Benteen Battle-field Memorial, Rosebud Battlefield State Park, Tongue River Reservoir, Wolf Mountains Battlefield National Historic Landmark, St. Labre Mission/Cheyenne Indian Museum, Tongue River

GETTING THERE: The Warrior Trail begins at the US 212 exit off I-90 (Exit 510) just south of Crow Agency, about 70 miles east of Billings. If you're coming from Billings, consider taking the Detour first: you'll explore some extraordinary country and avoid the monotonous 80-mph hum of the interstate between Billings and Hardin, and you can take a shortcut to the start of the Warrior Trail at Crow Agency.

OVERVIEW

No journey through Montana is complete without an immersion in the rich Indian culture that remains today. That experience best comes to life on the Warrior Trail through the Crow and Northern Cheyenne reservations in the south-central part of the state—if you take the time to look. This is not an adventure for the ill-prepared or naïve. A large section of the route is on gravel roads—albeit well maintained—through remote country that lacks the services to which travelers are accustomed, even by backroads standards. Life looks and feels decidedly different, and while the tribes are striving to overcome two centuries of cultural upheaval, the challenges are daunting. Alcoholism, unemployment, and general hopelessness are rampant, and even Indian leaders concede the reservations are reminiscent of Third World countries. It's readily apparent in the small, colorful, box-

A LARGE, HOGAN-STYLE STRUCTURE AT BUSBY LETS YOU KNOW YOU'RE IN NORTHERN CHEYENNE COUNTRY

THE TONGUE RIVER, WHICH MEANDERS ALONG THE EASTERN EDGE OF THE NORTHERN CHEYENNE INDIAN RESERVATION, IS THE ONLY STREAM IN THE STATE TO HOLD ROCK BASS

shaped, one-size-fits-all homes with the rusting skeletons of old cars in the yards filling the landscape. All the inherent risks of driving rural Montana roads at night—wildlife, alcohol, fatigue—are compounded here.

Yet, there are many more reasons to make this journey than not, starting with the people themselves. You can explore their cultures anytime, but to catch the Crow, Northern Cheyenne, and other Plains Indians in full celebratory regalia, visit during the Crow Fair Powwow in Crow Agency every August. A less boisterous affair is the Northern Cheyenne 4th of July Chief's Powwow & Rodeo in Lame Deer. At Crow Fair, the rolling grasslands in and around Crow Agency become a jovial, sprawling teepee city with thousands of revelers drumming, dancing, and telling tribal stories.

Of course, there's also the Little Bighorn Battlefield National Monument just outside Crow Agency, where the Lakota Sioux and Northern Cheyenne outwitted General George Armstrong Custer and, ironically, his Crow and Arikara scouts in the Indians' most famous military success. The Crow believed if they sided with the U.S. government against the Sioux, Northern Cheyenne, and Nez Perce, they would get to keep much of their vast historic homeland for a reservation. Like every other tribe that signed treaties with Washington, they were sadly mistaken. At 2.3 million acres, their reservation is the largest in Montana, but the Crow lost their prized Stillwater River drainage, the wildlife-rich Paradise Valley, and their sacred Absaroka Mountains.

The Northern Cheyenne Indian Reservation is about one-fifth the size and was born out of desperation. After the Northern and Southern Cheyenne were subdued and finally surrendered in 1877, they were sent to a reservation in Oklahoma, where the hot and muggy climate was deadly for the unacclimated Northern Cheyenne. When a small band tried to escape, most were killed, but about 125 made it north to Montana and settled near the Tongue River, not far from their traditional homeland in South Dakota's Black Hills. Eventually, the government provided the small reservation that exists today.

Much of the route hugs the Tongue River on the edge of the Northern Cheyenne Indian Reservation and traverses rugged prairie, range, and badland country with sharp geological features. Consider bringing a canoe and fishing rod. The meandering Tongue might be Montana's best warm-water stream fishery, with prolific numbers of smallmouth bass, sauger, chub, the prehistoric paddlefish, and the state's sole population of a Midwest fish called the rock bass.

HITTING THE ROAD

For the sake of lodging and dining options, we actually start the Warrior Trail in **Hardin** (pop. 3,730), a mixed agricultural community of Anglos and Indians on the edge of the Crow Reservation.

Starting the loop, Hardin is largely nondescript but does have a **Custer's Last Stand Reenactment** in a field northwest of town every June. Some historical buildings are worth seeing, too, including **St. John's Catholic Church** and **Hardin Depot**, but the area's history is best captured at the **Big Horn County Historical Museum & Visitor Center** (406-665-1671). The 22-acre site features more than two dozen outdoor structures and two buildings with exhibits—one focusing on the region's farming traditions, the other on cultural history.

Arriving in **Crow Agency** (pop. 1,616) is not unlike visiting a Mexican border town. The differences between cultures are almost that dramatic, starting with the language. The exit sign reads "Bauxuwuaashee"; weathered buildings featuring similar tongue twisters are interspersed with such newer buildings as those at Little Big Horn College and the Crow/Northern Cheyenne Hospital. When embarking on your journey along the Warrior Trail, which starts at the US 212 exit off I-90, stop at the **Custer Battlefield Trading Post and Cafe** ($, 406-638-2270, B/L/D, shorter hours winter/fall) for a bite and a look at the compelling collection of gifts ranging from the usual jiggers and coffee mugs to fine American Indian art, jewelry, and intricate beadwork. If you're lucky, owner Putt Thompson will be on hand for history lessons. Listen carefully, and you're likely to hear the service staff communicating in Crow. Say "Kay-Ha" (hello), and if they're not busy, ask for the Crow perspective on the nearby **Little Bighorn Battlefield National Monument** (406-638-2621), so named after it was appropriately changed from Custer Battlefield National Monument in 1991. Every American elementary school student knows the story of Custer's Last Stand or, as the Indians call it, the Battle of Greasy Grass Creek. Led by Sitting Bull, the Lakota and Northern Cheyenne overwhelmed Custer and his troops, killing 268 in a battle that galvanized the Anglos against the Indians. The most poignant way to experience the scene is to walk amid the markers where Custer, his 7th Cavalry soldiers and scouts, and the Indians fell. In the better-late-than-never department, a memorial has been erected that offers the Lakota, Northern Cheyenne, Crow, and Arikara versions of the battle. Most people are content to see Little Bighorn, but about 4.5 miles to the southeast of the main battlefield on a paved road is the **Reno-Benteen Battlefield Memorial**, now part of the 765-acre Little Bighorn Battlefield complex. The

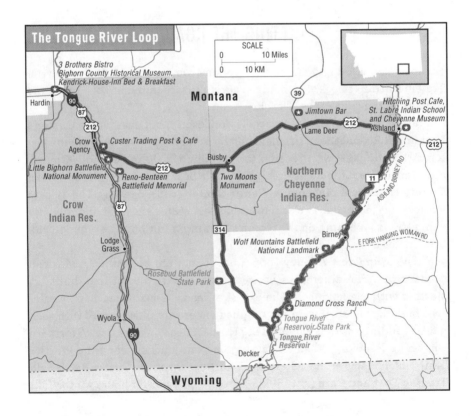

COLORFUL CROW TEEPEES MARK THE ENTRANCE TO THE CUSTER BATTLEFIELD TRADING POST AT CROW AGENCY

Reno-Benteen site is a tribute to soldiers who tried and failed to arrive in time to assist Custer.

Back on the Warrior Trail (US 212) heading east, you can see the stone monument to Custer on a hill as you look out the passenger side of the car. At that point, you begin to get a sense of why the natives cherish this country. There is a gentle beauty in the rolling grasslands and coulees where ponderosa pines poke out of distant ocher rimrock like many thousands of green pushpins. Painted ponies graze in pastures around the colorful array of small homes, where aging minivans, pickups, and sedans swallowed up by grasses paint a living history.

The north–south Wolf Mountains, visible on the passenger's side, serve as a rough border between the Crow and Northern Cheyenne reservations. At **Busby** (pop. 745), just inside the Northern Cheyenne boundary, look up a hill on the south side of the highway for a stone pillar. This is the **Two Moons Monument**, a tribute to the great chief who led the Northern Cheyenne at Little Bighorn. The pillar is locked behind a chain-link fence, but you can still read the inscription and wander through a circular graveyard commemorating Northern Cheyenne killed in 1879.

At Busby, you have a choice to continue east on US 212 and the Warrior Trail, or turn south on Big Horn County Road 314 along Rosebud Creek toward the Tongue River Reservoir. To stay in the battlefield flow, go 20 miles south on the paved road to **Rosebud Battlefield State Park** (406-757-2298). This is the place where a fierce battle on June 17, 1876, pitting Chief Crazy Horse's Sioux and the Northern Cheyenne against General George Crook's forces, kept the cavalry at bay long enough to prevent Crook from helping

INDIAN PAINT PONIES EYE RARE VISITORS ALONG THE TONGUE RIVER SOUTH OF ASHLAND

Custer at Little Bighorn eight days later. Unlike Little Bighorn, which has a visitor center and interpreters, this is a primitive area intended to retain the look and feel of 135 years ago. A short gravel road through private land leads to a kiosk describing the events and a gravel road for touring. The park also has a buffalo jump, rock cairns, and clearly visible teepee rings.

As with other great tracts of eastern Montana and northern Wyoming, the prospect of coal-bed methane gas drilling is a threat to the site. Though the state owns surface rights at Rosebud, an energy company owns rights to the valuable minerals underneath and eventually could turn the area surrounding this extraordinary historical site into an industrial zone.

Continuing southeast on the county road, the Tongue River Reservoir eventually comes into sight. This alluring 12-mile-long, caterpillar-shaped lake in the boonies, a short cast from the Wyoming border, has such extraordinary fishing that the sprawling **Tongue River Reservoir State Park** (406-234-0900) annually lures 50,000 visitors, mostly boaters from Billings and Sheridan, Wyoming. There are numerous places to camp, many with full hookups, and a marina to provide all the necessary supplies for a day chasing northern pike, crappie, catfish, bass, and that eastern Montana delicacy, the walleye. The shallow and narrow reservoir has produced state records for four types of fish.

As the reservoir draws nearer, a railroad appears on the right. A spur from

Sheridan was built to service two huge open-pit coal mines west of the reservoir at **Decker** (pop. 96). Unless you're into seeing how some of America's energy thirst is quenched, there is little reason to make the 6-mile trek from the state park to Decker, about a mile north of the Montana-Wyoming border.

Heading north along the lake's western shore on a well-groomed gravel road, you'll pass the dam. The road then hugs the lazy Tongue River, winding past red scoria rock and ranches north to Ashland. As you follow the river, look for deer, eagles, herons, and sandhill cranes. You'll surely notice ornate log gates for many miles—part of the vast **Diamond Cross Ranch**, which owns tens of thousands of acres east of the Tongue River (the Northern Cheyenne Reservation is on the west side).

A few miles before **Birney** (pop. 106), and on the west side of the gravel road, hangs a large wooden sign that creaks in the wind. "The Battle of the Butte—Jan. 8, 1877," it reads. Below it is a small commemorative stone erected by the U.S. Department of the Interior. This windswept place, nearly forgotten in history, is on private lands, but you can try to imagine what happened here at the **Wolf Mountains Battlefield National Historic Landmark** and ponder its historical significance.

Seven months after Little Bighorn, Chief Crazy Horse—the hero of the nearby Battle of Rosebud—and 800 warriors tried to mount a surprise attack on Colonel Nelson Miles one frigid winter morning. Miles fended off the Indians and sent them scurrying into the nearby hills. It was to be the last skirmish of the great Sioux Indian Wars; within four months, all the Sioux were relocated to distant reservations, and a huge chunk of the West was open to white expansion. Given the battle's magnitude, it's surprising that there isn't more to commemorate it.

Birney is almost entirely populated by Northern Cheyenne. There isn't much here except a few well-kept homes, a school, a church, and a post office kept dust-free by a short section of pavement between the shady cottonwoods. Judging by the ramshackle remnants of what must have been a mercantile, there haven't been services for a while. If you're not pressed for time, turn right on the East Fork Hanging Woman Creek Road past Poker Jim Butte for about 25 gravel miles to the **Blacks Pond Drive Route** on the Custer National Forest. In the spring and fall, this man-made pond and its associated wetlands are a favorite stop for birdwatchers who admire ducks, turkeys, herons, warblers, and that Montana favorite, the Lazuli bunting. A campground-and-picnic area is nearby.

About six miles north of Birney, you'll have to choose between the gravel Ashland-Birney Road on the east side of the river and the paved Bureau of Indian Affairs Road 11 on the reservation on the west side. If you cross the Tongue through a small Northern Cheyenne settlement, you can continue north along the river to Ashland or save some time and drive overland to Lame Deer. We suggest staying the course to **Ashland** (pop. 464), best

A SIGN SWAYING IN THE WINDS IS ALL THAT MARKS THE BATTLE OF THE BUTTES—WHERE THE SIOUX INDIAN WARS ENDED

known for the **St. Labre Indian School**, established in 1884, and the **St. Labre Mission/Cheyenne Indian Museum** (406-784-4500 Mon.–Fri.) slightly north of town. Once a three-room cabin, the school is now a campus that reflects Catholic roots and the Plains Indians lifestyle. The museum, which has a gift shop, is almost an exclusive showcase of Cheyenne history. The school and museum represent a dedicated effort by the Northern Cheyenne to stay close to their roots; their native tongue is taught in the school and at Chief Dull Knife College in **Lame Deer** (pop. 2,052). Ashland also has a mercantile, gas station, and small diner.

Back on the Warrior Trail heading west, US 212 rises out of the Tongue River bottoms and into pretty ponderosa forest. The Northern Cheyenne economy once was dependent on logging, which is apparent in some of the small cuts and reforestation visible from the highway. You'll see signs prohibiting the shooting of prairie dogs, once considered a varmint—it still is in many circles—but now valued by many as a symbol of the plains. Look for the telltale mounds in the fields behind barbed-wire fences. Following Alderson Creek, the highway eventually reaches Lame Deer, capital of the Northern Cheyenne nation. Don't expect your typical small-town diners and motels; they aren't here. There is a casino, expensive gas, and the Lame Deer Trading Post, a.k.a. "The Big Store." Also in town are the sleek and modern Chief Little Wolf Hospital and Chief Dull Knife College, both named after one of two chiefs who brought the Northern Cheyenne here from Oklahoma to meet up with a group led by Two Moons.

If you've got real adventurous spirit, drive about 7 miles north of Lame Deer on MT 39, cross the reservation line, perch yourself on a log stool, and have a beer and burger at the notorious **Jimtown Bar** (406-477-6459)—after which you'll be able to boast that you've survived the toughest tavern in Montana. Don't take our word for it; the *Guinness Book of World Records* has officially made the claim. If that seems a little intimidating, just go during the day when it's decidedly tamer.

Returning to US 212, the highway follows Rosebud Creek upstream about 25 miles to Busby, where the Warrior Trail tour is complete.

Best Places to Bunk

HARDIN: We don't usually recommend chains, but the **Super 8 Motel** ($$, 406-665-1700) is well-maintained and includes continental breakfast, Wi-Fi, and flat-screen TVs (yes, this is considered an amenity in these parts). Likewise, the **Rodeway Inn** ($, 406-665-1870) is similar to the Super 8, but if you have kids in tow, you'll probably appreciate the waterslide that's open during the summer. For personality, though, nothing in the area tops the **Kendrick House Inn Bed & Breakfast** ($$, 406-665-3035), an immaculately manicured 1915 Edwardian boarding house with five guest rooms/suites furnished with English and French period fixtures. A garden house was made from bricks salvaged from old Fort Custer when the Smiths restored the property some 20 years ago. The breakfast is typical fare, except for the lingonberry pancakes. We hope the Kendrick stays open, but as of press time the owners were debating whether to call it quits.

Best Alternative Bunking

BIRNEY: All of this vast country seems at your feet—or at your horse's shoes—when you stay at the all-inclusive **Lodge at Diamond Cross** ($$$$, 406-757-2220), a 1930s working cattle ranch that blends the old and the new with a renovated lodge in the heart of 100,000 private acres. The Tongue River snakes its way through what was once a camping area for the Crow Indians. Laurie and Dick Hosford, licensed outfitters, can accommodate up to thirteen guests and offer a hands-on experience with the muscle, sweat, and simple pleasures of a modern-day cattle operation.

CAMPING: The **Tongue River Reservoir State Park** (406-234-0900) has every option and amenity for campers, ranging from forty busy paved sites

THE 'LITTLE PEOPLE'—LEGEND OR LEGACY?

The Crow call them *awwakkulé*. To folks who grew up on the forested flanks of the Pryor Mountains, they're simply the Little People. Like Bigfoot and the Loch Ness Monster, nobody actually has any proof of the existence of these mysterious peoples who are said to exist somewhere between the real and spiritual world. The Crow chief Plenty Coups said the *awwakkulé* provided him with a vision of cooperation with the white people that prevented great Crow tragedy during westward expansion. A bar owner in Fromberg swears she has been visited by the Little People and had relics on display in the back of her building that, alas, perished in a fire.

No absolute evidence of the Little People has ever been established, and many Native cultures have legends of pygmy-sized peoples in their midst. But among the believers there is no doubt about the existence of these 18-inch-high humans with sharp teeth and remarkable strength, who fiercely protect the integrity of the Pryors, a little island range with more than 1,000 plant species, 200 types of birds, and plentiful remnants of vision quests made by Natives. Even Meriwether Lewis wrote about seeing 18-inch-high "deavals" that so frightened the Sioux in South Dakota they refused to go anywhere near them. Adding to the legend of the Little People was the 1932 discovery of the mummified remains of a 14-inch-tall human in a mountain range south of Casper, Wyoming. Pedro The Mummy, which (or is it who?) was found in a sitting position with arms crossed, was taken to the University of Wyoming. X-rays were taken in 1950 and again in 1980, with conclusions ranging from identifying the entombed human as a violently beaten 65-year-old man to a preserved infant. Other such mummies have been found as far north as the Pryors as well.

Plenty Coups had two dreams involving the Little People. The first, when he was nine years old, was of a leader telling him he'd one day be a great chief. The second altered the course of Crow history. When he was 11, a Little People chief presented visions of white people one day swarming the land, replacing the buffalo with cattle. Crow chiefs helped him interpret the dream, saying it meant if the tribe listened to what was coming they would survive. The Crow were more cooperative with the coming whites than other tribes, and wound up with one of the country's largest reservations because of it. Plenty Coups eventually became a farmer.

Legend or legacy, many in the Crow Nation and in area communities are adamant that the Little People exist in the Pryors. Indians traveling the Pryors leave tokens, claiming that Little People have protected them in the wilds, and that they've healed sick tribal members. And many Anglo hunters, campers, and hikers report some strange goings-on whenever they're in these mysterious mountains.

with electrical hookups along the reservoir to a peaceful tent-oriented campground along the river about a half-mile below the dam.

FOREST SERVICE CABINS/LOOKOUTS: For a primitive retreat under the stars, the Custer National Forest's **Diamond Butte Lookout** (406-784-2344, $25/sleeps four) about forty miles east of Birney is an attractive 30-foot masonry tower. It's a pretty steep 60-yard hike from the end of the road to the lookout, but there's a wagon for hauling gear. Also nearby, the 1930s **Whitetail Cabin** (406-784-2344, $25/sleeps four) is easily accessible from the road even in winter, though in snow you'll probably have to hike the length of a football field to the front door.

Best Eats

HARDIN: Kerri and Greg Smith are back in the theatre and food biz. After leasing the restaurant side of the historic Lee building downtown, they're now running **3 Brothers Bistro** ($/$$, 406-545-5133, Tues.–Sat.), formerly Pizza & Java Company, as well as **Centre Cinema** next door. Their goal: provide a complete entertainment complex in which to nosh, imbibe, and play. Special touches include homemade pizza dough and sauce, house-smoked pork, tri-tip and salmon, 10 Montana craft beers on tap, a wine list (no box wine here), modern casino games, and first-run movies. Oh, and you can get your grub to go and eat while watching a flick next door. The bistro's name is a nod to the Smiths' three sons. The **Ranch House Grill** ($/$$, 406-665-1900, L/D) is a friendly and country-comfortable place, sans alcohol, completed by an active fireplace for cold winter days and an outdoor patio for warm summer evenings. When breakfast sandwich and burger prices are less than $10 and the most expensive dinner entrée is a hand-cut, smoked, and grilled 12-ounce rib eye with all the necessary sides for less than 20 bucks, you definitely have our attention. However, as we've learned the hard way, if you're in Hardin after 8 PM on a Sunday night, you won't find much open except **Pizza Hut** ($/$$, 406-665-3334, L/D).

CROW AGENCY: The **Custer Battlefield Trading Post** ($, 406-638-2270, B/L/D) has a variety of road food that comes in sit-down form or to-go boxes. We recommend the Bear Paw (Indian fry bread stuffed with taco meat, beans, cheese, and large enough for two hungry people), the potato or cowboy soup, or what they proudly call the "best Indian taco in the West." While you wait for your food, shop for authentic Crow and Northern Cheyenne art, souvenirs, and crafts in their remodeled gallery.

ST. LABRE MISSION ON THE OUTSKIRTS OF ASHLAND IS A CENTURY-OLD BOARDING SCHOOL FOR CROW AND NORTHERN CHEYENNE

ASHLAND: The first restaurant you'll see on the trail after Crow Agency is the **Hitching Post Café** ($/$$, 406-784-2779, B/L/D Mon.–Sat.), which doesn't offer anything fancy—just solid home-style cooking such as fried chicken, burgers, and a sirloin steak dinner that comes with a potato, salad, veggies, roll, and dessert. But it's the rich Crisco-crust homemade pie you'll remember (especially if you order the peach variety).

DETOUR: ONE FOR THE ROAD

The Other Warrior Trail
Billings to Crow Agency

ESTIMATED LENGTH: 152 miles

HIGHLIGHTS: Sacrifice Cliff, Pictograph Cave State Park, Plenty Coups State Park, Pryor Mountains, Bighorn Canyon National Recreation Area, Bighorn Lake, Bighorn River

GETTING THERE: Take I-90 Exit 452 (Old US 87) just east of Billings and make an immediate right on Coburn Road.

Coming from I-90, consider this loop as a memorable tune-up before hitting the Warrior Trail. Bring your camera. And your fly rod. This is a warrior trail in its own right, given that much of it traverses the Crow Reservation—and all of it crosses what was entirely Crow country, including the flanks of the mysterious Pryor Mountains.

Start the drive by taking Exit 452 off I-90 on the far eastern edge of Billings and making a quick right on Coburn Road. This short side trip up the ochre-tinted limestone rimrock—probably the genesis of Yellowstone National Park's name—leads to two extraordinary pieces of Indian history: **Sacrifice Cliff** and **Pictograph Cave State Park**. There are two versions of the tragedy that took place at Sacrifice Cliff in 1837. Story number one is that two Crow teenagers returned from an outing to find their sweethearts stricken with smallpox; the grieving young warriors subsequently blinded their ponies and rode off the cliff. The second version says that as many as sixteen Crows did the same after finding their entire village stricken. To reach Sacrifice Cliff, drive for a mile on Coburn Road, turn right on Canyon Trail Road, and go about a half-mile to the rim. Returning to Coburn Road, turn right, and head another three-plus miles to the Pictograph Cave Visitor Center.

The 500- to 9,000-year-old drawings in yawning Pictograph, Middle, and Ghost caves are faded but still visible, revealing the hopes, dreams, and

THE CROW CHIEF PLENTY COUPS SLEPT IN HIS TWO-STORY FARMHOUSE WHEN WHITE VISITORS CAME, BUT HE'D MOVE TO A NEARBY TEEPEE WHEN THEY DEPARTED

MANY FISHERMEN SAY THE 13 MILES OF THE BIGHORN RIVER FLOWING OUT OF YELLOWTAIL DAM ARE THE BEST TROUT FISHING SPOT IN THE WORLD

fears of lost civilizations. Paths take you through box elder, sage, and grasses to sheltered rimrock, where more than 30,000 artifacts have been discovered. It is believed that a perfect storm of climate conditions has enabled these paintings to survive.

Return on Coburn Road to Old US 87 (Hardin Road) near the freeway exit, and turn right. Drive about 12 miles to the junction of Pryor Creek Road and turn right toward **Pryor** (pop. 628) and **Plenty Coups State Park**, a picturesque day-use area that honors a visionary Crow who became a chief at age 28. Plenty Coups was a great warrior, but he began farming in 1884 and continued to do so until his death in 1932. The two-story home in which he slept when he had white visitors—he stayed in a teepee otherwise—is now a museum that's open May 1 through September 30, or by appointment.

After leaving the park, veer west on BIA 91 across the rolling coulee country toward **St. Xavier**. Off to the right are the Pryor Mountains, famed today for Montana's best-known herd of wild horses. As the road continues west, it forks about one-third of the way to St. Xavier, and then reconnects 20 miles later. For the more improved of the two, take the left fork, which follows Beauwais Creek. St. Xavier is the site of a Catholic mission that became a boarding school. It was here that the tribe was introduced to basketball in the late 1800s by Jesuit priests as a means of providing exercise and restoring a sense of community.

At St. Xavier, you'll enter the **Bighorn Canyon National Recreation Area** and cross the Bighorn River. Turn right on MT 313 and continue to **Fort Smith** (pop. 122) and Yellowtail Dam. It's worth continuing through Fort Smith and up the winding road into some pretty Bighorn Mountain foothills to the dam and a dead end at the marina. **Bighorn Lake** is one of the most popular places in the state for motorboaters, jet skiers, and water skiers, and the views of the canyon are spectacular. Below the dam, cold water from the bottom of the lake pours into the **Bighorn River**, creating what many believe to be the finest 13 miles of trout fishing in the world (after 13 miles, the water typically warms too much to support trout). Stop in at any of the fly shops in Fort Smith or hire a guide; success isn't as easy as it might seem, given that the 16- to 20-inch fish you're pursuing are visible near the shores, and you'll no doubt have plenty of company despite the area's remoteness. But the right flies and technique will ensure a memorable day.

After a few hours of fishing, retrace your steps to St. Xavier on MT 313 and continue along the Bighorn River toward Hardin. About 10 miles from town, just before the Two Leggins Creek river access, you can take a shortcut east on BIA 1 over the ridge to **Crow Agency**—and the beginning of the Warrior Trail.

PRONGHORN, ALSO COMMONLY CALLED ANTELOPE, LOOK FOR WINTER FORAGE IN THE TERRY BADLANDS

11

THE BIG OPEN
Big Sky Backcountry Byway

TERRY TO WOLF POINT

ESTIMATED LENGTH: 105 miles

ESTIMATED TIME: 3 hours to 2 days

HIGHLIGHTS: Terry Badlands, Cameron Gallery, Prairie County Museum, McCone County Museum, Fort Peck Dam Interpretive Center and Museum, Kempton Hotel

GETTING THERE: Veer off I-90 a few miles east of Billings onto I-94. Take Exit 176 from I-94 at Terry. On the northernmost point, Wolf Point is on US 2 and the Amtrak line, and it is served by Big Sky Airlines as well. The closest major regional airports are in Billings, 175 miles to the southwest of Wolf Point, and Williston, North Dakota, 130 miles to the northeast.

OVERVIEW

Some call it the Big Open. Some call it the Big Dry. Others think of it simply as the forgotten Montana. Whatever it's called, the Big Sky Backcountry Byway is a memorable experience as much for what it once was—and could be again—as it is for what little there is to see and do in this vast country that's largely devoid of humans and their trappings.

With only the slightest imagination, you can gaze from the windows of your car and envision bison outlined against amber hillsides, grazing on the short-grass prairie. Or picture a band of Sioux sitting astride horses above a coulee, scouting for a camp or warily scanning for a wagon train of settlers. Even in our modern world, neither image is overly far-fetched. For it was in the Big Open that the hooves of great bison herds last thundered across Montana, before wanton slaughter in the late 1800s rendered the shaggy beast extinct in the Northern Rockies in all but a remote valley in Yellowstone National Park. And it's here where some dreamers see bison roaming this undulating country again as part of a vast national park called the Buffalo Commons. Here also was where the legendary Sioux made a last stand, the most stubborn of the "hostiles" relegated to the arid and inhospitable Fort Peck Indian Reservation north of the Missouri River. At a forgotten place called Cedar Creek, about 35 miles north of Terry, the Sioux chief Sitting Bull—best known for orchestrating Custer's demise at Little Bighorn—surrendered to General Nelson A. Miles in the autumn of 1876 and permanently returned to the rez. The Indians were treated nearly as shabbily as the bison, and similarly what remains of a shattered culture today bears little resemblance to that of yesteryear.

This is some of the country that inspired great Western writers. It also was the inspiration for Montana's best-known name outside the state: Big Sky Country. The byway bisects the Big Open from south to north—through McCone and Prairie counties, from Terry on the meandering Yellowstone to Wolf Point on the mighty Missouri. It's part of an old trade route connecting Regina, Saskatchewan, with Yellowstone. Lonely windmills seem to outnumber lonelier trees, and you're as likely to see a pronghorn or mule deer as a cow or horse—or human. All of 1,700 people live in McCone County, which covers 1.7 million acres. In the 105 miles between Wolf Point and Terry are two towns: Circle and Brockway, once thriving cattle communities now clinging to their legacies in a region rapidly losing its youth to urban areas. Cattle and sheep outnumber humans about 100 to one in rugged country where the annual rainfall is only slightly higher than in Arizona's deserts and winter temperatures of minus-30 degrees aren't an aberration. On the north end of the byway, Wolf Point is a half-Indian, half-white community on US 2 that serves as a regional hub. In these parts, what suffices for a hub is an Albertson's grocery store, a few gas stations, and three serviceable motels.

If you're looking to be wowed, you've come to the wrong place. The beauty here is stark, subtle, and nuanced. There are no towering mountains, no glistening rivers, no thick forests rich with wildlife, no scenic vistas in the traditional sense. Stop and listen to the silence, broken only by the rustle of breezes massaging the sagebrush. Stop and look at the hardy flora and fauna in small coulees in the Terry Badlands. Or just sit and admire a fiery sunset that seems to go from here to eternity, and then marvel at the night lighting up with more stars than you'd ever imagine. This is Big Sky Country.

HITTING THE ROAD

Chances are your adventure will start in **Terry** (pop. 605), a blip on I-94 between Miles City and Glendive. About one-third of vast Prairie County's residents live here. The town, named for a general who was instrumental in winning the Indian Wars, is largely built around agriculture, though it becomes noticeably more crowded during hunting seasons in the fall. Terry's arrival is announced by the sight of the barren, erosion-pocked hills rising immediately to the north of town above the Yellowstone River. These are the **Terry Badlands** (406-233-2800), and if you appreciate unusual geologic formations sculpted by years of wind, rain, and heat, you'll want to spend a day exploring here.

Before heading into the badlands, though, there is at least one mandatory stop in Terry: The **Cameron Gallery** (406-635-4040). Lady Evelyn Cameron was a strong-willed British woman who moved to the Wild West to homestead in the late 1800s, including a year in Prairie County. She brought a camera and began capturing the unvarnished black-and-white essence of prairie life in eastern Montana. Though Cameron's keen eye generated some fame in her new home and some interest back in England, her compelling photos weren't brought to full life until the 1970s, when boxes full of negatives were found in the basement of a friend's home—nearly a half-century after she died. Soon after, the book *Photographing Montana 1894–1928: The Life and Work of Evelyn Cameron* was published, and today her riveting photos are on display in the Cameron Gallery.

For others who are history minded, the **Prairie County Museum** (406-635-4040) next door is full of the type of homesteading equipment Cameron was so adept at capturing on film. The museum also reflects the town's connection to the Northern Pacific Railroad and offers attractions you'll surely see nowhere else—a steam-heated outhouse, for example. The museum is in an old stone bank building next to the Cameron Gallery and is open every day except Tuesday from Memorial Day Weekend through Labor Day Weekend. After lunch or breakfast, peruse the byway kiosk at the 4 Corners convenience store before crossing the Yellowstone River on MT 253 and rising into the bleached, scoria-capped buttes of the badlands.

The Terry Badlands is a federal wilderness study area managed by the Bureau of Land Management, meaning the government has deemed the area wild and scenic enough to consider including protecting it under the 1964 Wilderness Act. Until that happens, the spires, natural bridges, and other extraordinary landforms in the 45,000-acre area are accessible by motor vehicle. One access point is a left turn off MT 253 3 miles north of Terry, though an unimproved road enters from the west on an abandoned Milwaukee Road grade. This is rugged travel on dirt, and the primitive roads turn to tire-grabbing muck on rare rainy days. It's a mecca for rock hounds and fossil enthusiasts, and there is a rainbow of vivid colors among the sandstone hoodoos and prairie potholes. Translucent agates of varying shapes and colors are found in the badlands and along the Yellowstone, many destined to be shaped into jewelry with a diamond saw (see Side Track).

Out of the badlands, MT 253 rises gently over the Big Sheep Mountains, mere molehills by Montana standards. The Big Sheep represent the conti-

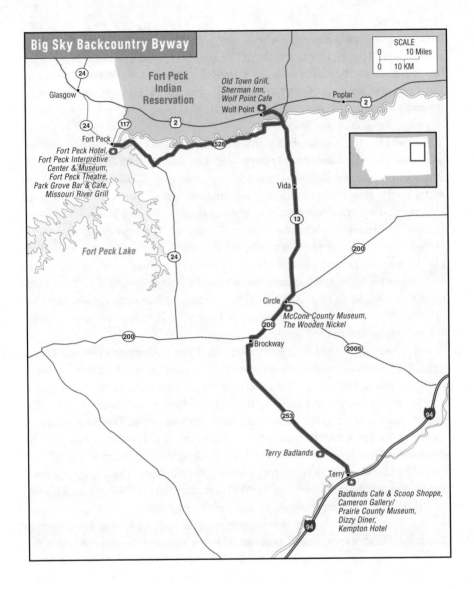

Big Sky Backcountry Byway

SCALE
0   10 Miles
0   10 KM

Glasgow

Fort Peck
Indian
Reservation

Old Town Grill,
Sherman Inn,
Wolf Point Cafe

Wolf Point

Poplar

Fort Peck
Fort Peck Hotel,
Fort Peck Interpretive
Center & Museum,
Fort Peck Theatre,
Park Grove Bar & Cafe,
Missouri River Grill

Vida

Fort Peck Lake

Circle
McCone County Museum,
The Wooden Nickel

Brockway

Terry Badlands

Terry

Badlands Cafe & Scoop Shoppe,
Cameron Gallery/
Prairie County Museum,
Dizzy Diner,
Kempton Hotel

nental divide between the Yellowstone and Missouri Rivers, which eventually meet about 80 miles away on the Montana–North Dakota border. To the west is Big Sheep Mountain, a 3,625-foot bump that's the range's apex. Aside from an occasional distant ranch and windmill, there is little sign of activity until **Brockway** (pop. 140), at the junction of MT 253 and 200. You'd never guess it from its weary facade, but Brockway was the country's number-one livestock shipping port in 1934 and even featured a drive-in movie theater as recently as 1962. Northern Pacific Railroad cars arrived empty and left full of livestock and wheat, barley, and hay. Look closely amid the weeds, and you'll see the abandoned railroad grade, a microcosm of a town that says it's "proud of its past and optimistic about its future." On the third Saturday each July, the town returns to its robust roots with the **Brockway Dairy Days Rodeo** (406-485-2543), which began in 1918 and can boast qualifying no fewer than 21 cowboys and cowgirls in the annual National Finals Rodeo in Las Vegas.

Turn right on MT 200 and venture another 10 miles along the nondescript Redwater River into the agricultural community of **Circle** (pop. 584), another town that clearly has seen more vibrant days. Arriving from the south, you'll see the **McCone County Museum** (406-485-2414, May–Oct.) on the right. Inside are more than 7,000 historical items, including more than 200 mounted animals and birds that call the Big Open home. In recent years, a Northern Pacific Railroad depot and caboose, homestead, church, and prairie school have been moved to the grounds. You'll also notice a statue of a *Brontosaurus* in town, a nod to the many fossilized dinosaur bones found in the area. If the creatures that roamed what had been swamps 65 million years ago pique your interest, take a side trip from Brockway about 70 miles west to Jordan on MT 200. Aside from being known as the most remote county seat in the nation and the site of a standoff between the FBI and a group called the Freemen in 1996, Jordan is also dinosaur central in Montana. A virtually complete *Tyrannosaurus rex* skeleton was discovered here in the late 1990s, and has since been moved to the Museum of the Rockies in Bozeman.

Circle, named for the brand on a nearby ranch, has several gas stations, all offering diesel. The town also has the only two cafés—the Wooden Nickel and Lunch Box—between Terry and Wolf Point. At the north end of town, continue straight on MT 13, toward Wolf Point.

The only community between Circle and Wolf Point is the unincorporated **Vida** (pop. 243), which has two churches, a post office, and a dance hall. By this point, you might feel as if you've been transported from Big Sky Country into central Nebraska. The land is flatter, and distant grain elevators are visible in both directions along US 2. **Wolf Point** (pop. 2,663) is the largest town on the byway and has long served as an Indian trading post on the north bank of the Missouri. Long gone are the days when wolves were common here. Reviled by the European culture, wolves were hunted and trapped relentlessly, and their hides were stacked here waiting for steamboats to take them for sale in the Midwest and East. Wolves were eradicated by the 1880s, but the name remains. When the **Fort Peck Indian Reservation** was created in 1912, with Wolf Point as its largest town, the buildings were moved away from the river to the Northern Pacific line. If you happen to be in Wolf Point the second weekend in July, the **Wild Horse Stampede** (406-653-1770) is considered "the granddaddy of Montana rodeos" because it's the state's oldest.

Perhaps the most interesting human-created attraction in the area is the **Fort Peck Dam**, 35 miles west of Wolf Point—reached either by taking US 2 on the north side of the Missouri or the more interesting County Road 528 to MT 24 on the south side. Start your visit at the **Fort Peck Dam Interpretive Center and Museum** (406-526-3493) between the huge dam's powerhouses and campgrounds. Built over seven years at the height of the Great Depression (1933–40), Fort Peck is one of the world's largest earthen dams and employed more than 11,000 workers at the apex of construction, turning quiet villages into 18 raucous Wild West boomtowns overnight—as many as 50,000 people lived here. The numbers for the nation's fifth-largest man-made lake are staggering: a dam 21,000 feet long and 250 feet high, 1,520 miles of shoreline, a lake 134 miles long, 18.7-million-acre-feet of water, and a drainage area of 10,200 square miles. The interpretive center explains the magnitude of this endeavor in photos and journals. Also on display are dinosaur

Step *Way* Back in Time on the Montana Dinosaur Trail

Human history has its Olduvai Gorge. Dinosaur history has its Montana. And it all comes into sharp focus on the 15-stop Montana Dinosaur Trail, which includes the Fort Peck Field Station of Paleontology and the Garfield County Museum in Jordan.

Dinosaurs once roamed the entire earth, but few places combine the necessary ingredients for discoveries like Montana. The state still has open spaces and boasts a wide variety of exposed rocks from every geologic era in the planet's history. The result is a potpourri of dinosaur types—from the land, air, and even a sea that once covered parts of the state.

The *Guinness Book of World Records* calls Leonardo, a mummified *Brachylophosaurus* found near Malta, the best-preserved dinosaur anywhere. The first, largest, and one of the most complete *Tyrannosaurus rex* fossils in the world, respectively, have all been unearthed here and now reside at Fort Peck. A duckbill dinosaur's eggs from the ancient Bearpaw Sea are on display on the H. Earl Clack Museum in Havre. The motherly *Maiasaura* is Montana's state fossil.

In all, the preserved remains of at least 25 types of dinosaurs have been found across the state, and their actual fossils or replicas are the centerpiece of museums in the tiniest of towns. The Dinosaur Field Station in Malta, Fort Peck Field Station of Paleontology, Garfield County Museum, Two Medicine Dinosaur Center in Bynum, and Makoshika Dinosaur Museum in Glendive all offer the opportunity to get your hands dusty on guided field digs.

The Montana Dinosaur Trail is a marketing effort by the state to attract tourists to places that don't see many visitors and often struggle economically. But the exhibits are impressive and the concept isn't gimmicky, other than perhaps the Montana Dinosaur Trail "passport" in which stamps from all 15 sites results in a free T-shirt.

bones unearthed during the construction, including yet another skeleton of a *Tyrannosaurus rex*. Fort Peck Reservoir, surrounded by the **Charles M. Russell National Wildlife Refuge** (406-538-8706), has become a recreation hub for boaters, fishermen, and hunters.

If you want to see this area at its wildest—it's the fourth-most visited place in Montana—come in early July for the **Montana Governor's Cup Walleye Tournament** on Fort Peck Reservoir. More than 50 types of fish swim the waters of Fort Peck, but there's little question that the walleye ranks number one, as evidenced by the hundreds of anglers lured from around the country and Canada for the tournament. While visiting the Fort Peck area in the summer, plan an evening around the ornate **Fort Peck Summer Theatre** (406-526-9943), which has been graced by the likes of Will Rogers, Joan Crawford, William Powell, Shirley Temple, and, to this day, Floyd the Friendly Ghost. Shows, which run Memorial Day Weekend through Labor Day Weekend, included *Steel Magnolias* and *The Best Little Whorehouse in Texas* in summer 2015.

Unlike the Terry Badlands and other points along the Big Sky Backcountry Byway, Fort Peck will test your ability to imagine what it was like before the Euro invasion. Long gone are the days when the Sioux and Assiniboine hunted the cottonwood bottoms along a free-flowing Missouri. Yet even here, what was once unimaginable might soon become reality. Today, the grounds of the Fort Peck Indian Reservation are thundering again under the hooves of wild Yellowstone National Park bison, returning a slice of long-lost history and restoring a frontier spirit to the Big Open.

Best Places to Bunk

TERRY: There are no traditional or chain motels in town; those are 38 miles to the southwest in Miles City or 40 miles to the northeast in Glendive, both on I-94. Terry's most notable lodging offering is the **Kempton Hotel** ($, 406-635-5543), built in 1912 and the oldest continually operating hotel in Montana. Calamity Jane and former president Theodore Roosevelt are among the more celebrated guests in a structure that looks as if it came from a military outpost. The Kempton's walls are adorned with old black-and-white photos. There's an adjacent antique shop and the place does exude a certain charm, but luxurious it isn't. Like all century-old hotels, the Kempton reputedly is haunted. Rooms are available by the night, and well-worn cabins out back are rented by the week or longer for hunters or residents. They also have 18 RV spaces from May until hunting seasons end in October. For the more traditional traveler, the **Diamond Motel & Campground** ($, 406-635-5407) is a 1950s-style motor-court operation just down the street and is the only other game in town. It's only open April to October.

CIRCLE: Circle has one motel, **The Traveler's Inn** ($, 406-485-3323), and the fourteen rooms are serviceable if you need a roof over your head on a route where lodging options are far apart.

WOLF POINT: The best option is the forty-four-room **Sherman Inn** ($$, 406-653-1100) on the edge of Old Town. It has a remodeled restaurant, lounge, casino, and 24-hour fitness center, and renovations were underway in 2015. On US 2, it's probably the most appealing lodging between Williston, North Dakota, and Glasgow.

FORT PECK: The old **Fort Peck Hotel** ($$, 406-526-3266, Apr.—Dec.) has earned a spot on the National Register of Historic Places. It's a throwback to the 1930s, when the nearby dam was built and folks swarmed the area. Things are much quieter now, except in the summer, and also when the occasional ghost reputedly wanders the creaky halls. Rooms are smallish, with older beds, and you won't find televisions, telephones, and, in some cases, showers (some have clawfoot tubs)—hence the modest rates.

Alternative Bunking

CAMPING: Fort Peck Reservoir has ample camping opportunities, most in appealing locations. If you don't mind having the earthen dam looming over you, **Downstream Camp** (406-526-3224) is set amid leafy cottonwoods and has by far the most amenities. There are eighty-six sites with electricity, another thirteen for tents. Play basketball, walk a mile-long nature trail, and turn the kids loose in the play area; you'll likely need advance reservations for this popular campground. The **West End Recreation Area & Campground** (406-526-3411) has twenty-four sites with views of the lake, including fourteen for RVs. Outside Circle you'll find the most intriguing lodging and the best way to fully grasp the subtle rhythms of the region—the **Wolff Farms Vacation Home** ($$/$$$, 406-485-2633). Wolff Farms is a sprawling working farm about 15 miles northwest of Circle, between MT 13 and Fort Peck Reservoir. The rooms are intimate and filled with antiques, and you'll get three hearty meals. But the draw is the wide-open spaces, horseback riding, deer and game-bird hunting, access to fishing and boating on the reservoir, immersion in the prairie way of life, and peace and quiet. They might even let you lasso a calf.

Best Eats

TERRY: The cash-only **Dizzy Diner** ($, 406-635-4666, B/L/D) is bright, has wireless Internet, and is a comfortable place to get a burger or chicken strips, fries, shake, and salad. In an area where you're always feeling as if you've stepped back in time, the new **Badlands Cafe & Scoop Shoppe** ($, 406-635-2233, L/D, Mon.–Fri.) harkens back to the 1950s. You can't miss it: the hindquarters of a red 1955 Chevy are part of the marquee above the entrance. Note: the café was for sale in the summer of 2015.

CIRCLE: The **Wooden Nickel Bar & Restaurant** ($, 406-485-2575, L/D), as you might expect in a place surrounded by cattle, is known for locally produced burgers and steaks. For solid wraps, sandwiches, smoothies, and baked goods, there's the **Lunch Box** ($, 406-485-2386, B/L/D).

WOLF POINT: Highlights are the **Old Town Grill** ($, 406-653-1031, B/L/D) and **Wolf Point Cafe** ($, 406-653-1388, B/L/D), both with traditional lineups. The **Sherman Restaurant** ($/$$, 406-653-1100, B/L/D) makes it possible to sleep and eat without leaving your hotel. The chicken carbonara and the pork chop dinner are highly recommended, along with prime rib on Wednesdays and ribs on Saturdays.

FORT PECK: The **Missouri River Grill** ($/$$, 406-526-3266, B/D, Fri.—Sun., May—Nov.) in the Fort Peck Hotel offers upscale environs unique to these parts. Naturally, one of the local favorites is the walleye, crusted with Parmesan cheese.

Best Bars

PARK GROVE: Just about every joint says they have the best hamburger in Montana, but the otherwise nondescript **Park Grove Bar & Cafe** (406-526-3252, L/D), downstream from the dam, can back it up with a burger once deemed best in the state by *Montana Magazine*. That led to the bar's burgers being featured in a "Get Lost in Montana" television commercial. The freshground patties are hand-pressed each day by the owners. The weathered bar and café, in an old farmhouse set amid the shade of giant cottonwoods, is the only business still operating in the one-time boomtown of Park Grove. The café has lunch specials daily. The remains of a few abandoned shanties are scattered nearby, relics still clinging to existence eight decades after the heady days of the Great Depression.

MONTANA MAGAZINE ONCE DUBBED THE BURGERS AT PARK GROVE BAR NEAR FORT PECK THE BEST IN THE STATE

FORT PECK: The **Gateway Club** (406-526-3557, L/D) dubs itself "The Best Dam Bar by a Dam Site," and who's to argue, given the locale? The Gateway has a meat-centric menu and is a happy gathering spot for folks who've just pulled their boats out of the reservoir at the nearby marina. If looks were everything, this place would be a Best Bar, hands down. But it tends to run inconsistent in food quality and service. Too bad, because the setting is the kind of place where you want to take a drink outside and watch the sun set over the vast sea of water. Take a chance, we say—you might hit it on a good night. The Gateway is open daily in summers and Wednesday through Saturday during the winter.

DETOUR: ONE FOR THE ROAD

The Far East
Miles City to Ekalaka (115 miles)

The landscape surrounding I-94 at Miles City doesn't look like much, so you might be surprised at what awaits once you exit onto US 12 east. The road quickly rises past Strawberry Hill into country pocked with ponderosa pine, sage and chiseled badlands on a route offering some unique diversions that include Ismay (pop. 26)—or, as the town was known for a month back in 1993, Joe—Medicine Rocks State Park, and the forests above little Ekalaka. Bisecting this stark country is the turbid Powder River, whose meandering subservience to agriculture and the coal industry upstream belie its pristine beginnings in Wyoming's Bighorn Mountains.

After crossing the Powder on US 12, it's 20 miles to a sign pointing the way to **Ismay**. Turn left and navigate the dusty red-rock gravel road 6 miles to the two grain elevators marking this lonely and weather-beaten stop on the old Milwaukee Road railway line. Plucked randomly from a map, this was the second little community in Montana to receive a call from a Kansas City, Missouri, radio station in 1993 wondering if it would be interested in changing its name as part of a promotion marking the acquisition of a quarterback of some renown by the city's National Football League team, the Chiefs.

The once-thriving community, which needed a new fire truck, voted unanimously—21-0—to change its name for a summer to "Joe, Montana"

ISMAY VOTED 21-0 IN 1993 TO CHANGE ITS NAME TO "JOE" AS PART OF A PROMOTION BY A KANSAS CITY RADIO STATION AFTER THE NFL'S CHIEFS ACQUIRED QUARTERBACK JOE MONTANA. THE TOWN RAISED ENOUGH MONEY TO BUILD A NEW FIRE HALL AND THIS COMMUNITY CENTER.

in hopes of rekindling its flame, however briefly. The town spent a summer selling Joe Montana memorabilia and made enough money not only to purchase a fire truck but also to construct a community center, which now says "Joe Montan" after losing an 'a' to Mother Nature's fierce winter ways. Today Ismay, which once boasted two car dealerships and numerous other businesses, has no services and, other than the pigeons congregating on the grain elevators and the occasional passing train, offers little more than what your imagination can conjure up.

SIDE TRACK

Terry Badlands (12 miles)

Generally when you think of wilderness you think of towering mountains, clear and cool streams tumbling over boulders, and iconic wildlife. The **Terry Badlands** will encourage you to adjust your thinking. These multi-hued formations just a few miles north of Interstate 94 at Terry offer a different perspective, but with at least one element in common with the more traditional perception of wild country: solitude.

The Terry Badlands are 44,000 arid acres of sedimentary rock that has eroded over millions of years to form dramatic hoodoos, arches, spires, washes, and other camera-friendly formations. The area is so uniquely wild that the federal government has designated it as a Wilderness Study Area, meaning it features characteristics worthy of protections under the 1964 Wilderness Act. Pronghorn antelope, bobcats, and prairie rattlesnakes are frequent sights among the wildlife, and the blooms on spring wildflowers, prickly pear cactus, and yucca are spectacular. Yet experiences here are so much more nuanced than in traditional wilderness that locals have lived in Terry for years without fully appreciating what they have in their backyards.

There are two ways to access the Terry Badlands: off MT 253 a few miles north of Terry, or due west of town on the Calypso Trail. The former is a short drive to an overlook; the latter is on a primitive dirt road offers more intimate glimpses of the landscape. Drive west of Terry on old US 10 for almost two miles to the old Milwaukee Road and turn north across the Yellowstone River on a rickety old one-lane railroad bridge until you reach a Bureau of Land Management kiosk. In all, it's about seven miles of high-clearance dirt road on the Calypso Trail to its end at the Natural Bridges trailhead.

Fair warning: You'll want a high-clearance vehicle, preferably 4-wheel-drive, if you intend to explore the Calypso Trail in a vehicle. And don't even think about entering during or immediately after a rainstorm. These roads quickly turn into the dreaded "gumbo," and at that point it's not "if" but "when" you get stuck. The good news is the gumbo dries quickly and you might only have to wait a few hours before the road is navigable again.

AN ABANDONED HOMESTEAD CREAKS IN THE WIND NEAR ISMAY

Plevna (pop. 182) is only slightly more vibrant, but the town named for Bulgarian railroad workers does have a bar and small store, though any fuel needs for your body or your car will be met 13 miles down the road in Baker. If you hadn't gassed up in Miles City or found a place to overnight, **Baker** (pop. 1,875) is the place, for it'll be chancy in Ekalaka. Baker has a couple of cafés, motels serving the oil and gas boom in the nearby Bakken formation, and a mid-sized lake that looks—from the right angle—as if it had been plucked from Minnesota and dropped onto the prairie. As the location of one of the largest lakes in the area, Baker lures boaters, fishermen, and snowmobilers from miles around. Baker has a trio of restaurant/casino combos for dining, the best of which is the **Tavern Big Game Casino**. Because of the energy frenzy in western North Dakota and parts of eastern Montana, Baker has added more motel rooms, most recently the **Red River Inn & Suites**.

The highlight of this route is **Medicine Rocks State Park**, a jumbled collection of sandstone hoodoos where Indians came on vision quests. The Sioux called it "Ina-oka-la-ka," or "rock with hole in it." Upon seeing the giant pocked boulders for the first time, former President Theodore Roosevelt, who traveled the West extensively remarked, "as fantastically beautiful a place as I have ever seen." The 330-acre park features trails and 12 isolated campsites scattered amid the boulders, some of which rise to 80 feet. You'll also notice that it seems everybody who's ever visited Medicine Rocks—from ancient cultures to contemporary local teen-agers—has carved their initials,

names, pictures, and/or messages into the vulnerable sandstone. Park officials estimate the number of inscriptions at more than 15,000, allegedly
including Roosevelt's.

Ekalaka (pop. 343) originally was called Ijkalaka, named for an Oglala
Sioux Indian whose hand in marriage was given to David Russell, the first
white settler in the region, for eight horses and a 100-pound bag of sugar.
Ekalaka's pleasant setting in an agricultural valley belies perceptions most
folks—including Montanans, few of whom have ever been here—have of eastern Montana. Though its primary function is to serve the ranching community, there's plenty in the way of visually appealing landscapes, especially
to the south. More sandstone buttes sculpted by wicked prairie winds and
driving rains rise above 4,000 feet in the pine-studded Eklalaka Hills. Car-
pets of these ponderosas rise to flat-topped prairies with views of North
Dakota, South Dakota, and Wyoming, all of which are within 60 miles. Most
noteworthy among the natural formations are the Chalk Buttes and Capitol
Rock National Natural Monument, which looks remarkably like a famous
building in Washington, D.C. Look for little falcons called merlins darting
across the sky.

There isn't much to do in Ekalaka proper other than admire the white-
washed wood county courthouse, but be sure to visit the **Carter County
Museum**, which is famed for its two-headed calf and nearly complete duck-

THE SIOUX INDIANS CONSIDERED THE SANDSTONE HOODOOS NEAR EKALAKA SACRED. SOME OF THE BOULDERS AT
MEDICINE ROCKS STATE PARK RISE 80 FEET

THE CARTER COUNTY MUSEUM IN EKALAKA IS FAMED FOR ITS TWO-HEADED CALF AND A NEARLY COMPLETE DUCKBILL DINOSAUR

bill dinosaur. Though other places in Montana get more fanfare for dinosaur digs, it's arguable that Ekalaka is the choicest locale. The first and most complete Tyrannosaurus Rex was found near here, along with sea reptiles and ancient shells. Either replicas or real bones are on display throughout the museum. Ekalaka does have a café, bar, and gas station, but all are open or closed on a whim—not surprising for a community that was at the end of the paved road until a few years ago, when asphalt was laid heading south to Alzada.

WEATHERED GRAIN ELEVATORS TOWER ABOVE THE HI-LINE'S MOSTLY FLAT LANDSCAPE EVERY 10 MILES OR SO

12

MONTANA'S ENDLESS HORIZON
The Hi-Line

GLASGOW TO SHELBY

ESTIMATED LENGTH: 260 miles

ESTIMATED TIME: 5 hours to 3 days

HIGHLIGHTS: Dinosaur trail museums and field stations, Sleeping Buffalo Hot Springs, Sleeping Buffalo Rock, Bowdoin National Wildlife Refuge, Blaine County Wildlife Museum, Bear Paw Battlefield, Havre Beneath the Streets, Havre Railroad Museum, Fort Assinniboine, H. Earl Clack Museum, Wahkpa Chu'gn Buffalo Jump, Marias Museum of History & Art

GETTING THERE: We recommend starting your Hi-Line adventure in Glasgow, in part because you will end up at Glacier National Park's doorstep. You can include the Big Sky Backcountry Byway tour by leaving I-94 at Terry and continuing north to Wolf Point on MT 263, MT 200, and MT 13. From Wolf Point, it's 47 miles west on US 2 to Glasgow. The west end of the Hi-Line is accessed by taking I-15 north at Butte and continuing through Helena and Great Falls to the US 2 East exit at Shelby. In addition, Amtrak parallels US 2 on the busy Burlington Northern Santa Fe route, with twice-daily stops—one each direction—in Glasgow, Malta, Havre, and Shelby. Glasgow is served by Great Lakes Airlines with flights from Wolf Point, Miles City, Billings, and Denver; Havre has Great Lakes flights to and from Lewistown, Billings, and Denver.

OVERVIEW

In Montana, where rugged individualism is almost as much a part of the human experience as breathing, even the most leathery residents tip their hats to the weather-toughened residents of the Hi-Line. A hardy constitution is required to carve a life and livelihood out of the wind-sculpted prairies shouldering the turbid Milk River just south of the Canadian border.

This was the last area of Montana to be settled and the first to be deserted. At first glance, there is little here but cattle, barbed wire, and lonely whistle-stop grain elevators to blunt the winds from the north as they roar unchallenged across the prairies from the Arctic and Canada. If it weren't for the distant "island" mountain ranges rising like protective shadows on the horizon, you'd think you'd taken a wrong turn and landed in Nebraska. The reward for residents' fortitude is hot summers amid cottonwood trees in oasis towns 8 to 10 miles apart, lazy days angling for warm-water fish, and evening breezes that may or may not fend off the prodigious mosquitoes. The towns, all but a handful with fewer than 1,000 residents, are some of Montana's loneliest. By the time they sprang up as sidings along the Great Northern Railway (now Burlington Northern Santa Fe), creativity for new names of water stations was tapped out. So most monikers on the Hi-Line came from an office at the Great Northern headquarters in St. Paul, Minnesota, where a railroad employee was blindfolded, a globe was spun, and a finger was randomly aimed. The result was such incongruous post office addresses as Glasgow and Inverness (Scotland), Zurich (Switzerland), Malta (island in the Mediterranean Sea), Saco (Maine), Hinsdale (Illinois), Harlem (New York), Fresno (California), Dunkirk (France), and Joplin (Missouri). Folks in Chinook did localize theirs—they named their comfortable little town for the winter winds that blow off the Rockies with such ferocity that a minus 20-degree day can turn to plus-30 degrees in a few hours, or vice versa.

The Hi-Line is so-called because the railroad and then US 2 cut a gradually rising straight east–west line that begins at the North Dakota border and slams into the Rocky Mountains about 450 miles later. This came to be in the 1890s, when the discovery of Marias Pass between present-day Glacier National Park and the Bob Marshall Wilderness enabled James J. Hill to push his Great Northern from Minot, North Dakota, across Montana's northern tier. As one of the few regions of Montana where towns are actually shrinking, spending a day strolling Main Street along the Hi-Line is like stepping into a Rockwell painting. Rusting farm implements, battered grain elevators with flocks of pigeons, and the whistle of frequent trains provide much of the character.

Even the Hi-Line's contemporary tourism marketing is tied to a very distant past—many of the museum stops on the Montana Dinosaur Trail are located here. This area has produced some of the world's greatest dinosaur finds, and many are on display. Most of the museums, dinosaur or otherwise, typically are only open in the summers—though managers will give private tours if you twist their arms.

To know the Hi-Line is to take your time exploring it. The 260 miles from Glasgow to Shelby can easily be driven in five hours, but treat yourself to a

THE GREAT PLAINS DINOSAUR MUSEUM AND FIELD STATION IN MALTA IS HOME TO LEONARDO, A DUCKBILL DINOSAUR

slower pace. Take a closer look with each passing mile, and you'll begin to see the subtle differences in landscapes and people, both with more personality than meets the eye.

HITTING THE ROAD

Glasgow (pop. 3,253) is the starting point for your Hi-Line journey. It's also the gateway to the Fort Peck Dam and Reservoir area covered in the Big Sky Backcountry Byway chapter. Glasgow is unique among Hi-Line towns in that for two decades it had a third major economic influence after agriculture and the railroad: the U.S. Air Force. Glasgow Air Force Base was built during World War II, then shut down in the 1960s. This history is reflected in the fighter jet in the front yard of the **Pioneer Museum of Valley County** (406-228-8692), which has an extraordinary collection of memorabilia ranging from nearly a century of military artifacts to the stories of the area's Indians and homesteaders. The giant teepee just inside the entrance is part of the impressive Joshua Wetsit collection; it purportedly is one of three buffalo-

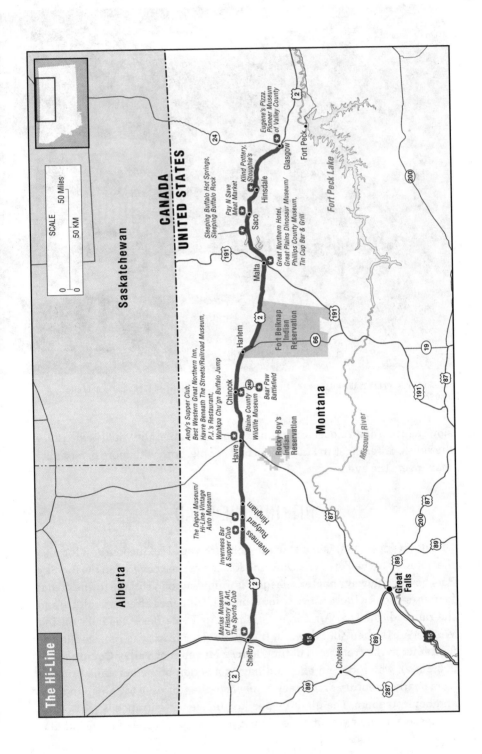

The Hi-Line

SCALE
50 Miles
0
50 KM
0

Alberta

Saskatchewan

CANADA
UNITED STATES

Montana

Missouri River

Fort Peck Lake

24

2

200

191

19

87

191

87

89

200

87

89

89

287

66

191

240

Glasgow

Fort Peck

Eugene's Pizza,
Pioneer Museum
of Valley County

Hinsdale

Klind Pottery,
Stoughie's

Saco

Pay N Save
Meat Market

Sleeping Buffalo Hot Springs,
Sleeping Buffalo Rock

Malta

Great Northern Hotel,
Great Plains Dinosaur Museum/
Phillips County Museum,
Tin Cup Bar & Grill

Harlem

Fort Belknap
Indian
Reservation

Chinook

Blaine County
Wildlife Museum

Bear Paw
Battlefield

Rocky Boy's
Indian
Reservation

Havre

Andy's Supper Club,
Best Western Great Northern Inn,
Havre Beneath The Streets/Railroad Museum,
P.J.'s Restaurant,
Wahpa Chu'gn Buffalo Jump

Hingham

Rudyard

Inverness

The Depot Museum/
Hi-Line Vintage
Auto Museum

Inverness Bar
& Supper Club

Shelby

Marias Museum
of History & Art,
The Sports Club

15

Great
Falls

Choteau

LATE NBC NEWS ANCHOR CHET HUNTLEY SPENT PART OF HIS CHILDHOOD IN SACO, WHERE HE WAS EDUCATED IN THIS ONE-ROOM SCHOOLHOUSE

hide teepees left in the world. Any bar in Montana would be thrilled to have the Pioneer Museum's mahogany cherry back bar—bullet hole and all.

Heading northwest out of Glasgow on US 2, look for **Klind Pottery** (406-364-2263) in **Hinsdale** (pop. 609). Gloria Klind has been hand-throwing pottery for more than three decades, starting in an old homestead without running water. She attempts to capture the state's wildness in what she calls "Montana's Spirit of the Clay." **Saco** (pop. 225), 14 miles west on US 2, is the best place on the Hi-Line to stock up with meaty snacks for the journey. For a quarter century, **Pay N Save Grocery and Meat Shop** (406-527-3361) owner Robert Plouffe has been winning awards for his cured meats, especially his ham, bacon, and 20-plus flavors of bratwurst. Saco is unique on at least four other counts: it's a childhood home of the late NBC News anchor Chet Huntley, its school system is nationally recognized for its progressive education, it owns natural gas wells that provide residents with a virtually free heating source, and *National Geographic* once dubbed it the Mosquito Capital of the World.

About 10 miles west of Saco on US 2 is **Sleeping Buffalo Hot Springs** (406-527-3370), a developed area that features a 109-degree indoor hot pool, a larger indoor swimming pool with 93-degree waters, and a 48-degree cold pool. The main building has been beautifully renovated, an anomaly amid a collection of buildings in need of a similar makeover. The waters are tinted red from iron oxide—"rust-ic," they call it—but because the water is now drained nightly by new owners, unsightly stains are no longer an issue. The iron oxide is one of the minerals reputed to have healing powers for local Indians and cowboys. The hot springs are named after **Sleeping Buffalo Rock**, one of two boulders under a three-sided shelter at the junction of US 2 and the road to fishing-rich **Nelson Reservoir**. These glacial erratic rocks are considered sacred because they were once mistaken for sleeping bison at a time when herds were scarce. Upon discovering that the sleeping buffalo were rocks, the Indians saw *real* bison in the distance, ensuring food, clothing, and shelter. Now that the rock resides near the highway alongside Medicine Rock, carloads of Indians and others regularly pull alongside and pray before leaving tobacco, colorful flags, coins, and other trinkets as offerings.

After passing the **Bowdoin National Wildlife Refuge** (406-654-2863), a paradise for waterfowl, upland game birds, and big game, you'll arrive in **Malta** (pop. 1,922), a peaceful and shaded hamlet on the Milk River that once was one of the most lawless towns on the frontier. Kid Curry and Butch Cassidy's Wild Bunch made off with $40,000 from a train robbery here. The town has two museums in one—the **Phillips County Museum and H.G Robinson House & Gardens** (406-654-1037) are across a gravel parking lot from the **Great Plains Dinosaur Museum & Field Station** (406-654-5300). A $5 fee will get you into both. The Phillips County Museum focuses on the area's homesteading, Indian, and outlaw history. Part of the Montana Dinosaur Trail, the Great Plains Museum offers more than a glimpse of active archeology with its participatory dig programs and has remarkably preserved dinosaurs that were unearthed locally, including either the real mummified Leonardo or a replica—depending on whether the world's most complete dinosaur is at home or on the road. Leonardo is one of four *Brachylophosaurus* in the world and the first largely intact "subadult" dinosaur ever found.

About 20 miles west of Malta along the Milk River is the **Fort Belknap Indian Reservation**, created in 1888 as a home for the Gros Ventre and Assiniboine tribes; today, about 5,000 Indians live there. Before arriving in Fort Belknap, just past Three Mile Reservoir, an abandoned pink mission and colorful cemetery appears on a small hill just north of the highway. Though you can't enter the boarded-up and reputedly haunted **Sacred Heart Mission**, the scene provides a classic Hi-Line photo op. A respectful walk through the cemetery will reveal Native stories to those who look closely. Fort Belknap has a small park and clean rest area just off the highway where you can read historic markers about how the Assiniboine tribe split from the Yankton Sioux and learn about vision quests on Snake Butte. Leaving the reservation, **Harlem** (pop. 806) has a public picnic area that serves as a memorial to two Air Force pilots who crashed near here.

Twenty-five miles farther west on the Hi-Line is **Chinook** (pop. 1,386),

GHOSTS REPUTEDLY HAUNT THE ABANDONED SACRED HEART MISSION ON THE EDGE OF THE FORT BELKNAP INDIAN RESERVATION

home of the famous Sugarbeeters high school teams. The skinny smokestack and abandoned factory on the eastern edge of town serve as reminders of futile attempts to raise sugar beets. Wheat is the crop of choice now, but the town clings to a sports team nickname that former late-night television host Jay Leno once rated the second strangest in the nation. Sugarbeeter jokes aside, Chinook—originally called Dave's Station—is a sweet place to spend an afternoon (great tennis courts) or even a night. The **Blaine County Wildlife Museum** (406-357-3102, Memorial Day–Labor Day) has five vivid exhibits, including a 25-foot-high diorama of a buffalo jump with four full-sized bison plunging to their deaths in front of two life-sized Indians. The **Blaine County Museum** (406-357-2590, Memorial Day–Labor Day) is clean and polished, with collections ranging from prehistoric times to World War II, a remarkable assortment of books for sale, and a multimedia theater where one film explains the tragic 1877 events at the **Bear Paw Battlefield** some 15 miles south on MT 240 (see Side Track).

Back on US 2, it's 21 miles to **Havre** (pop. 9,390), which will feel positively cosmopolitan with its stoplights, strip malls, chain stores, restaurants, and Montana State University Northern campus. Originally called Bullhook Bottoms, the town was built as a trading post not far from Fort Assinniboine. Given that it's at the halfway point between Minneapolis and Seattle, this was to be an important stop on the Great Northern's line, and so the railroad man Hill asked the town fathers to change Bullhook Bottoms' uncivilized name. They obliged, and because many hailed from France, they called it

A SMALL STEEL POST AND TOKENS MARK THE SITE OF CHIEF WHITE BIRD'S TEEPEE AT THE BEAR PAW BATTLEFIELD

LeHavre, after a harbor town where the parents of a prominent early home-steader lived. They eventually shortened it to Havre, and a statue of Hill stands in front of the Amtrak station.

Havre is one of many small towns across the West that had two faces: The above-ground face it wanted the rest of the world to see and a sordid below-ground face where gentlemen went to gamble and imbibe, ladies of the evening hung their red lights, and Chinese residents did laundry and provided opium in a web of tunnels and open rooms. Where Havre differs is that in 1904 a fire leveled virtually the entire city. Legitimate businesses moved underground, and today that history is kept alive at **Havre Beneath the Streets** (406-265-8888, $8). Daily guided tours take visitors past a dentist office, bordello, haunted meat market, livery, drugstore, saloon, Chinese laundry, the wax caricature of booze purveyor Shorty Young in his dank office, and more. Tours start at the **Havre Railroad Museum** (406-265-8888). Though focused primarily on the Great Northern, the spacious museum has artifacts from other railroads that opened the West and features a mesmerizing model railroad display.

Six miles southwest of Havre on US 87 are the remnants of **Fort Assin-**

niboine (406-265-8336/406-265-4000, June–Sept.), where as many as 500 soldiers were stationed on 700,000 acres—the largest military fort west of the Mississippi River. The soldiers presided over north-central Montana and ensured that there would be no trouble from Indians, smugglers, and bootleggers from Canada, and that the new settlers could plow the prairie safely. The fort, built as a direct result of the Sioux rout of General Custer at Little Bighorn in 1876 and the flight of the Nez Perce a year later, had more than 100 buildings in its heyday. Most were torn down when the fort was ceded to the Rocky Boy's Indian Reservation in 1916. Its most famous resident was General John J. "Blackjack" Pershing. Today, a handful of buildings remain, and daily tours are offered in the summer. To sign up for a tour, go to the **H. Earl Clack Memorial Museum** (406-265-4000) in the Holiday Village Shopping Center on Havre's west end. The Clack Museum squeezes a lot into a small space, including a diorama of the Bear Paw battle, dinosaur eggs dating back 75 million years, and artifacts from the **Wahkpa Chu'gn Buffalo Jump** (406-265-6417/406-265-4000, June–Sept.). The buffalo jump seems out of place directly behind the shopping center—or maybe it's the mall that's misplaced. Buffalo jumps are scattered throughout the Northern Rockies, but none is more extraordinary than Wakhpa Chu'gn. Bison bones from 600 to 2,000 years old are stacked 20 feet high precisely as they were discovered in 1961 by a 12-year-old boy named John Brumley. Daily one-hour walking tours ($9 for adults) in the summer also reveal arrowheads and other artifacts.

West of Havre at the one-blink blur of **Fresno**—where do you suppose the railroad employee's finger landed on the globe for that one?—the Milk River disappears over the horizon to the north behind Fresno Dam. For the next 104 miles to Shelby, while the river spends a few hundred kilometers visiting Canada, the Hi-Line becomes a relatively flat and treeless string of wheat and lentil fields stretching even farther to the horizon than they had from Glasgow to Havre. Six miles up the road from **Hingham** (pop. 157), little **Rudyard** (pop. 596) is home to the best greeting sign on the Hi-Line: "Welcome to Rudyard, Home of 596 Nice People and One Old Sorehead." The "sorehead" is a complete *Gryposaurus* dinosaur discovered nearby, and it's displayed in **The Depot Museum** (406-355-4356, Memorial Day–Labor Day) along with dinosaur trail denizens and homesteading equipment. Down the street is **Hi-Line Vintage Auto Museum** (406-355-4356, Memorial Day–Labor Day), with cars from as far back as 1905.

Shortly after passing through **Inverness** (pop. 103) and virtually vacant **Joplin**, you'll arrive at a small rise in the highway. For miles, the outline of a striking island mountain range has been visible in the distant northwest: the Sweet Grass Hills, sacred grounds for the Blackfeet, who believe their creator, Napi, made the range from boulders left over from his work on the Rocky Mountains. Now, as the highway begins a slight southwesterly bend, you'll make out the faint outline of much larger mountains to the west—the

UNDERGROUND FRONTIER HISTORY COMES TO LIFE AT HAVRE BENEATH THE STREETS

Rockies. Soon, **Chester** (pop. 811) will appear in a broad bowl below, an oasis of trees amid the wheat prairie. Chester features the smallish and neatly kept **Liberty County Museum** (406-759-5256, May–Aug.), with its homesteading history tucked inside a red barn, and the year-round **Liberty Village Arts Center & Gallery** (406-759-5652), which showcases a variety of Montana artists. Also on a street corner here is the studio of Philip Aaberg, an internationally renowned composer and pianist who grew up in Chester.

The remaining 44 Hi-Line miles to **Shelby** (pop. 3,216) offer a last look at the sweeping prairie as the mountains to the west draw ever closer. The "Welcome to Shelby" sign is noteworthy for featuring a small, sculpted outline of two boxers, a nod to an unforgettable chapter in the town's history. In 1923, Shelby had visions of being the commercial hub of a bustling oil region and all the trappings that come with it. In an effort to shine a spotlight on the fledgling town, city officials convinced heavyweight boxing champion Jack Dempsey to stage a fight there, against Tommy Gibbons. Shelby built a 40,000-seat arena on a farm and acquiesced to every demand made by the iconic champion Dempsey, thinking that revenues from a recent oil strike and ticket sales would ensure financial success. Instead, fewer than

10,000 attended the Fourth of July bout, which Dempsey won in 15 rounds, and Shelby was fleeced by promoter Doc Kearns. Four banks and other businesses went bankrupt trying to cover the $300,000 guarantee, and the town hasn't been the same since. To get a closer look at an event that's still a part of the Shelby psyche, visit the **Marias Museum of History & Art** (406-424-2551, May–Sept.), which has more than 10,000 artifacts. Today, Shelby is a rural stop on I-15, with the obligatory chain motels and restaurants.

Best Places to Bunk

GLASGOW: The **Cottonwood Inn & Suites** ($$, 406-228-8213) has 145 rooms and is the closest to an upscale choice. On site is a casino/lounge and Willows Restaurant, which sports a typical steakhouse menu plus a tasty chicken or beef stir fry. The Cottonwood is the only motel in town with an indoor swimming pool. The **Star Lodge Motel** ($, 406-228-2494) isn't much for adornment, but it's a solid choice for those who like a quiet, clean, mom-and-pop kind of place. **Rundle Suites** ($$/$$$, 406-228-2800), in the heart of downtown, is typically booked as corporate lodging, but overnight stays are okay. They've got two-room suites with kitchenettes.

SACO: In 2014, Dennis and Michelle Simpson took on the daunting project of breathing new life into the **Sleeping Buffalo Hot Springs Resort** ($$, 406-527-3370). The result: the main facility has been beautifully renovated, including the four remodeled motel rooms. The floors are retiled, a new sauna was installed, the locker rooms have been updated, and the water is drained from the three pools nightly. Next on Simpsons' agenda: renovating the outdoor pools. The area surroundings, including a campground, are anything but eye candy, though the Murphy's Landing bar next door—not affiliated with the spring—provides a colorful diversion.

A BURLINGTON NORTHERN SANTA FE TRAIN RUMBLES PAST THE GRAIN ELEVATOR AT ZURICH

MALTA: The adorable and colorful **Maltana Motel** ($, 406-654-2610) has park-at-your-door spotless, spacious, and newly renovated rooms with lovingly maintained flower boxes in the windowsills. It's just far enough from the main drag to offer some quiet. A half-block away is the two-story brick **Great Northern Hotel** ($/$$, 406- 654-2100), which is owned by the same couple that runs the Maltana. At the Northern you'll find the same impeccably clean rooms, and it's the place to be if you like to enter your room from a hallway. Built in 1904, the Great Northern reveals its colorful railroad history in the form of photos on the walls. On site for convenience are a solid restaurant, lounge, mini-store, and an underground parking area for those wicked winter nights.

CREATING AN 'AMERICAN SERENGETI'

At first glance, the sweeping vistas between Malta and the Missouri River east of US 191 don't look like much. But *National Geographic* describes what's happening on these untilled grasslands and in the rugged coulees as one of the most ambitious conservation efforts in the world.

A Bozeman-based nonprofit organization called the American Prairie Foundation is working to create a 3.5-million-acre reserve the group likes to call "The American Serengeti." The goal is to protect, preserve, and expand one of the most threatened ecosystems on Earth—the prairie. When APF is finished, an endless horizon of native plants will again host nearly all the native species that roamed these lands when Lewis and Clark floated past the southern boundary. That includes a projected herd of about 10,000 wild bison thundering across the plains and coulees. By the summer of 2015, the reserve had more than 600 bison, compared to the original 16 imported from South Dakota's Wind Cave National Park in 2005. In 2010, another 94 with genetic roots in Montana—the so-called Pablo herd, one of the last in the lower 48 states—was imported from a national park in Alberta, Canada.

APF's approach is to buy area ranch lands with the goal of stitching them together with neighboring public lands to create a reserve nearly the size of Yellowstone, Grand Teton, and Glacier National Parks combined. The group has secured seven-figure donations from people around the world and uses public-relations firms in New York and London in an effort to shine an international spotlight on this American outback, but its primary tool is first-hand experience. APF's biggest donors are out-of-staters who were smitten by the wide-open spaces, solitude, and plight of vanishing prairie ecosystems. It's a primitive world with no services, though APF opened an eleven-site

Buffalo Camp campground in 2011 and a plusher Kestrel Camp with five temperature-controlled suites in 2013.

Though one of the APF's talking points is the promotion of economic vitality in area communities, local resistance to the effort is stout. Fueled by the fact that APF's headquarters are in trendy Bozeman, many believe the group's ultimate agenda is to remove ranchers from lands they've homesteaded for more than a century. They also fear the creation of a national monument that would restrict such historic uses of the land as grazing and hunting. A few even envision herds of wild bison leaving paths of wanton destruction. In Malta, front yards are pocked with green-and-white signs saying "No Free-Roaming Buffalo," "No Monument" and "Don't Buffalo Me."

To combat these perceptions, APF is reaching out to local ranchers with a program called "Wild Sky Beef," which pays a premium to livestock producers willing to meet certain wildlife-friendly protocols. That includes no longer shooting or poisoning such native creatures as prairie dogs, and installing fencing that, for example, enables pronghorn antelope to migrate easily. The beef is marketed as healthy and wildlife-friendly to consumers willing to fork out a little extra money in the name of conservation. As of 2015, the fledgling program, based on a similar model in Africa, had four area participants with a goal of 50 by 2018.

As you might guess of such a remote landscape, reaching the American Prairie Reserve requires some effort. From Malta, head south on Central Avenue and turn left onto MT 364. Shortly after the road turns to gravel, look for a fork in the road and take Regina Road to the right. It's another 30 bouncy miles to a T-intersection, where you'll turn left and drive another 6 miles to yet another "T," this time turning right. American Prairie Reserve signs will guide you in from there to the headquarters.

CHINOOK: The pleasant and reasonable **Chinook Motor Inn** ($/$$, 406-357-2248) is centrally located to other businesses and also has the Chinook Grille & Bar (B/L/D) as an anchor. The thirty-eight rooms with queen beds are basic but clean. The restaurant is known for Chinese food and freshly ground burgers.

HAVRE: Most of Havre's motels are located on US 2, the major artery through town. **TownHouse Inn of Havre** ($$, 406-442-4667), and **AmericInn** ($$/$$$, 406-395-5000) are some of the more corporate-style, locally recommended places to stay. The **Best Western Great Northern Inn** ($$, 406-265-4200) is another good choice, but like so much of the lodging on the Hi-Line, it's near the busy Burlington Northern Santa Fe railroad tracks—so you might want to bring earplugs.

SHELBY: Similar to Havre, you can find a decent night's stay at a couple of chains. **The Best Western** ($$, 406-424-4560) has a slight edge over **The Comfort Inn** ($$, 406-434-2212), though both are consistent in quality. To get away from the cookie-cutter variety, consider the **O'Haire Manor Motel of Shelby** ($, 406-434-5555), which remains a throwback to the 1950s, when oil and gas execs used it as a base to oversee the workers in the energy fields scattered across northern Montana.

Alternative Bunking

CAMPING: The **Lake Shel-Oole Campground** (406-434-5222) north of Shelby, is tucked beneath an earthen dam, has nearly 70 sites for RVs and tents, and decent fishing.

Best Eats

GLASGOW: Chef Scott Redstone raises the bar at the **Durum Restaurant & Bar** ($$, 406-228-2236, L/D Tues.–Sat.). It's a classic Montana-style steakhouse named for a type of wheat grown on the Hi-Line. They're known for their excellent pasta and battered walleye, and their wine-by-the glass selection with a decent selection of apps (garlic mussels, bacon poutine) lift Durum above the norm. Look for bar specials like their 2-for-1 burger and brew night. **Sam's Supper Club** ($$, 406-228-4614, L/D, Mon.–Sat.) began as The Club in the 1930s, when Fort Peck Dam was under construction. Sam's has credible steaks, but locals love their chimichangas, served with a side of history. People from as far away as Malta, Wolf Point, and even Billings— seriously—rave about **Eugene's Pizza** ($$, 406-228-8552, D). Eugene's, a community mainstay since 1962, specializes in thin-crust pizza basted with a house-made sauce. But it's much, much more than pizza. One highlight is their ribs smothered in Sam & Jeff's Sweet Montana barbecue sauce made— and now bottled—onsite. They're also proud of their half-cooked pizzas that they send across the West in the form of "care packages." **Soma dis Deli** ($, 406-228-4700, L) is good for a light bite, sandwiches on rich bread, thick hearty soups, and many flavors of cheesecake by the slice.

HINSDALE: Stoughie's ($/$$, 406-364-2132, L/D), a community gathering place complete with a screened front porch, is famed for huge burgers plated with hand-cut fries, prime rib on Saturdays, homemade soups, and tasty daily specials.

MALTA: In a town not known for its dining options, locals tend to opt for the tried and true **Great Northern Hotel**'s ($$/$$$, 406-654-2100, B/L/D; breakfast only Sundays) restaurant. Mornings greet you with great omelets or great biscuits and gravy. Lunch and dinner give way to fresh ground burgers, hand-cut steaks, and the locally ubiquitous walleye. New on the scene is **Ray Jay's BBQ** ($$, 406-654-2159, L/D). The pulled pork and brisket are meticulously rubbed, smoked, and slow-cooked by Ray himself, resulting in BBQ you won't be afraid to share with your Southern relatives. Ray Jay—a nickname he acquired in his younger days—and his wife do all the work, sometimes with the help of their kids.

SACO: The **Cabin Café** ($, 406-527, 3353, B/L) is a proud little café in a proud little town that, like Saco, keeps reinventing itself. The café opened in 1950 as O'Brien's (or O.B.'s) but became the Cabin Café when Chinook native Nena Malmend took over for her mother-in-law in 2013. Breakfast sandwiches and omelets are popular, and so are the juicy burgers with hand-cut French fries for lunch. Malmend gets her fresh beef from the Pay 'N Save Meat Shop two doors down.

HARLEM: **KB's Deli** ($, 406-353-4435, L) has a terrific chicken salad sandwich, chili nachos, and homemade soup; seal the deal with a shake, malt, or ice-cream float.

CHINOOK: Looking for a cool summer-time snack break? **The Creamery** ($, 406-357-4260, Apr.–Sept.) ice-cream parlor has milkshakes, malts, soft-serve ice cream, banana splits, and more toppings than you could ever want. They also serve burgers two nights a week.

HAVRE: Dining options here are more diverse than anywhere else on the Hi-Line. For more than 30 years, locals have been heading to **Uncle Joe's** ($$/$$$, 406-265-5111, L/D Tues-Sun) for supersized steaks, the onion blossom, and broasted chicken. Joe's has two menus, one for finer dining downstairs (opens at 5 PM) and pub grub upstairs in the bar. **Andy's Supper Club** ($$/$$$, 406-265-9963, D) would fit right in an older Rat Pack movie, with its half-circle bar and red tuck-and-roll wall behind it, the huge saltwater fish tanks separating the darkened bar from the dining room, and spaghetti as a side starch. Andy's reminds us of the Midwest steakhouses of our youth. Joyce (81 years old in 2015) and Jim have owned the joint for years, and have finally turned it over to their daughters, Dorothy and Judy. Although not so

Irish, a little more roguish is **Murphy's Irish Pub** ($$$, 406-265-4700, L/D). Murphys diversifies the menu—which changes twice a year—by adding beef or chicken Asian dishes, gyros, and similar menu items. But never fear; they still serve pasties, a wide selection of Irish whiskeys, and micro beers. For a pizza pie, meatball sandwich, and fresh pasta specials prepared with care in their kitchen to enjoy at home, on the road, or in your motel, it's **Nalivka's Original Pizza Kitchen** ($/$$, 406-265-4050, L/D Tues.–Sun.). It's take-out or delivery only, and no credit cards are accepted. Their famous cannelloni Florentine, lasagna, spaghetti with meatballs, and soups go out frozen.

HINGHAM: At **Hi-Way Bar & Quick Stop** ($, 406-397-3266, L/D) you can treat yourself to inexpensive, good eats while marveling at your luck for finding such a bargain in the middle of seemingly nowhere (see Best Bars).

INVERNESS: The **Inverness Bar & Supper Club** ($$, 406-292-3801, L/D) is not much to look at from the outside, but it's what's on the inside that counts. Bank on reasonably priced steaks, supreme walleye, steamed cod with drawn butter, and a good stiff drink from the bar. Dining room opens at 5 PM; if you're there for lunch it's soup and sandwiches from the bar side (see Best Bars).

CHESTER: The **Grand Bar & Grill** ($/$$, 406-759-5582, D) was once called the Chic N Coop because of its great broasted chicken, which is still their top seller. If you're not a chicken fan, mow down one of their burgers (with homemade fries) or an entrée salad (steak, grilled chicken, taco). Weekends are crowded, and so is Monday night during football season.

DUNKIRK: Ten miles east of Shelby is yet another well-loved steakhouse, the **Frontier Bar & Supper Club** ($$$, 406-432-3600, D Wed.–Sun.) Owners Michelle and Loren Billdeaux bring a note of gourmet to standard steakhouse cuisine. He's a classically trained chef, and she knows her market. Your choices aren't limited to huge, hand-cut steaks. You can also order fresh seafood (salmon, mussels and oysters). Try those oysters in a shot of vodka! Extra touches such as the sauces, soups, and dressings are made in-house, making this a destination-dining experience.

SHELBY: For one more Hi-Line slice of life, it's **The Griddle** ($/$$, 406-434-7260, B/L/D), the place where men in their John Deere and Massey Ferguson ball caps come for their morning coffee and stacks of bacon and eggs. For lunch, the roast beef for French dip is prepared in-house and the hoagie bread fresh-baked. That The Griddle is always busy is all you need to know about the food, service, and ambience. And you can't miss it—just look for the giant frying pan on the sign above the diner.

Best Bars

HINGHAM: The **Hi-Way Bar & Quick Stop** (406-397-3211) is a respite from sore-derrière syndrome, and it appeals to families, bikers, and John Deere drivers alike. Sit a spell, chill with a beverage, or load up on good food for less than you'd expect. The husband-and-wife team of Mike and Kyle Spencer have a good thing going: She runs the kitchen while he works the front. Lunch is blue-plate style, and although limited in selection, it isn't short on tastiness.

INVERNESS: Boots, buckles, and cowboy hats balance well in the **Inverness Bar & Supper Club** (406-292-3801). On the bar side, it's comfortably cramped, with slightly dusty dark wood, a functional back bar, and faded turquoise barstools. Around the corner is the dining side with tables dressed in gray, blue and white tablecloths. The buzz is as genuinely congenial as the servers. The place has been in the Dahlke family for 50 years; daughter Shawn and her husband, Elton, have had it since the late 1990s. The bar has entertainment that crosses generational lines: big screen TVs, gaming machines, a foosball table, and darts. The prices are just as friendly: a burger will run you less than $5, and the supper club is popular for its walleye, fried shrimp, and the "keep 'em coming back" steaks. We like the steamed cod served with drawn butter and a salad topped with house-made blue-cheese dressing.

HAVRE: A little more upscale yet still Montana-style laidback is **Vic's Place** (406-945-9026) in the Park Hotel in the heart of downtown. Kurt Johnson has owned the building for many years, but four years ago got into the bar biz. His lessee next door needed a liquor license, and so it began. The theme of his small intimate bar with barrel furniture and comfortable couches is "Budget Premium." Blended cocktails, stiff martinis, microbrews (many local), and good wines by the glass are to be expected. The unexpected includes Vic's extensive lineup of Crown Royal (nine varieties), Jim Beams (seven), Bailey's (newest is Espresso-flavored) and Johnny Walker Blue— the only place on the Hi-Line with it. Look for wine tastings and whiskey samplings at Vic's, where you can order bar menu appa-teasers like bacon-wrapped shrimp, or sample authentic Mexican cuisine. What's Kurt most proud of with this place? The compliments he gets for how clean it is, and the overall ambience: never a fight, never foul language and always fun. It's a place where you can hang out with the premium beverage of your choice, have a business meeting, or just stare into your sweetie's eyes over a romantic meal. Check out the photo on the wall of the namesake's 85-year-old crossed hands. Vic Spindler was the longtime maintenance man for the Park Hotel and was retired when Kurt asked for his help in starting up. Vic put in a few more years and Kurt gave him his due with the name of his business. Like a parent who can't admit which child is their favorite, we can't say Vic's is our favorite bar in Montana. So we'll just say it's our kind of place.

DETOUR: ONE FOR THE ROAD

The Missouri Breaks
Winifred to Charles M. Russell National Wildlife Refuge

ESTIMATED LENGTH: 92 miles

HIGHLIGHTS: Missouri Breaks, Charles M. Russell National Wildlife Refuge, Winifred Museum, McClelland Ferry, Woodhawk Trail

GETTING THERE: From the south, each route that leads to the byway starts at Big Timber—Exit 367 if you're coming from the west, 370 from the east. Drive north on US 191 through Harlowton and Lewistown to Hilger. Here you'll have to decide between taking County Road 236 directly north 23 miles to Winifred or continue on US 191 to just before the Missouri River. Looking west on Knox Ridge Road you'll quickly be able to tell whether the dirt road is navigable; it can be extremely soupy here after a rainstorm.

It doesn't take much imagination to contemplate bygone eras on the snow-white coulees of the **Missouri Breaks**. After all, little has changed in the two centuries since Lewis and Clark arrived at these forbidding badlands, and barely a century has passed since the flight of the Nez Perce ended a few miles to the north. The modern world doesn't spend much time here, except in canoes, kayaks, and rafts plying the lazy waters of the **Wild and Scenic Missouri River** and the occasional pickup kicking up dust on the **Charles M. Russell National Wildlife Refuge**. In a state renowned for its solitude, ruggedness, and raw beauty, the Missouri Breaks has few peers.

First, a warning: The entire route might not be navigable, even in July or August. A good rainstorm can turn parts of the road to gumbo, and even if you have a high-clearance and/or four-wheel-drive vehicle, you could wind up stuck a long way from anywhere. The closest town of any size is **Lewistown** (pop. 5,813), 37 miles from the route's hub in **Winifred** (pop. 156). If the weather has been rainy or it's threatening to storm, save your trip for another day. If negotiable, however, this route provides a marvelous glimpse of the famed White Cliffs of the Missouri and vast grasslands of both the wildlife refuge and the **Upper Missouri River Breaks National Monument**.

Bear Paw National Battlefield (32 miles round-trip)

In the "Land of the 10,000 Haystacks" chapter you read about Chief Joseph and the valiant march of 800 Nez Perce as they tried to escape the U.S. Cavalry in 1877. Here, on grassy shoulders above willowy Snake Creek and in the shadows of the Bear's Paw Mountains, is where Joseph, uttering his famous "I Will Fight No More Forever" speech, surrendered to Generals Nelson A. Miles and Oliver O. Howard on a frigid October day after a 1,710-mile journey spanning four months and four states.

A 1-mile interpretive trail offers a haunting look at the events that signified the end of the Indian wars, in this case 40 miles from freedom in Canada. Engraved inch-high metal posts mark the sites of teepees, including Chief Joseph's, and show where the warriors Ollokot and Looking Glass fell to cavalry bullets. But the best way to fully appreciate the scene is to stop first at the **Blaine County Museum** in Chinook. Pick up a brochure and watch "40 Miles From Freedom" before venturing 16 miles south on MT 240 through pastoral countryside with the Bear's Paw Mountains rising in the near distance.

Bear Paw is one of three Nez Perce National Historic Parks and the end of the 1,310-mile Nez Perce National Historic Trail, which begins in Joseph, Oregon. Guided tours by rangers are available.

Here are the goose-bump-raising words of perhaps the most famous Indian speech ever given: "Tell General Howard I know his heart. What he told me before I have in my heart. I am tired of fighting. Our chiefs are killed. Looking Glass is dead. Tu-hul-hul-sote is dead. The old men are all dead. It is the young men who say yes or no. He who led the young men (Ollokot) is dead. It is cold and we have no blankets. The little children are freezing to death. My people, some of them, have run away to the hills, and have no blankets, no food; no one knows where they are—perhaps freezing to death. I want to have time to look for my children and see how many of them I can find. Maybe I shall find them among the dead. Hear me, my chiefs. I am tired; my heart is sick and sad. From where the sun now stands I will fight no more forever."

The drive has earned a Backcountry Byway designation in part because of its historical significance: Lewis and Clark camped here in 1805 and dubbed it "The Deserts of America." The Nez Perce came through on their unsuccessful flight to Canada in 1877. Appreciation of a stark natural world is a must. There are no services along the route except at Winifred, a bright agricultural town with an extraordinary little museum.

The Missouri River is most responsible for this spectacular rock sculptures in the White Cliffs and badlands areas. For it was the river that cut through alternating soft shale and hard sandstone, creating an array of tall, thin, and eerie rock features called hoodoos and crops of pedestal rocks that look like toadstools. Montanans have an abiding affection for this arid area, and a journey in a river craft is a popular pastime.

Though the Missouri Breaks Backcountry Byway can be reached from US 191, begin your trip in Winifred, a proud and tight-knit gateway to the region and a necessary stop to appreciate local history and culture. The **Winifred Museum** has the requisite assortment of historical homesteader, Indian, and dinosaur artifacts, but the primary reason to stop here is for what the town claims—and after seeing it, who's to doubt?—to be the largest collection of Tonka trucks anywhere. The museum is open only in summers, but if you're there during the off-season give them a call and they'll gladly come by and open up.

Winifred is also the only place on the route to grab a bite to eat, either at the **Winifred Tavern & Cafe** or **Trails Inn Bar**—both of which serve what you'd expect in rural Montana—and you can gas up at the Cenex. The historic building that houses the **Winifred Grocery** underwent renovations that stayed true to character, dating to when it was known as Stafford's. You're in the middle of nowhere here, but the grocery has purchased a cellphone range extender so townies and out-of-town customers alike can now make calls, text, or use the Internet.

As you drive about a mile east from Winifred on Knox Ridge Road to begin the byway, go off the beaten byway about 12 miles to the free **McClelland Ferry**, one of three left crossing the Missouri. The McClelland Ferry, also called the Stafford Ferry, is nearly a century old. Make the detour just to experience a vanishing piece of frontier history and talk to the operators of the diesel-powered craft.

Back at the junction near Winifred, head east again and drive another 11 miles to the next junction: Two Calf Road. Here begins the byway loop. The more improved Knox Ridge Road continues to the east; the more scenic but slower Two Calf Road route goes north and eventually reaches the rim above the Missouri. If you're feeling especially adventurous, take some of the two-track trails veering off toward the rim for some spectacular views of the river, distant mountains, and a look at geologic history, peeled away one era after another in the cliffs. Fourteen miles into Two Calf Road is the **Woodhawk Trail**, which leads to a dramatic overlook. Continue another 2 miles on Two Calf Road, and you'll reach Woodhawk Bottoms Road, which leads down to the river. Two miles beyond Woodhawk Bottoms Road is Power Plant Ferry Road—this one to the site of an old ferry, the only crossing in the area until Fred Robinson Bridge on US 191 was built. And that isn't the last road to the Missouri: five miles beyond Power Plant Ferry Road is 2-mile-long Heller Bottom Road, which might be the most scenic of the bunch.

About 30 miles into the northern route is the western end of the 125-mile-long, 1.1-million-acre **Charles M. Russell National Wildlife Refuge**, a small portion of which is west of US 191. The refuge was created in 1936 to preserve habitat for the pronghorn and sharp-tail grouse. Some 60 mammals and 220 bird species are here year-round, and if conservationists have their way, there'll be one more mammal—the bison.

The byway loop roads reconnect about 5 miles west of US 191. The return 23-mile trip across sage plains will surely be quicker, but take your time—even though you're away from the river there's still plenty of wildlife to see.

13

BONUS DRIVE
Glacier's Going-to-the-Sun Loop

WEST GLACIER/ST. MARY/EAST GLACIER/ESSEX

ESTIMATED LENGTH: 132 miles

ESTIMATED TIME: 7 hours to 2 days (summer/fall)

HIGHLIGHTS: Wildlife viewing, hiking, Middle Fork of the Flathead River, Lake McDonald, Bird Woman Falls, Weeping Wall, Logan Pass, St. Mary Lake, Two Medicine, Marias Pass, Walton Goat Lick Overlook, Essex

GETTING THERE: The fastest way to Glacier National Park from I-90 is the US 93 exit west of Missoula. Take US 93 north to Ravalli and continue through the Flathead Indian Reservation to Polson. US 93 continues around the west side of shimmering Flathead Lake. You can skirt the traffic through Kalispell by taking County Road 206 around the southeast end of town to the junction of US 2 west of Columbia Falls. From there, it's 16 four-lane miles through the eclectic mountain towns of Hungry Horse, Martin City, and Coram into West Glacier.

From Missoula, take MT 200 east through Ovando and Lincoln over Rogers Pass to the junction of US 287, then turn north. Stay on US 287 until it meets US 89 at Choteau, and continue northwest on US 89 to Browning, where three roads lead to Glacier National Park. Another way is to leave I-90 at Butte and travel north on I-15 through Helena to Wolf Point, where US 287 veers to the north and begins the Rocky Mountain Front tour to Browning.

Glacier International Airport in Kalispell is served by Delta (SkyWest), Alaska (Horizon), United, and Allegiant. Amtrak's Empire Builder has one stop daily each direction at East Glacier, Essex, and West Glacier.

OVERVIEW

It's difficult to classify a road piercing a busy national park as a backroad or byway, but no book about spectacular drives in Montana is complete without

GLACIER NATIONAL PARK OFFERS SOME OF THE MOST BREATHTAKING VIEWS IN ALL OF MONTANA

Railroad Magnate Made Blackfeet Part of Glacier Vision

Great Northern Railway president James J. Hill had a unique idea when he schemed to create a new national park in 1910.

As part of Hill's grand vision for what would be called Glacier National Park, he wouldn't banish the Blackfeet Indians who lived on the nearby plains. No, he would *welcome* them. In what the *New York Times* labeled "Tourism of Doom," Hill's brilliant see-it-before-it's-gone marketing plan included luring nostalgic tourists west on his railroad by touting a vanishing wilderness— most notably the last place to see real Indians living much as they had before the western migration changed their lives forever. The Blackfeet hunted wild animals, rode their ponies, slipped into teepees at night, and moved in and out of the park's shadows.

In addition to moving freely across the eastern flanks of the park as they had for centuries, the Blackfeet also served as greeters at the train station in Midvale (now East Glacier), at the massive Swiss-style lodges, and at other key tourist spots. At many places, they sang, danced, and told Blackfeet stories for eastern tourists who couldn't get enough of this faux frontier.

This exotic marriage between the Anglo culture and Indians lasted about two decades, until the stock-market crash of 1929. Short of funds for advertising and marketing, the railroad no longer could afford the Blackfeet, who were sent back to their neighboring reservation on the prairie. By the time the economy rebounded during World War II, the Going-to-the-Sun Road had been completed, and more tourists were entering the park from the west.

Historians concede that the railroad's use of the Blackfeet was blatant exploitation, but they note it did have one benefit: By singing, dancing, and telling stories, the tribe retained an oral history at a time when fellow tribes' traditions were disappearing. Today, the Blackfeet have a bittersweet relationship with Glacier, partly because they feel disenfranchised, partly because what few park jobs they have are largely menial, and partly because they still struggle with the concept of political boundaries drawn across sacred earth on which they have lived for centuries.

the Going-to-the-Sun Road in Glacier National Park. It is matched only by the Beartooth All-American Highway between Red Lodge and Cooke City for sheer jaw-dropping magnificence. This dramatic, cliff-hugging ribbon of pavement surely leads the state in photo-ops per mile, whether it's the grandeur of its serrated mountain peaks, the sweeping views of U-shaped valleys, a distant melting glacier shimmering under a bright sun, or the people-tolerant mountain goats nibbling on grasses peeking through snows.

Here, slightly south of the Canadian border, the Rockies are squeezed into a 50-mile-wide spine, forced skyward by the prairie on the east and Flathead Valley on the west. The Blackfeet who roamed this sacred country called it "The Backbone of the World." Early conservationist George Bird Grinnell labeled it "The Crown of the Continent."

Slightly more than a century ago, the park was envisioned by both the naturalist Grinnell and a railroad tycoon named James J. Hill, albeit for polar opposite reasons. Grinnell saw a national park as a way to preserve unparalleled beauty and a precious source of water spilling off the Crown toward the Atlantic, Pacific, and Arctic Oceans; for Hill, it was a marketing tool to lure passengers west on his Great Northern Railway. "See America first" was Hill's rallying cry in coaxing Easterners to explore a last vestige of untamed wilderness. Hill envisioned an American Swiss Alps without livestock and villages, and dreamed of building magnificent chalet-style hotels in the wilderness. Today, those chalets are as much a part of Glacier's persona as pointy mountains and ice fields.

In 1910, less than a decade after a park was first seriously proposed, Glacier joined the National Park System. "See it before it's gone," the Great Northern implored in its advertisements, referring to the wilderness and the choreographed routines of the Blackfeet that Hill placed in the park (see Sidebar). Today, the same mantra applies to the park's namesake feature— the glacier. Over millions of years, glaciers have come and gone, and they have been melting since about 1850. But global warming has accelerated the pace to such a degree that climate models show the remaining twenty-three glaciers disappearing within a decade. Now is indeed the time to see them before they're gone—though even without glaciers, this region will retain its grandeur.

Going-to-the-Sun is the only road bisecting the park, and it's an experience not to be missed. As you'll soon understand, the 48.7-mile road was an engineering marvel when completed in 1932 after 11 years of construction. It was conceived in 1917, the result of a mandate to make parks accessible to a newfangled contraption called the automobile. To this day, the road ranks at or near the top of the most challenging road-building projects in American history. Though one might guess that the name comes from the seeming rise to the sun at Logan Pass, it's actually a nod to a nearby mountain—named for a Blackfeet legend about a celestial being called Sour Spirit, who would come down from the sky to assist the tribe in dire times and go back to the sun when his mission was accomplished.

The miracle we see today is how the road over 6,646-foot Logan Pass is kept open. Plowing snow that can get as deep as 80 feet requires up to 10 weeks of work.

The grandeur doesn't end when the Going-to-the-Sun Road drops into St. Mary. The stretch through aspen and foothills to East Glacier on the eastern fringes of the Blackfeet Indian Reservation is also spectacular, and US 2 between East Glacier and West Glacier offers peeks at mountaintops while splitting Glacier and the Great Bear Wilderness Area.

HITTING THE ROAD

In Glacier's early days, most visitors arrived via rail at **East Glacier** (pop. 396). Today the busiest entrance is West Glacier. Tourists still come by train on both sides, but air access to Kalispell, access from I-90, and the generally more aesthetically pleasing landscapes to the west have turned the blue-collar communities of **Kalispell** (pop. 19,927) and **Columbia Falls** (pop. 4,688) into working towns catering to tourists. Kalispell was the fastest growing city in Montana in 2015. Also alluring is **Whitefish** (pop. 6,649), a destination village not unlike Sun Valley or Vail that has a year-round economy due to the Whitefish Mountain Resort at Big Mountain ski area.

As you come toward **West Glacier** (pop. 227) from Kalispell or Columbia Falls, explore the canyon area or, as the locals call it, "up the line"—a reference to the string of one-time trapping communities between Columbia Falls and the park. **Hungry Horse** (pop. 826), **Coram** (pop. 539), and **Martin City** (pop. 424) are home to a once-reclusive and sometimes-lawless collection of folks who came to help build the Hungry Horse Dam on the South Fork of the Flathead River—and never left. Today, these towns have mellowed with an influx of new blood, and are more inviting to tourists.

As you approach the loop's beginnings in West Glacier, you'll know you're in a national park gateway community. Motels, campgrounds, lodges, helicopter tours, rafting companies, trading posts, and an assortment of Coney Island-esque activities are dead giveaways. That doesn't mean some aren't redeeming. For a mountain state, Montana is surprisingly shy of whitewater rafting thrills, but the Middle Fork of the Flathead River provides some of the best Class III splash-and-giggle runs in the state; no fewer than three outfitters in West Glacier offer day trips.

West Glacier itself has retained a pre–World War II feel with its throwback shops, restaurant, bar, motel, and cabins. In fact, the company that owns the businesses in West Glacier and Apgar, Glacier Park Inc., is responsible for avoiding the cheap T-shirt and cheesy-photograph environments that plague so many national park gateway towns.

On US 2 at West Glacier, once called Belton, cross the Middle Fork to the village of **Apgar** (pop. 426), which sits at the southern end of picturesque, glacier-carved **Lake McDonald** and is home to the park's headquarters. Before starting the Going-to-the-Sun Road into the park's interior, consider a detour on the 23-mile paved and gravel Inside Road along the astonishingly wild North Fork of the Flathead River. It leads to the commune-ish

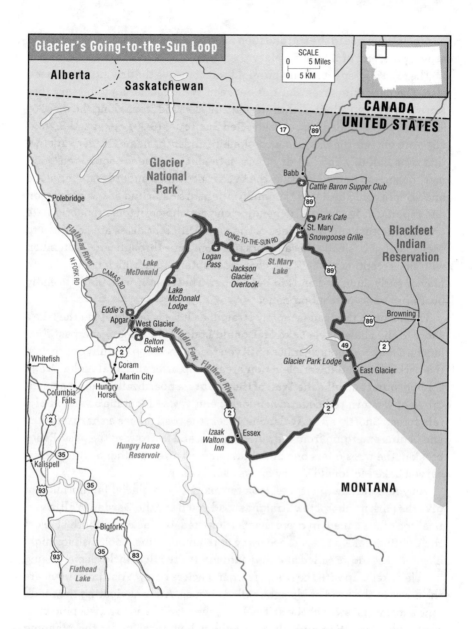

Glacier's Going-to-the-Sun Loop

SCALE
0   5 Miles
0   5 KM

Alberta
Saskatchewan

CANADA
UNITED STATES

Glacier
National
Park

Polebridge

Babb

Cattle Baron Supper Club

Park Cafe
St. Mary
Snowgoose Grille

Blackfeet
Indian
Reservation

GOING-TO-THE-SUN RD

Logan
Pass

Lake
McDonald

Jackson
Glacier
Overlook

St. Mary
Lake

Flathead River

N FORK RD

CAMAS RD

Lake
McDonald
Lodge

Eddie's

Apgar
West Glacier

Browning

Belton
Chalet

Middle Fork Flathead River

Glacier Park Lodge

East Glacier

Whitefish

Coram
Martin City

Columbia
Falls

Hungry
Horse

Hungry Horse
Reservoir

Izaak
Walton
Inn

Essex

Kalispell

MONTANA

Bigfork

Flathead
Lake

village of **Polebridge** (pop. 90) and its rustic century-old mercantile, home of the best fresh-baked bread and bear claws in the region. Polebridge doesn't have electricity, so the mercantile and neighboring Northern Lights Saloon are powered by generators and solar panels. The only public bathroom is a one-holer behind the mercantile, but it adds to the charm. Don't debate whether to take this 7-mile Side Track. Just go.

Apgar Village signals the beginning of the Going-to-the-Sun Road, which hugs the forested shores of 470-foot-deep Lake McDonald before beginning its precipitous rise to the sun and then making a less-dramatic descent to the aspen, pine, and prairie at St. Mary.

The road is so spectacular you might want to leave the driving to someone else. The park offers free shuttles between West Glacier and St. Mary that run every 15 to 30 minutes, with strategically located stops along the way. For an informative guided trip, consider **Red Bus Tours** (855-733-4522, U.S., 303-265-7010 outside the U.S.), a concessionaire under the name Glacier Park Inc. that runs half-day and full-day tours in the historic, open-topped red "jammer" buses—so named because the buses once had standard transmissions and drivers could be heard "jamming" the gears—starting at $30 per person and capping at $95 in 2015, depending on your choice of tours that originate on both the east and west sides of the park. Different dates are assigned to each tour, but basically the jammers run from June through mid-September, with the exception of the Huckleberry Mountain Tour, which begins in late May or early June and ends in September. These environmentally friendly buses run on 93 percent propane.

From Apgar, the road is mostly straight as it rises gently along the lake's shore to the chalet-style **Lake McDonald Lodge** (May–Sept.) and past Avalanche Creek for about 25 miles until you reach The Loop. To fully appreciate the park's forested lower-elevation areas, stop after the **Avalanche Creek Campground** and hike the **Trail of the Cedars**, a boardwalk amid an ancient grove of western red cedars, hemlocks, and yews—Montana's version of a rain forest. Shortly after Avalanche Creek, the road makes a sharp left turn and begins emerging from the pines, cedars, and firs toward the pass. Every break in the trees offers one breathtaking view after another as the glacier-carved Lake McDonald Valley grows ever deeper.

As you continue to elevate, look for many of the glacial landforms that give the park its character. Straight ahead you'll see the **Garden Wall**, a vertical rock face called an *arête* that was created as glaciers on both sides of the Continental Divide scraped away at the mountains. Look also for high-elevation meadows called hanging gardens, the result of little glaciers being unable to keep up with the work of larger glaciers below. Also prominent are the bowls at the head of glaciers, called cirques. After navigating the road's lone substantial switchback at The Loop, the road opens to a sweeping view of 492-foot **Bird Woman Falls** across the valley, eases under the **Weeping Wall**—where a waterfall lands on the road, its volume dependent upon the season—and **Big Bend**, perhaps the most popular viewpoint on the west side of Logan Pass. Just past Big Bend is **Triple Arches**, the best stone-and-mortar example of the massive challenge faced by Depression–era road builders.

Crowds notwithstanding, you'll want to spend a few hours at **Logan Pass**, the road's climax. Open mid-June through mid-October, the **Logan Pass Visitor Center** (406-888-7800) is where you'll learn about the fragile plant and animal life at high elevations before striking out on one of the two hikes that depart from the summit. The 6-mile **Hidden Lake Nature Trail** on pavement, boardwalk, and then gravel is the park's most popular hike. Bring a fly rod to fish for Yellowstone cutthroat trout in the lake. Across the road from the visitors center, the **Highline Trail** cuts across the Garden Wall and isn't for the weak-kneed—for about 100 yards early in the hike there is a sheer drop off, and you might have to—or get to, depending on your perspective—share the trail with a single-minded mountain goat.

Heading down the east side of Logan Pass, you'll notice a drier forest with more pine, aspen, and eventually sagebrush. Highlights of the backside include the 408-foot **East Tunnel** through Piegan Mountain and a stop at the **Jackson Glacier Overlook,** 4 miles below the pass. This is the only place on the road where a glacier is still visible. Snap a photo and then compare the current size of the glacier to visitor center pictures from the 1930s, 1950s, and even 1980s. Look to the north side of the road, and you'll see its namesake mountain, Going-to-the-Sun, which rises to 9,642 feet. The road down to **St. Mary Lake** offers a number of worthwhile short hikes, including an easy 3.6-mile round-tripper to St. Mary and Virginia falls, a short walk to 75-foot **Sunrift Gorge,** and the 1.2-mile **Sun Point Nature Trail** to views of the lake. One more stop to make is at the **Wild Goose Island Overlook,** where a tiny island is a striking contrast in St. Mary Lake against a mountain backdrop.

Five miles before St. Mary is **Rising Sun** (866-875-8456, June—Sept.), which offers the first services since Lake McDonald, including boat rides across the lake. Take a look around at the prairie and aspen landscape and ponder just how much it has changed in the 35 miles since the ancient cedars on the west side. St. Mary has a visitor center and a congested conglomeration of restaurants, motels, gas stations, and gift shops.

Turn right on US 89 for the pretty 33-mile drive through aspen and sage foothills toward East Glacier, keeping an eye on the majestic mountains visible on the passenger's side. Look for Blackfeet ponies high on benches in scenes reminiscent of 150 years ago. At a little outpost called Kiowa, turn right on MT 49 for 13 miles of zigging and zagging through the **Two Medicine** country to **East Glacier,** which has a few smaller motels, motor inns, eateries and gift shops, an Amtrak station, and the massive **Glacier Park Lodge.**

Just under the railroad bridge is the junction of US 2, which begins a quick if not as dramatic ascent to 5,220-foot **Marias Pass** to the west. The views at the summit—including 8,770-foot Summit Mountain to the north—are enticing. Pull into a large parking area that features a miniature version of the Washington Monument dedicated to J. F. Stevens. He was a Great Northern Railway engineer who discovered the route across the Rockies with the help of a Blackfeet scout. Also at the pass is a tribute to a Slippery Bill Morrison, who donated a portion of his 160-acre spread to create the only year-round passage through the Rockies between Rogers Pass and the Canadian border.

When US 2 descends to the Flathead River and bends north, look for the

Walton Goat Lick Overlook on the left side. A short walk to a new viewing platform reveals a natural salt lick where as many as 50 mountain goats at a time regularly convene for an energy boost, alongside bighorn sheep, deer, and other wildlife. A few miles beyond are the communities of **Walton** and **Essex** (pop. 223), where the extravagant **Izaak Walton Inn** is worth exploring even if you're not staying in one of its railroad-oriented lodging options. The 29-room hotel, often called Inn Between because of its location deep in the mountains between East Glacier and West Glacier, was built as a possible southern entrance for Glacier. The hotel has survived numerous disappointments—and nearly perished in a wildfire in the summer of 2015—and has evolved to become a destination for visitors desiring unusual year-round lodging. It has become a twice-daily hotel tradition to wander onto the porch to wave at Amtrak passengers.

The next 25 miles back to West Glacier offer some of the wildest paved-road country in America. Glacier rises above the Flathead River on the north side and the Great Bear Wilderness looms to the south.

Index